A
Divine
Confrontation

Birth Pangs of the New Church

A
Divine
Confrontation

Birth Pangs of the New Church

Graham Cooke

Destiny Image® Publishers, Inc.
P.O. Box 310
Shippensburg, PA 17257-0310

"We Publish the Prophets"

ISBN 0-7684-2039-3

For Worldwide Distribution
Printed in the U.S.A.

This book and all other Destiny Image, Revival Press,
and Treasure House books are available
at Christian bookstores and distributors worldwide.

For a U.S. bookstore nearest you, call **1-800-722-6774**.
For more information on foreign distributors, call **717-532-3040**.
Or reach us on the Internet: **http://www.reapernet.com**

Dedication

*T*his book is dedicated to Tony and Hannah Morton and to the guys and girls on the leadership team at the Community Church, Southampton, England. You took us in as a family during our own time of fiery transition and have made us welcome and honored. My family has prospered under your love, acceptance, and guidance. Thanks for being so kind and for making it all work.

I dedicate this book to Tony in particular; he has become a good friend and father figure to me. I enjoy our times and our travels together. I appreciate being included in on all that is happening.

Also, this book is dedicated to all the c.net (Cornerstone) churches in hundreds of places in dozens of countries, and to all of us who strive together for the purpose of the Kingdom despite trials, suffering, and persecution. May we all transition to a new level and discover afresh the majesty, supremacy, and sovereignty of our incredible Lord Jesus Christ.

Acknowledgments

*M*y thanks and gratitude to all the following:

Carole Shiers, my personal assistant, who continues to be a stalwart support in everything we do together in the ministry. Her friendship, skills, and influence are an incredible asset in an increasingly busy office.

Elsie Bataille, our secretary, who painstakingly typed the manuscript, the corrections, and the updated changes with good humor and much grace!

Julia Pomeroy for a brilliant job at proofreading.

Dave Botma for all his assistance with art and graphics.

Our friends in the USA with their cheerful support, financial backing, and sheer patience with the English guy.

Pat, Susan, Cherie, and *Denise* for the outstanding ministry support developing our resources.

Our prayer coordinators in the UK, USA, and *Canada* who intercede for the ministry.

All who financially support the ministry, enabling me to go into places that could not afford to host an event or a school...brilliant job, guys!

Lance Wallnau, who is my friend, fellow thinker, and strategist. I hope you recognize yourself in the book.

John and Melly, Patrick, Tim, John, Mark, and *Danny and Dena* who have all helped with establishing the ministry in the USA.

Mike and Karen, good friends and faithful givers from Florida.

Duncan and Jane, still giving after all these years.

Tom, Barbara, and *the Sword Church in Sooners territory*, what a neat bunch.

My mother, *Gladys*, who taught me about perseverance and not quitting. Her heart is in this book.

My wife, *Heather*, and children, *Ben, Seth,* and *Sophie*. What a funny, odd, quirky, zany, intelligent, artistic, and spiritual lot we all are. The Bee fits right in with our hearts.

My personal thanks to *Don Milam, Marsha Blessing, Elizabeth Allen, Jeanette Sprecher,* and *Tony Laidig* of Destiny Image Publishers for their gracious support, personal kindness, enthusiasm, and profound belief in this book, which have made me dare to believe on a deeper level that the Lord really has given me some things to say on transition.

Endorsements

In the Books of Ezra and Nehemiah, a work of "rebuilding" took place that radically affected not only individuals, but also society. The "builders" of the day (Ezra, Nehemiah, and Zerubbabel) were encouraged by the help that the prophets brought to them. Ezra 5:2 states, "...and the prophets of God were with them, helping them." In this book, Graham helpfully stands with the "builders" in today's Church, bringing encouragement, challenge, and revelation. His prophetic insights shed light on the Church that is yet to emerge.

Stuart Bell
Christian Fellowship, Lincoln, England
Author of *In Search of Revival*

I joyfully recommend this book to any church desiring to enter fully into the next move of God. With practical wisdom and insight, Graham Cooke speaks of the glorious dimension of the move of God and does not draw back from the sometimes painful process needed to allow God to do His complete work. He puts a specific emphasis on how to develop strong relationships. He then outlines practical ways for equipping warriors in the battle for the Lord Jesus! This book will impart encouragement and hope to a weary Church.

Mike Bickle
Friends of the Bridegroom

Someone once said, "Constant change is here to stay." In a time of profound transition for the Church throughout the world, this book will comfort as well as challenge, heal as well as hurt, and equip as well as expose so we can "keep step with the Spirit" in these historic days. Great job, Graham!

Larry Tomczak
Christian leader, church planter
Author and teacher at the
Brownsville Revival School of Ministry

With prophetic insight and apostolic strategy Graham navigates the course of transition in the Church. Pioneering the way, he clearly marks the trail for us to follow. Local churches and individual Christians would benefit from the practical experience and fresh revelation in this book. It is a must read for any individual or church going through the difficult and rewarding process of transition. Graham Cooke is one of the most perceptive individuals I have met in my travels around the world in understanding the context of the Church in today's world and how to take a church through the difficult times of transition.

Randy Clark
Global Awakening

Contents

Foreword

This book has the potential to help us all as well as unsettle us. With Graham's charismatic, radical insight there is both a spirituality and a practicality that leaves no stones unturned. His passion for the Church and how it responds to God's purposes is stimulating. Portrayed in fresh and unpredictable ways, his wisdom and prophetic urgency will sound a "wake-up call" to many. Do not settle down to read this book; it bristles with heart-searching demands for a people who will be found ready in a day of God's power and prevailing presence.

Tony Morton

Foreword

*G*raham Cooke is an agitator, and this book is trouble look-ing for a place to happen! Can you believe his audacity to state that God wants to interfere with the Church? You would almost think that God owned the Church.

I say, "Go for it, Graham. Point out the places of *divine confrontation*. God is on your side. A holy confrontation can bring about a blessed birth. Ask Mary, the mother of Jesus!"

If you choose to read this book, you should probably throw out your old ecclesiastical dictionary. Nothing is as it seems...it's bigger and better. Only we didn't know it! And Graham Cooke told us.

Thank God for men like him. Their vision elevates the process above the destination (because where we're going is out of this world anyway). Men like him make hamburgers out of our sacred cows—and at the same time make us say, "This tastes good!"

Change is coming! The spiritual climate is about to be radically altered. Thank you, Graham, for "forthtelling" the spiritual weather patterns.

Bring on the babe of revival!

Tommy Tenney
Author of *The God Chasers*

Chapter 1

Discovering the Internal Catalyst

Enjoy the Paradox

I must apologize if my words in this book are not what you are used to. I really do not know any better. I am a pragmatist at heart. I am interested in what works and what is beautiful. I want to marry them together. The Church is a paradox. It is not what the world thinks it is. It is contrary to received conventional opinion. Sadly, that also may be true for large sections of the Church.

The Church is a house and a city, an army and a bride, a building and a body. Each of these concepts is designed to shake us and stretch our thinking and practice beyond our current capacity. Most of the ways that God operates are paradoxical. His ways are not ours and His thoughts are radically different from our own (see Is. 55:8-9). Everything He does is to display His glory and majesty. He is not seeking a powerful people to represent Him. Rather He looks for all those who are weak, foolish, despised, and written off; and He inhabits them with His own strength. He has not come to give strength but to be strength to us as we relate to

Him in weakness. He fills everything with Himself. He is our joy, our righteousness, and the power of salvation.

That means we must understand the difference between vulnerability and insecurity. All God's dealings with us are to create maximum dependence upon Him. He calls us to do the impossible. He demands that we see what is invisible. He thrusts us into situations that would overwhelm us. It could be rescuing more than a million people from bondage to the most cruel, occult, and oppressive regime of the day. (Moses managed to do it.) Or it could be building a huge boat when there is no body of water large enough to float it, then populating it with every species of life imaginable. (No wonder it took Noah more than a hundred years!)

How would we feel about taking the most fortified city in our world by ordering a week of silence followed by a single shout?! (Joshua did it.) Would we cheerfully stand by as God reduces our army to one percent of the original number because He liked the way those guys drank their water? (Gideon had to!) This effectively raised the odds from 4:1 to 400:1 in favor of the enemy, making vulnerability and dependency a very real issue!

Insecurity produces unbelief. A paralysis occurs where there needs to be movement and faith in action. People see their own smallness rather than the majesty of God. (The Israelites in Numbers 13:33 said, "We were like grasshoppers in our own sight.") Such people are prevented from achieving breakthrough because they cannot translate their weakness into power.

Vulnerability is knowing that God is happy to send us out as lambs amongst wolves because He is hugely confident in His own ability to watch over us and work through our weaknesses. When we are vulnerable, we see our inadequacies in the light of God's sovereignty and power, and we discover hope and faith. Like Paul, we rejoice in our weaknesses that the power of Christ may rest upon us (see 2 Cor. 12:9-10). The whole point of vulnerability is to bring us to a place of restful dependence in a powerful and overcoming God.

> *God's majesty is concealed within our vulnerability.*

Vulnerability is given by God to release His presence, which builds self-esteem and confidence in God's sovereignty. Insecurity occurs when the enemy twists our soul to reduce our self-esteem and cause us to focus on our shortcomings.

What Are We Giving Birth To?

God looks for a catalyst among His people—someone who will enter into a purposeful relationship with Him and who is capable of suspending disbelief as he discovers the majesty of God. The Lord is always on a treasure hunt, finding something precious in the unlikeliest of places! We look at the earthen vessel; God sees the treasure. We are more concerned with the rubbish it is buried in than the innate value of the real find itself. We see the rough edges; He sees the cut and polished jewel. Thank God for Jesus!

I love the way that God esteems us in Christ...the way He cherishes the bride in us...the value that He places on our lives because of His Son. He always sees the treasure within and then works to extract the precious from the worthless. Humans do the opposite. We take the worthless away from what is precious. Therefore our focus is on rubbish removal and not on the glory of the Christ-life that is present though hidden in every believer.

God always speaks to our potential while simultaneously showing us Himself. I AM is with you! Gideon was a frightened, inadequate, resentful, questioning, and angry young man with severe low self-esteem. God looked beyond all that and spoke to the latent capacity that was hidden within the man. He said, "The Lord is with you, mighty warrior" (see Judg. 6). In the face of Gideon's initial alarm, He would only restate: "I will be with you!"

God did not deal with Gideon's inadequacies. The Lord established the warrior in him by showing Gideon His own nature and sovereignty. Whatever we speak to in people will rise up, for good or for bad. Speak to the flesh and it will bite you. Speak to the Christ-life and it will bless you. Always speak to what is noble in people and nobility will emerge. The Holy Spirit is present in people, so if we speak to the fruit of His character and not to our misgivings or suspicion about them, we will save both ourselves and others from bitter confusion and possible rejection.

God will inhabit only what is compatible with His purpose. He comes to tell us that there is a new way of looking, being, walking, and doing. The Lord is not coming to do what we want but to fulfill His desire to become our Bridegroom. It is vital that we be ready to pursue God's desire.

The Lord lives only with what is pure, holy, and consecrated. He cohabits with the virgins who have jars of oil. We are in a season of grace where God is covering us to give us time to repent. How will God come to you? In mercy because of your desire for Him? Or in judgment because of His desire for you?

We want to be a dwelling place of God by the Spirit and therefore compatible to the image of God. He is compatible with humility and brokenness. He gives grace to the humble. Grace is His empowering presence flowing out from the crucible of brokenness and humility. We are a people seeking identification with God through crucifixion, humility, servanthood, obedience, and suffering; having the same mind in us that Jesus had in His compatibility.

How desperate are we to be a dwelling place of God in our lifestyles? People must have a goal for sanctification. Sanctification is not necessarily coming to a place where we never sin but to a place where the practice of sin is not normal. Sanctification precedes revival. We need teachers and prophets combining together in the process of sanctification, acting as midwives to deliver a purity that will bless the Lord. Many charismatics do not know the difference between legalism and self-discipline. Real accountability is provoked from below and promotes self-control, a fruit of the Spirit. Imposed accountability is dealt from above and can produce shame, fear, and inertia as well as controlling, domineering leadership.

Who Are the Midwives?

What kind of house are we building and what type of wineskin do we want? Who are the external catalysts and builders who can shape our design and destiny? Who are the internal movers and shakers who will respond to what the Spirit is saying to the churches? Who are the people who can be positive agents for change just by the quality of their life in the Lord?

The womb represents a place of growth and stretching as the life within takes shape. Every church has a womb. Some churches are capable of giving birth to multiple life forms; others are able to deliver a single aspect of vision. Some churches cannot conceive while others cannot produce. Every church needs a midwife who can deliver the vision into a specific form capable of interacting with God and humanity.

In Scripture, the midwives are the fivefold ministries mentioned in Ephesians 4. They are given as gifts to train, equip, empower, and release the Body of Christ into ministry. There is a greater depth of spiritual reality that emerges in the combined company of apostles and prophets. New foundations have to be laid if we are restructuring the building for a different use or a more dynamic purpose. Apostles and prophets are the only ministries that can release the dynamic of the presence of God that turns a church from an organization to an organism. The church must become cloud-sensitive, not crowd-sensitive. The new wineskin must be defined prophetically. The new structure of the church requires apostolic strategy. Many churches have become a memorial to what God did. Raising up and renewing the prophetic in our midst will enable us to preserve the revelation that will rebuild the house and keep the wineskin soft. We can pass on our church style or we can release prophetic successors. To do the latter, we need the Father's touch as a wise master-builder.

Good leadership releases the fruit of the Holy Spirit in the lives of people by continually encouraging the flock back into the arms of Jesus. Apostles are the Eliezers of the church sent out to prepare a Bride for the Son (see Gen. 24). We must distinguish between leadership of the church and management. Leaders are proficient in the art of going somewhere and taking people with them. Managers maintain what they have.

> *Potential is never invisible; it is merely disguised.*

Leaders go out to get something more. They know they have to give something to gain something more.

Shipbuilders will tell you that a vessel is built to take the roughest waters. They are built with the surrounding seas in mind—to be unsinkable in the foulest weather and highest waves. Many churches are not built for the battleground. If we are truly walking with Jesus, then we will partake of all the warfare that He provokes (see Lk. 22:28). We must be ready for the storm that is to come. The anointing of the fivefold ministries is to add layer upon layer to the revelation and release of a warrior bride.

Fivefold Ministries Are Consultant Gifts

It is not my intention to produce anything more than an overview of the role of all the fivefold giftings in these next few pages. To do anything more would completely unbalance the nature and purpose of this book.

I need to be brief and succinct. The premise I want to operate from is this: The fivefold ministries are consultants sent by the Lord not necessarily to *do* the job, but specifically to train and equip the Body of Christ to fulfill God's purposes through grassroots body ministry. So I am going to put their ministry into a pragmatic context of apostolic practice. (I am using the word *apostolic* as an umbrella term to denote the function of all the fivefold ministries operating together in the life of a church.)

Apostolic ministry operates according to the measure of the grace gift given by Christ. Some of the main ingredients of apostolic ministry are for...

- Perfecting and maturing the saints.
- Edifying and building up the Body of Christ.
- Producing saints for the effective work of the ministry.
- Bringing the saints into a unity of the faith.
- Creating knowledge of the Son of God to produce a perfect man.
- Attaining the measure of the stature of Christ's fullness.
- Raising spiritual children to adulthood.

(Key Scriptures in support of this general theme are Ephesians 2:19-22; 4:11-16; Colossians 1:25-29; and Hebrews 6:1-2.)

Apostles

Apostles are father figures who produce quality leaders who, in turn, nurture and strengthen the flock. They are wise master-builders who lay the correct spiritual foundations. They will ensure that the Church is built on the sure foundation of Jesus Christ (see 1 Cor. 3:9-16). The Church is built upon the apostles and prophets relating to Jesus as the Chief Cornerstone.

In bringing change that confirms the new vision and direction the apostle may, where necessary, give input to the restructuring of the leadership. New foundations may need to be re-laid to enable us to overcome the roots of our history. New beginnings are a powerful motivator to a church going through a profound season of change.

There is a dynamic in the corporate life of a church that simply does not exist in one's personal life. We must ensure that our leaders can cope effectively with the corporate stress of a company of people engaged in active service.

It is not the title that people give to themselves that defines who they are; it is the fruit of what they produce. Apostles have a concern for the house of God, particularly in relation to people being fitted and framed together. Relational church is vital.

As the work grows, apostles set in place a leadership that will represent the oversight and that will effectively produce the quality people required for the coming days. They develop the partnerships that are required to run the local church and the wider vision of the corporate Body of Christ in the area. Apostles are Kingdom people concerned with the whole Church in the region, not just their particular network's representative.

Apostles provide the ethos and the atmosphere of the church by the way they relate to leaders and by the way those leaders are trained to relate to the church. Apostles are facilitators

Many churches will not develop apostolic teams or ministries, but it is vital that they have access to that fathering initiative.

enabling good communication and the growing of the vision from the ground up, not the top down. They are sending ministries, releasing others into specific times of building and blessing within the local church. Everyone who is sent in with the next building block is a representative figure of that apostolic character and strategy.

There is a school of thought that says every church has embryonic apostolic potential. I don't believe this.

Prophets

The chief role of a *prophet* is not to prophesy. It is to teach everyone how to hear the voice of God for themselves. "My sheep know My voice," Jesus said (see Jn. 10). We want everyone to be trained effectively in hearing the voice of the Lord and in distinguishing between that, their own opinions, and the disrupting influence of the enemy.

The setting of protocol as a framework for moving in revelatory prophecy in the church is extremely vital. There is a huge difference between the simple inspirational prophecy that exhorts, edifies, and comforts (see 1 Cor. 14:1-5) and the more revelatory words that can carry overtones of new direction, correction, warning, or judgment. The former can be given a fairly free hand because it is highly unlikely anyone will be damaged or upset by inspirational prophecy. At its heart is a desire to bless, encourage, support, and build up the people around us. The worst that may happen is that we get a blessing in an area of our lives that does not exactly need one!

> *Radical churches are built, not just blessed.*

The latter, however, may be incredibly damaging and hurtful if we do not set appropriate guidelines. Revelatory prophecy may lead us across governmental boundaries in church life that are inappropriate and unscriptural. Whatever we hear from the Lord that is of a revelatory nature must be shared with the leadership first. There is a governmental principle at stake. The operation of certain spiritual gifts often requires defined cooperation and relationship with the leadership of the work. Prophets promote such partnerships. They also help to create a framework for ongoing development of prophetic people. We want leaders willing and able to pastor the prophetic, not merely police the ministry.

Ongoing training in the gift, the ministry, and the office of a prophet can be laid down over a period of many years. It takes between 10 and 15 years to make a prophet, depending on his access to a good prophet/teacher who can model and mentor him effectively. Without that key person in place, many people will never make it or will take twice the time.

Finally, a prophet will prophesy and model how the gift should be correctly used. There are too many blessing prophets and not enough of the building type in today's Church. Blessing prophets do a good job in one-off or onetime situations by preaching and ministering prophetically to people. They do not, however, leave a deposit in terms of raising up a local team of prophetic people who can be trained and discipled in the gift and ministry. They do it *for* you rather than teaching you how to do it!

Teachers

Anyone who can stand up and speak with a reasonable degree of motivation, encouragement, and exhortation skills is called a preacher. Anyone who can stand up and speak consecutively on an issue or provide some in-depth explanation from Scripture is called a *teacher*. However, just because we can speak for 60 minutes on the "eschatological significance of the frog in Leviticus" does not make us a teacher. Teachers are builders also. They put flesh, sinew, and muscle onto the bones of our experience of God. They want to build a mature man who by training, modeling, and equipping (all the role of the teacher) can grow up into all things in the Lord. Teachers are a solid part of apostolic strategy in building the church. Scripture has a vital part to play in building an effective church model.

It is always theology before practicality. Most leaders focus on the behavior of people. They look at what they are doing and how they are living in order to try and bring change. This may have some effect in the short term, but eventually people will go back to their old habits or just drive them underground with secrecy.

Teachers want to establish people's lives based on what they believe, not on how they behave. Our behavior is based on what we believe about God, ourselves, or the church. Our lifestyle, how we tackle problems and setbacks, is the by-product of a solid belief system—whether positive or negative.

We need a firm grip on theology before we can experience any success at practical Christianity. Part of the problem is the failure to marry teaching to discipleship and the way that Scripture is used in the church. People base their spiritual growth and maturity on the practical sections of Scripture without internalizing the doctrinal elements. The apostle Paul's letters are in halves: one-half doctrinal and one-half practical.

For example, Romans chapters 1–8, Ephesians chapters 1–3, and Colossians chapters 1–2 reveal what we need to know doctrinally about God, ourselves, sin, and salvation. The central theme is "in Christ." They teach us regarding our position and inheritance in the Lord Jesus. The practical sections of Romans chapters 12–15, Ephesians chapters 4–6, and Colossians chapters 3–4 describe what we need to do to live out our faith in daily experience.

Leaders try to correct people's behavior by jumping to the practical sections of the Bible. We get speakers to come, who may be mainly preachers with a blessing ministry, to minister to the church. We want a "quick fix," or we are looking for something to happen. We want some instructions or an event to use like sticking plaster to cover the cracks and make things better.

We don't have time for theology and thought. We want a practical solution and we want it *now!* But if people do not understand the doctrinal truths regarding our position in Christ and are not taught to enter in and experience them, they will have no grounds for success in the practical arena of life in God. It is actually this attitude that leads churches to abuse prophetic ministry in particular. By not understanding the role of teachers, we also make life harder for the prophets. Churches invite prophets to come to bless, motivate, and encourage the very people who have never learned to stand on the revealed word of God in Scripture.

I have heard many leaders over the years denigrate prophetic ministry. The usual comment is that they were good, the meetings were exciting, but there was little lasting fruit. The other main criticism is that some of the prophetic words never come to pass.

All personal prophecy is conditional. If we obey the Lord and live in the truth of Scripture, then God's word—prophetic or otherwise—will come to pass. The truth will set us free—if we live in it and depend on God. If we do not, if we sin, then the truth cannot set us free.

I have sat in many leaders' groups and heard their horror stories about prophetic ministry. I have acted as a troubleshooter between the prophetic and other ministries. I have campaigned for the prophetic ministry to get its house in order. I have unraveled problems with prophetic people for more than two decades.

I have also sat with prophets and heard their horror stories of being treated like magicians, being put into situations and expected to pull rabbits out of hats. People think that prophets can cure years of bad leadership, abuse of power, lack of vision, and lack of development with a few meetings and some choice prophetic words. I have been to the cross so many times personally over this kind of treatment, I may as well have a house built on Golgotha.

> *Apostolic ministry has three goals in the church... maturity, maturity, and maturity!*

The best way to ensure a person's failure in God would be to make sure that...

- We did not insist on biblical foundations in doctrine and practice.
- We failed to marry training with discipleship.
- We never created opportunities to serve.
- We impose vision and accountability onto people rather than inspire its growth from below.

- We never give loving, effective feedback to people.
- Our leaders are not mentored into becoming fathers and facilitators.
- The majesty and sovereignty of God is not magnified in the hearts of key people (we model what we move in).

I am quite sure that we could all add to the list. An example of doctrine and practicality working together would be the following:

Practical: "Stand firm against the enemy" (see Eph. 6:11). This is a wonderful injunction! But how can we practice this if we do not understand the doctrinal truth of...

Doctrine: "Seated with Christ in heavenly places" (see Eph. 2:6).

Doctrine precedes practice. So the truth of being victoriously raised in Christ precedes power over the enemy. In the violence of spiritual confrontation with an implacable enemy, the assurance of our position in Christ enables us to make a firm stand.

Pastors

Pastors are part of the apostolic strategy to build the church. Taking this ascension gift ministry out of its apostolic context and putting it into local leadership has devalued the role and the gift enormously. Using the term *pastor* out of context has meant in many cases that the other fivefold ministries have been pushed out of local church leadership involvement. This has resulted in an almost exclusively pastoral maintenance emphasis in the lives of church members. We have produced a lopsided, safe church leadership that often lacks a cutting edge and the ability to evangelize effectively. Most of our ministry is spent on the church, producing a dependency culture of introspective and powerless believers who live from week to week. We have spawned an industry within the church that has had a direct impact on evangelism, social action, and church planting.

Pastors are concerned with people development. Firstly, they teach the whole church to care for one another. The Body of Christ must befriend itself and practice the "one anothers" of the

New Testament family. Secondly, pastors help to build a relational body of believers by helping us learn how to handle tension, conflicts, and disputes. Thirdly, their goal is to develop specialist ministries in counseling, marriage guidance, parenting, and family in order to produce a healing, deliverance community. Fourthly, they work with evangelists to survey the region and develop practical goals to help the poor and bring the community into the grace and experience of God.

They are the main initial disciplers working with teachers to implement doctrinal truth into good practice at the foundational level of our walk with God. They enable people to get rid of excess baggage and walk in the light with the Lord Jesus. They help to shepherd people from passivity to an active role in discipleship.

Pastors train and raise up large pastoral teams who are on hand for new believers and soon-to-be Christians. Pastors help to shape people's lives. They are the physical trainers here to get the church into shape. They interact with teachers, evangelists, and prophets to get people ready for advancement in truth, practical ministry, and supernatural anointing.

Fivefold pastors visit churches to help set up, model, and monitor pastoral systems in the local body. They are a consultant traveling ministry that is based and active at home but sent out under apostolic direction to put various building blocks into churches to develop the pastoral initiatives.

Evangelists

The main role of an *evangelist* is to equip the saints to do the work of witnessing and evangelizing. Most people become Christians through one-on-one personal contact. How many of our people have actually been taught the basics of witnessing? Do they know how to spot when someone is interested in the gospel? What are the stages that take a person from initial interest to actual confession of faith? Do our people know how to lead people to Christ? Do they know how to get someone filled with the Holy Spirit?

Conduct an occasional workshop with your main leaders without announcing it. It is a safe bet that if they cannot rise to it properly, then your people may be just as slow and awkward. Do your people understand basic apologetics? Can they give a satisfactory answer to difficult questions? Why does God allow suffering? What is the difference between Christianity and religion? Evangelists are made, not born; though some people may take to it more quickly. Every gift needs to be shaped and developed.

Evangelists will act as consultants to get the whole church on to a more effective and disciplined platform of witnessing and interacting with non-Christians. To be fair, there are lots of ways to gain people's attention for Christ. Some people are good at it relationally; others are better at reasoning with people; some prefer using good works and practical help; whilst others may be more at home praying with people and moving in the supernatural.

> *The role of church is King and Kingdom.*

This last expression fits my own temperament and lifestyle with all the traveling I do each year. My intercession team prays about people I may meet on planes, in airports, at hotels, or on the road as I travel. I often have God-encounters initiated by a word of knowledge, some prophetic insight, or simply seeing a situation requiring prayer combined with power. I readily admit that I would not be any good at reasoning with apologetics, nor could I come up with a standard way of presenting the gospel. I know that I can introduce people to Jesus at their point of need. The supernatural way fits me best. Evangelists help people to discover their most effective way of communicating the Lord Jesus.

Evangelists also help churches understand their community and its demographic spread. They enable churches to infiltrate the community at the most relevant point. There are many different types of evangelists. I have seen children evangelists who are outstanding at creating children's church—likewise with evangelists for youth churches. There are street evangelists, signs and wonders people, and ministries who are excellent at presentational-style events using music and drama.

Evangelists produce a breakthrough anointing by developing people and teams. Besides teaching everyone basic witnessing— how to give your testimony, spot the signs of interest, and lead someone to Christ—they also help to identify and fast-track for development and discipleship those people with a stronger, sharper evangelistic anointing and call.

Continuous activity over the same ground will produce a harvest. Some churches plow only once a year or even less. It requires a regular, consistent, and ongoing thrust into the community to achieve a breakthrough. The moment we limit the breakthrough to the timetable of a mission or event, we lose our objectivity in spiritual warfare and prayer over a defined geographic location. I believe in reaping events as part of a deliberate and continuous strategy within the community. It has been said that some people need to hear the gospel seven times before it penetrates to a place of response. The first few times may result in a negative response. Continuity breaks down the walls of objection and culture.

I sincerely doubt the efficacy of planning a reaping event when we have not plowed up the ground, sowed seed, watered and nurtured it for a season, and built relational bridges into the community. Continuous mission will result in two things. Firstly, people will respond to Jesus when they see us at work with honest endeavor and integrity. Secondly, it produces a large church fringe of potential Christians who are known to us. This group will enable us to change our practice and strategy as the Lord makes Himself known to them. Evangelistic strategy should at least be partially shaped by the potential response of "not-yet believers." What is the best way for them to enter the Kingdom?

Evangelists work with pastors and teachers in the integrating of new believers into the church. They are not an import simply doing a job for us. They are a consultant, a breakthrough ministry to help us plan, strategize, train, and equip the church to break into the world and rescue people from hell. In the course of their involvement with us, they will inevitably preach the gospel, pray for the sick, and be a catalyst for the Holy Spirit to move in power both from the platform and in the team of people they have raised up in the local church.

By not understanding the broader role of these ministries, we have created a professional anointed ministry emphasis in key people that not only has elevated them to a place of unrealistic pressure and performance, but also has relegated the main body of the church to sterile inactivity. These ministries then come under a system of abuse because of the pressure to perform and get results.

Playing the numbers game at evangelistic meetings is a fairly typical example of the peer pressure. We are looking for how many people were present and how many first-time responses to the gospel were realized. At times of extreme pressure these numbers can be very "evang-elastic!"

When is a person saved? Is it when he makes a decision at an event? When she puts her hand up in a meeting? When he fills out a card afterwards or when she has a general prayer and chat after the meeting? Or is it when, on a one-to-one basis with someone, the person repents of specific sin, receives Christ, and progressively decides to lead an unselfish life. Pastoral people act in support as new believers immediately begin the process of removing excess baggage from their life prior to baptism in water. I have found that if we can get new believers through a serious phase of confession and specific prayer before baptism, then their spiritual experience of the baptism becomes incredibly profound. The "new man in Christ" anointing that occurs at baptism is especially strong when we have teachers and pastoral people combining at this foundational stage. Salvation, of course, is progressive as we respond to the work of the Holy Spirit and "put on" Christ.

By not effectively releasing evangelists, pastors, and teachers in their equipping and discipling role, we have thrust them into a performance- and results-oriented presentation that has robbed the church of ongoing mature development. This has produced people with no thirst for depth, no long-term commitment to their own development, and no faith beyond feelings. We have created a church that is introspective with no sense of mission to a hurting world.

The thought of denying self and being equipped to touch the lives of others is like quantum physics to some people. If we have never felt the sting of repentance, we have never experienced true resurrection.

The poor preaching of the gospel coupled with no basic doctrinal foundations have resulted in many people being born into the Kingdom in a premature manner. If our preaching has been that Jesus will solve all your problems and give you a life of joy; if it has been that God wants you to have it all now, don't let satan rob you of your blessing; then what results is a needs-oriented gospel where people are passive—not active—in demonstrating their faith. People are born into a wrong perception of God and the Christian life. Then they are handed over to leaders for them to deal with the lives that have not really been handed over to Christ!

We have allowed a superficial mass production of people to come into the church where we are not adequately equipped to deal with the problems that keep arising. We produce a mutant breed of genetically engineered believers with a weird theology that is counterproductive to the work and practice of the Holy Spirit. It can take years to overcome this in most people. The real gospel is not "come to Jesus and get your needs met." Rather it is "Jesus Christ is Lord—what are you going to do about it?" Of course, as we live and walk out our salvation, we do get our needs met as we learn to give and sow into the lives of others.

> *The seeds of revival are sown in how we live for God on a daily basis.*

The basic early Church teaching was this:

- You have been snatched from eternal damnation to show forth the praise of Him who called you out of darkness.
- Live modestly, be vigilant, and be ready always to give an answer for the hope that is in you.
- Be in prayer and don't neglect true fellowship.
- Be soldiers, act like men, be strong in the Lord.
- Make disciples!
- Make Jesus Lord of everything.
- Give no place to the devil; fight the good fight of faith.

- Your body belongs to Jesus, so be a living sacrifice.
- Be servants of the Lord, for it is only reasonable.
- Crucify the works of the flesh.
- Being baptized in the Spirit enables you to be a witness and fulfill the Great Commission.

Apostles send out evangelists, pastors, teachers, and prophets to provide building blocks to train and equip the Body of Christ. They are consultant ministries to enable the development of leaders, key people, and church members with an anointed lifestyle. They stand in the gap between where the church is now and where it needs to be, assisting people into new levels of strategic growth, anointing, and spiritual power.

They facilitate the growth and development of the church in ministry and mission. They train people for the battlefield. They magnify Jesus to the Church and the world at large. They live by example, modeling all that God has bestowed on them in ways that are revelatory, faith-filled, and full of integrity.

What Causes Barrenness in Church Life?

When we talk about putting down roots or laying foundations, we often think of staying put in one place. Our God is not a camper. The tent of meeting in the Old Testament was a simple structure designed to be easily erected and dismantled as His people followed the cloud of His presence.

The more formal structure of the temple was designed to enable people to come to grips with the same phenomena. The presence of God was enshrined in mystery within the Holy of Holies. People waited with bated breath for the reemergence of the High Priest on the Day of Atonement. The smell and spectacle of the sacrifices added to the drama of coming into the very presence of God. People were brought to that place of awe-inspiring worship as they became involved with the ongoing pageantry of the manifest presence of God in their midst.

The supernatural was commonplace. Men and women both spoke with sharpness and clarity in their representation of God. Words were backed up with power and anointing that saved lives and brought deliverance from occult powers, famines, disasters, and human oppression.

This essence of pure relationship and raw power between God and His people has been the dominating theme of the Scriptures. Only the form and style have changed throughout the generations—from a handmade stone altar roughly put together with materials on hand by individual men such as Abraham, Jacob, and the prophets, to the designer places of worship expressed in the tabernacle and temple.

At times these places of worship were inspired by a revelation of God's grace, mercy, and calling, such as when Jacob-in-transition-to-Israel finally came to understand the desire that God had for relationship with him. In other times and places, altars were built upon the sites of intense spiritual warfare and upon battlefields as sacrifices were offered to God on the burning embers of false gods and idol worship. Mount Carmel and Gideon's hometown became places of cleansing and purification as the enemy was driven out and the name of the Lord revealed.

Continuity from the Old Covenant to the New was established in the person of Jesus, who became the temple of God wandering amongst a guilty and sin-ridden people. "Destroy this temple and God will raise it up in three days," He said, referring to Himself (see Jn. 2:19). Something had happened in the hearts of the people betweentimes. A creeping institutionalism had given way to form without power, to style without substance, and to a performance mentality that elevated men, not God, in the presence of the people. People did things to be seen of others; rules of behavior governed the lives of many. Leaders had become blind guides, searching the Scriptures without prophetic insight. Those who most desired the coming of the Messiah missed Him because their interpretation of Scripture was not mingled with worship, the manifest presence of God, and prophetic wisdom.

God walked among them, but they had not been trained to recognize His presence. All their teaching and distilled wisdom down through the years had left them without the faculty for discerning the glory of God. Even when they saw signs and wonders and Jesus graciously asked them to believe in those signs as part of their journey to a wider, deeper revelation of God's presence, they could not bring themselves to part from their institutional mind-sets.

So the early Church grew up next to a hidebound institution that continued thinking that it alone held the glorious tradition of the truth of God. The old persecuted the new, which in turn eventually came against the newer works, which in time grew to be the oppressors of new moves of God till the present day. The chronicles of the Church are littered with stories of new moves of God erupting in the earth through orthodox persecution and then settling back into conventional, narrow-minded religiosity.

> *The mystery and the majesty of God are not optional extras but the very proof of our life in Him.*

Only the presence of God can prevent institutional Christianity from reducing truth to a set of rules and worship or to a meaningless time of singing without awe. Only God's presence can enable believers to confront the enemy and the evils of mankind with a powerful expression of truth combined with supernatural power. Only God's presence is the glue that holds us all together through tensions, conflicts, and the violence of being on the front line of the battle against a depraved and intimidating foe.

We have lost the glory, the majesty, and the mystery of all that God is within Himself. The temple gave way to the synagogue and the mystery began to fade. Word stopped leading us to worship, and in time the dynamic revelation of God became a rote to live by as we waited for God to come in final deliverance. Today's worship precedes the Word and in many places has become the platform for the teaching and the ministry of people. Our churches have lost the art of ministering to the Lord in worship and discerning the voice of the Lord in our midst (see Acts 13:1-2).

People went to the temple to participate in the mystery and the majesty of God. They went for three main reasons: to worship, to make an offering, and to pray. In the synagogue they went to hear the word of God (i.e., for teaching), to get their needs met, and to have fellowship. In the temple, the instruction and communication of God's word always led them into an experience *with* God. In the synagogue, it often led them into debate and discussion *about* God. Meetings became man-centered instead of revolving around the presence of God. Even today in many of the newer churches, if the meeting has a lot of content and activity, it is often the worship that gets squeezed. People go to church for good teaching or fellowship. Our society has created intense loneliness, and people are hungry for companionship. Accordingly, it is easy to justify making our meetings into a designer-style atmosphere to attract people.

I am not against this in principle. I think all our meetings should be aimed specifically at God's desire to do particular things and achieve specific objectives. I am against stereotypes that do not bring us into the creative presence of God. We must regain the capacity to live in the manifest presence of God. The teaching of the Word must lead people into an encounter of God Himself, not just into an experience of the church.

God has always set people within the framework of tabernacle, temple, and church who would act as catalysts to cause breakthrough into the manifest presence of the Lord. When people look at us, they should see Jesus. They should observe His love in the way that we live together. The entrance of God's Word should produce hope, faith, life, and health to every part of our being. The presence of God is life to us. When we lose His presence or, even worse, if we have never grown up with the reality of His glory, it is inevitable that we would use the Word to relegate the supernatural to a future time of glory in Heaven rather than glory now.

God sits outside of time. He has never not been full of glory. He is altogether glorious. Everything He touches carries the fragrance and the passion of His manifest presence. He is wonderful, awe-inspiring, and magnificent. Our meetings must reflect the glory of His unchanging nature. I love to meditate on the nature and character of the Lord. For me, He has come to be the kindest person I have ever known. He is kindhearted, gracious, loving, good-natured, and benevolent. He is generous, cordial, approachable, and thoughtful. He is slow to anger and swift to bless. He sees the good, acknowledging the treasure and the worth in people. He inspires confidence, renews our self-worth, and puts a smile on our hearts. He is captivating, beautiful, and completely lovely. He is strong, powerful, a force to be reckoned with, a conqueror and overcomer. He is a paradox—a fierce and mighty warrior dressed as a lamb; the king of glory and a bruised reed; a son, a servant, a prophet, a priest, and a king. The fear of Him is the beginning of wisdom, yet His laughter makes us wriggle with pleasure. He continually brings us to points of vulnerability and weakness so that His sheer joy in Himself can be our source of strength.

Our meetings very often do not reflect His nature, but ours. They focus on our needs instead of celebrating who He is in our midst. How many of our people take time out during the day to spend just a few minutes in silent worship and awe of God? Whatever God is, He is—infinitely. It is impossible for God not to be everlasting, endless, and eternal. He is the greatest endless and eternal expression of goodness, kindness, and grace. He is everlastingly kind and merciful, eternally loving. He loves infinitely and without boundaries. There is no end to the kindness of God.

He is also totally perfect. He never does anything partway. He completes everything He starts. "He who has begun a good work in you will complete it [literally, perfect it] until the day of Jesus Christ" (Phil. 1:6). He does everything perfectly. He is infinitely good and perfectly good. He has perfect love and grace. His love is complete, wholesome, and endlessly perfect! He is always loving because He is infinite and perfect.

He is immutable. He never changes. What God was, God is and God will be. There is no shadow of turning within Him. He is unchanging. What a relief! We all have experienced the fluctuating fortunes of human relationships and been both blessed and burned. I love the ongoing continuity of God's affection for me. He put me in the one place where I could relate to Him in all of my changeableness. He put me into Christ so that His unchanging, infinite, and perfect love could become a constant to me as I grew up in Him.

He is never indifferent. His silence is just His silence. Never mistake His silence for detachment. He is never aloof and unresponsive. His silence is often a means to draw us into meditation, which becomes the prelude to worship and the entrance of revelation that then brings change to us. What changes us the most is the unchangeableness of God! Whenever I reflect on the unchangeable nature of God, I want to cry. His constancy and dependability always make me resolve to be like Him.

He brings peace to me by His constancy. I feel my heart settling down into Him in the turbulence of situations and events. In crises and conflicts I find myself wanting harmony and love rather than just resolution. To agree to disagree and remain loving friends is a sure sign that God is among us and that we are in love with Him.

> *Our spiritual house is built on the rock of what God is really like!*

God is endlessly enthusiastic about people. He has a boundless, unremitting energy. He never stops working, yet He exudes rest and peace. He rests in and through His work. I am never quite sure where my rest in Him gives way to His rest in me. (Oh, I love Him.) On the seventh day He rested from creating, but He never ceased from maintaining what He had made.

It is typical of God that man's first day of creation and life should coincide with God's rest. Our first day began with rest, and a prime part of our relationship with God is to enter His rest. One of my personal goals is to be one of the most restful, peaceful people on the planet. Since I have discovered rest as a major part of my relationship with the Lord, my output has increased significantly. Rest maintains worship, adoration, and focus. It promotes a God-consciousness by the Holy Spirit that increases productivity without detracting from fellowship. The more we rest, the more we get done. Time spent resting brings us into a place where God can do in seconds what we could not do in hours under the anointing.

The more we rest, the greater the power to break through. The greater the rest, the more God prepares things around us by His hand. His wisdom increases as we sit and relax in His presence.

I once was sent a complicated brief on certain conflicts and situations in a particular church. This was followed up by a meeting with the leaders where I was expected to give some kind of godly perspective and Solomon-like wisdom. I never read their pages of problems. For some reason I spent several days resting and meditating though that and other work were piling up. On the day of the meeting, I discovered that they were coming to visit only when I looked in my diary. (I am not normally like this—we run a very efficient office, though that is due more to Carole, my personal assistant, than myself.)

In the meeting with these guys it was clear there was a significant measure of conflict and tension. We can communicate peace only if we have it. I cannot remember what was said in that meeting—only that peace, love, and understanding broke out amongst the brothers. Harmony precedes resolution. I remember saying to the Lord afterwards that I wished I had taped the meeting because some of the things I said were brilliant! He smiled. He knew that I knew that the wisdom was His and that I was content just to be a vessel and vehicle for His presence.

He loves with a boundless consuming love. He hates with a terrible consuming fire. The anger of the Lord burns against unrighteousness and sinful activity. The mercy of the Lord in including us in Christ is eternally breathtaking and wonderful. To rest in the finished work of Calvary is a wonderful privilege. Lack of the presence of God is a major cause of barrenness.

Subverted by Our Strengths

Any strength taken to excess becomes a weakness. During World War II, Singapore was a very powerful military base. With a seemingly impenetrable jungle behind it, all its armaments were concentrated seaward. It was an incredibly difficult base to take for those two prime reasons. The city, however, was actually conquered by the Japanese, who cut single-track pathways through the jungle. Singapore was overrun by Japanese on bicycles! Its main strength— an impenetrable jungle—became its greatest weakness because no one mounted a thorough guard on that part of their defenses.

Similarly, one of the greatest strengths of our evangelical tradition has been our adherence to the Bible as the ultimate authority in terms of faith and practice. We believe the Scriptures are the inspired word of God regarding the person of Jesus Christ, salvation, and vital doctrines of truth. Evangelical Christians have done a superb job over many years in holding the line on biblical doctrine against rising levels of liberalism and erroneous teaching.

Schools of theology and Bible colleges sprang up as part of this battle for truth. Many churches began to look to these places to produce leaders who were excellent scholars and good teachers. A strong insistence and emphasis on studying Scripture and communicating its truth began to grow in the churches, which was a wonderful antidote to the wishy-washy, spurious teaching of those particular days. This has now become the normal practice and experience of many evangelical churches.

The ongoing training of people to do this has become a primary goal. People entering those places have then been sent out to pastorates to teach other people what they have spent years studying. On the surface this sounds great. However, it has led to a classroom situation in our meetings where church members have become the students and the leaders are the professors.

Churches have become almost mini-seminaries, many having several teaching sessions each week. Where there is no outlet for truth, decay sets in. We become expert listeners, but if our hearing does not progress to the point of our doing, then we are deceived. Deception does not have to be rooted in dishonesty or obvious sinfulness carefully coated with a veneer of respectability. Teaching that is not rooted in discipleship has no place to be birthed in the lives of people.

The whole point of leadership and ministry is to produce a body of people capable of doing the work. What we have produced from our colleges and schools is a leadership that does everything. Errancy occurs when truth and practice are not combined. Many church meetings are designed to carry out the objectives that the students lived under in Bible college conditions.

Preaching well-prepared sermons has now become the goal rather than producing disciples to do the work of the ministry.

> *The Truth is a person. Discipleship is interaction with Jesus by experience.*

Our rich, undiluted love for Scripture and communicating truth has caused some churches to neglect other significant aspects of life in the Kingdom. Body ministry is a fundamental biblical principle that is largely ignored in many places. If all we are is pew fodder for the teaching and preaching of a small number of "qualified" people, we are never going to grow up into all things in God. The questions that leaders must ask are "What?" and "Why?" "What are we doing, and why are we doing it? Does our church structure, culture, and model lend itself to drawing people into a deeper experience of God, the practice of truth, and into pathways of service and supernatural expression?" A key question concerns the development of worship and love for God. "Are we giving enough place to the scriptural and practical outworking involved in creating new expressions of adoration, devotion, and worship?" Worship must grow through ongoing development of devotion. "Do we actually train people how to worship in song, dance, and creative expression? Do we have devotional courses that develop people in their personal quiet times with God? Does our church know the difference between personal worship where we all sing together, and corporate worship where we deliberately enter into a communal and focused activity in order to minister to God?"

We are not good at balancing truth with experience and practice. We have emphasized correct doctrine and an understanding of Scripture but have neglected the importance of experience in the development of mature believers. Biblical orthodoxy has become a barren wilderness of organized religiosity. We defend the truth to the death, which is very admirable, but we do not live it out to the full. Our greatest strength has become our most telling weakness. Without experience our relationship with God has nowhere to go. It is like knowing everything about romantic loving relationships but never getting married. All your knowledge is merely study notes in a book. The experience of the relationship enables us to write the truth on the tables of our heart, which is a poetic way of referring to experience.

At Times God Is Deliberately Vague

I am always intrigued by what God does not say as well as by what He conveys in our lives. As humans we like structure, organization, form, and substance. We want detailed information because we like to know what God is doing and where He is taking us. Abraham, though, had to go out not knowing where He was going (see Heb. 11:8). Sometimes God does not give us detailed vision because He wants us to walk by faith. He will give us broad parameters rather than specific objectives. Vision is something we see in part and know in part, just like prophecy. God gives us enough to broadly see the next step or couple of stages but no more. When we fulfill those goals, we receive more insight and direction.

God is vague about meetings. He really says only two things. One of them is "not forsaking the assembling of ourselves together, as is the manner of some" (Heb. 10:25a). The second injunction just talks about creativity: "Whenever you come together, each of you has a psalm, has a teaching, has a tongue, has a revelation, has an interpretation" (1 Cor. 14:26; see also verses 27-33). This passage does not give detailed information on how to run meetings. If it did, most church meetings would be unbiblical! It talks about possibilities and what may happen if...! Interestingly, it is all concerned with supernatural utterance, which probably does not apply to a lot of churches. Does the lack of supernatural utterance in our churches make us unbiblical? It's just a question.

This passage does not speak of form or structure. There is no detail regarding when to sing, teach, pray, or otherwise. It only speaks of creativity and degrees of spontaneity arising out of our relationship with the Holy Spirit. I am *not* saying that every meeting must be open, creative, and totally spontaneous. There is a place for a more ordered meeting style—but only to fulfill specific objectives. I *am* saying that every meeting cannot be the same. By trying to fit people into a stereotypical meeting, we are not putting

God or them first. Meetings should be designed around objectives. If our objective is to teach people how to worship God corporately, then let us act appropriately.

Let us move the chairs aside (if we can!) and allow freedom of movement and expression in a workshop atmosphere. If our objective is training, let us have a seminar-type session in whatever style is appropriate for interactive learning. If our intention is to enable members to contribute openly what they feel the Holy Spirit is saying, then we need to set our stall out accordingly.

Most Sunday services are boringly familiar. In some places the order of service is made known before the meeting, rather like McDonalds or Burger King. Perhaps the only real difference between some churches and McDonalds is the fact that a fast food place is cheaper, the atmosphere is better, we are in and out in no time, and we've probably been better fed! Stereotypical services produce stereotypical believers. God is endlessly creative. His nature is a challenge to any one-dimensional state. The God who makes every snowflake different, who created millions of varieties of species, who controls climatic atmospheres and huge bodies in space, cannot be expressed through a stereotype. Who are the meetings for? If they are for God, then let us structure them as He wills, bearing in mind His creative nature. If they are for people, then let us form the meeting to suit the objective we have in mind.

If we arrange our meetings in a set formula because we have always done it that way, then we have missed the point entirely and become unbiblical in the process. If the stereotype is simply our best way to administrate people, time availability, and resources, then we need to drastically rethink what church is really all about.

God is vague about the operation of church at times, wanting us to learn sensitivity as we are led by the Spirit. The Scriptures often speak about task, operation, and purpose without specifying shape, patterns, or models. The reason for this is that the form we are working in will constantly change, whereas the task and operation may remain quite constant. The form is the wineskin that needs to be constantly oiled on the outside to retain its supple shape so that new wine will not crack it open. Similarly, the form and shape of the church need to be constantly adjusted to keep pace with the ongoing nature of the work of God.

Human beings will always set things in concrete for the sake of continuity, safety, and security. That is very laudable, but it actually works against us. Our security is only in God and one another. Security comes from relationships of grace and love, not from organizational structure. If our structure is set in concrete, it will have to be overthrown if God

> *Any form that inhibits growth must change.*

is to continue with us in power and purpose. It is so unfortunate that the Lord has to set in motion a whole series of events just to break into our structures! People misconstrue this as warfare and resist it, which often leads to church splits. It is never the Holy Spirit who splits the church. It is usually the wineskin that has become dry and cracked and cannot handle the new thing that God wants to introduce. We try our hand at compromise, which is like patching an old garment with new cloth—it will not work!

When our safety and security in the form of what we have produced is threatened, many people resist the change that God wants to bring. Even when the Bible does define a model or a pattern, the language it uses is not too descriptive. The model will be limited in terms of long-term identity. Models do not last for years; they change constantly. The changes may be subtle in order to take into account what is happening with people. Our goal is to make people change, to transform them into the image of Jesus. For that change to become complete, we must alter the model and form we build around them. As the people change, the wineskin must change. If people change but the form and structure of the church remains stagnant, we will be in serious trouble with the Holy Spirit. Leaders who do not change can only be replaced. The apostle Paul remarked that people should follow him inasmuch as he was following Christ.

God is vague about patterns, models, operation of church, and form and structure because He knows that the culture of different nations would make it impossible for a one-dimensional Church to exist. Clearly we cannot expect believers in atheist or anti-Christian countries to build a church the way we have in the western nations. They would be imprisoned and murdered for their faith as they are currently in many countries. Christians are forbidden to meet publicly in many nations. Does that make them unbiblical?

The Bible is vague about form and structure because the chief principle we are working to is one of being led by the Spirit. Churches will change as people respond to the Lord and grow into levels of maturity. Cultural restrictions also play a big part in the changing nature of church. Whether that culture is caused by different national characteristics or simply by the difference between youth and elderly; street people and upper middle class society; the intelligentsia or the illiterate—all will have a bearing on how we operate as a church.

I once spoke at a church in the north of England, which was affectionately known as the "cartoon church." Most of its members were unable to read and had poor educational experiences. They could relate well to a simple and profound message, the main points of which were illustrated in cartoon form and put on the overhead projector. These people were not unintelligent; their capacity to understand truth merely had to be expressed through a different form. I enjoyed it.

One of the biggest problems we have in building church is changing the stereotype that certain companies of people have produced. If we are wedded more to our structure than we are to the Lord, then we have made an idol of what we have produced. It will have to come down, for God will be against it. Anything that prevents God from moving amongst His people will be overthrown by the Holy Spirit. This happens when God demonstrates through willing people all that He wants to do and be to His bride. Sadly, these people are labeled disruptive, unteachable, and rebellious. To be fair, some of them may not have been able to contain their frustration, but that does not make them rebels.

Beware! Apostolic Ministries Can Bite!

The fivefold ministries of apostle, prophet, pastor, teacher, and evangelist will understand the pressures of growth, creativity, the development of maturity, and the production of anointed people who can fight. Each in his own way will contribute to the building of the prototype of a new church that needs to live on the battlefield. Each of them has a cutting edge that is designed to be attacking, stimulating, and provocative. Apostles are against mediocrity in any form. They will attack false ministries, false motives, and false lifestyles. Paul continually campaigned for moral purity, relational harmony, and doctrinal clarity. He attacked and opposed people who defied God in those areas.

Prophets attack injustice, unethical behavior, oppressive regimes, and stereotypical barriers to what the Lord wants to do. They are a stimulus to holiness of life and loving relationships. They provoke the Church to hear the "now" word of God and make all necessary adjustments. Teachers are given to stimulate the marriage of truth with discipleship and knowledge with experience. They attack ignorance and unbelief. They know that whenever the real truth is taught, it will cause a crisis. Anyone who is not living a life compatible with Scripture will come into conflict with the Holy Spirit. Teachers know that Spirit-induced crisis must lead to the process and development of mature response through repentance and obedience. That is why all truth must be followed up. If it is not, then condemnation will result because the enemy will fill the vacuum if no repentant response occurs.

Pastors will be a part of this process of change, working with teachers to produce a positive belief system that can terminally change our behavior. Pastors practice the art of loving confrontation as they deal with tensions, conflicts, acts of rebellion, and people's historical baggage. Evangelists have to stand against worldly value systems and spurious philosophies as they engage a sin-sick world with the gospel. The message of the gospel is contentious, controversial, and confrontational—one permeated with the revelation of the goodness, kindness, and mercy of a loving God who paid the price for us to enter His presence for all eternity.

> *Consultant ministries agitate for change and provoke us into new experiences with the Lord.*

How to Use This Book

I want this to be some kind of handy recall tool to aid our thinking. It is not a reference book; it is not good enough for that, and I am too limited a man to produce such a work. Rather, it is a prompt to make us think harder about what we are doing in relation to church and the ministry. The various chapters relate to specific ideas and concepts that will require some thought and corporate deliberation. There will be some ideas to get us moving and to help us build. My main hope is that we will all meet Jesus in this book; that we will encounter the happiness of God as well as understand His thoughts, His heart, and His way of doing things. I hope that we may understand process and the crisis that often precedes it.

In Chapter 2, "God Is Doing a New Thing," I want us to understand the dream that God has about the Church and why the Church is going through a profound change. The Church needs to put the right face of Jesus on the Body of Christ. Does God share our theology, or do we need a new paradigm? The conclusions we come to about our own work will be critical to our development and future.

In Chapter 3, "Conditions for Revival," we need to examine the principles of how revival starts. God is more concerned with habitation than visitation. Transformation comes by divine interruption, and God is clearly interfering with His Church. God will inhabit only what is compatible with His purpose. We need to understand the process of renewal, revival, and reformation.

With Chapter 4, "Understanding Church," we do need to understand that we can only be as strong as our concept of God. Only the corporate man of the Church can rise up to police the heavens. This chapter is concerned with the paradox of Church. It is a building and a body. At the same time, it is both rigid and fluid, unmoving yet constantly moving, inflexible yet totally flexible. Understanding these dynamics will prevent legitimate tensions from becoming unworkable friction.

Chapter 5, "Revitalizing Your Church," is concerned with identifying the internal catalysts within the work and developing key people. It takes a critical look at pioneering people, support personnel, and ways to release them into greater productivity. It also looks at the resistors in the Church who slow down our progress. It examines the vital role in leadership to turn all our people into productive individuals.

Chapter 6, "Implementing Change," examines the criteria for reforming people and situations that have gone stale. It looks at the process of changing mind-sets and details some of the ups and downs of the practice of bringing change. It will help us to understand the attitudes and fears of people resistant to transformation.

Chapter 7, "Building a Prototype Church," asks the relevant questions about Church and Kingdom. Is the structure of our church or network hindering a new Kingdom anointing from being birthed? It will enable us to recognize our time of visitation, change our mind-set and approach, and walk by faith in the new thing that God is doing.

Chapters 8 and 9, "The Process of Transition, Parts 1 and 2," relate to the means and the method that the Lord uses in bringing lasting change and birthing new things. In transition, the Lord gives us a road map to faith. This chapter details the journey of closure, conversion, and new commissioning. It will help us understand where we are and where we are going in the process of Church transformation.

Finally, Chapters 10 and 11, "Character and Transition, Parts 1 and 2," are concerned with understanding the mind of the Lord in change and transformation. They will provide us with a revelatory rationale for all that is happening. There is a pattern that God uses to bring order out of chaos. If your church is going in the opposite direction to your vision, or to prophetic words spoken over the corporate body, it is for a specific reason. This chapter details that reason in full and will provide you with enough revelation and information to halt the slide and begin to move forward with purpose and direction.

This book is about process more than anything. Hopefully it will help you to understand how God thinks and moves. My prayer is that it will be a word in season to you, no matter what type of church you are in, what culture you work in, or where you live.

Chapter 2

God Is Doing a New Thing

*T*hese days more than ever we need to pray for a depth of understanding regarding the purposes of God. We need the cobwebs of our mind swept away by the Spirit of God. The Church must be realigned with God's present purpose and break out of the things that have made us irrelevant in this day and time. We are in transition now whether we like it or not—indeed, we are in a process of change whether we want it or want to avoid it!

All change begins in the heart of God and makes its presence felt in our lives by His hand. There are times and seasons when God intervenes sovereignly in humanity to bring an end to one thing and a beginning to another.

> *Behold, the former things have come to pass, and new things I declare; before they spring forth I tell you of them* (Isaiah 42:9).

> *Do not remember the former things, nor consider the things of old. Behold, I will do a new thing, now it shall spring forth; shall you not know it? I will even make a road in the wilderness and rivers in the desert* (Isaiah 43:18-19).

One of the characteristics of an outstanding leader is to know when change is imminent, to know the proclamations and declarations of the Spirit with regard to new times and fresh seasons.

Happy is the church that has such an understanding of the ways of the Lord!

God has a dream about Church, and Jesus birthed that dream in the hearts of men. People under the influence of the Holy Spirit wrote concerning the dream in all its many forms. The Holy Spirit is given as our tutor and comes alongside as a friend to impart the dream and make it live within us.

What is this dream? It is that God would have a dwelling place amongst us...that the people, who make up the Church, would see themselves as living stones and allow themselves to be fitted and framed together in relationship and ministry...that God would inhabit our friendships to such a remarkable extent that His manifest presence would break out amongst all people groups everywhere.

Instead, we observe a Church corpulent with truth but impractical in revelation. We see an organization claiming biblical structure but manifesting a hierarchical world system of government. Leaders are bent on titles, status, and position; ignoring servanthood, sacrifice, example, and stewardship. We have churches where we enjoy worship but have not learned corporately how to minister to the Lord...assemblies where we exalt the power of God but do little to attract His presence. All around us are camps where we revere what God has said but have no clue as to what He is saying today. God used to speak, but since He has written a book, He lost His voice. In order to receive everything they need, some people have turned faith into an object of desire in itself.

> *God has a dream about Church.*

To some, spiritual warfare is a myth, a work of fiction. To others, the focus on the demonic and the power of satan has relegated the majesty of Jesus to a place of seeming inconsequence. Of course, the other side of this coin is quite different. Millions of people have faithfully stood their ground against dark opposition. Hundreds of thousands are being born again weekly throughout the earth. Countless numbers of churches have been renewed into a fresh awakening of God's love, mercy, and joy. There are profuse signs in every nation of the desire of God to break out in a fresh way to all people.

Here we have the paradox of the modern-day Church. (A paradox is the tension between two extremes.) The Church is a contradiction that can no longer be tolerated by Almighty God. We are being caught up into a new dimension of Kingdom activity that will jar us out of our complacency.

The universal Church is in a state of profound change. There is a shaking taking place as God moves through His Body. New alignments are taking place, new relationships are forming, and current friendships are re-forming in a higher spiritual dimension and purpose. There is an ongoing tactical shake-up taking place as God's new strategy for worldwide harvest comes off the drawing board and into our hearts for these last days. It is clear that the Lord is doing a new thing: He is presenting the Church with more new wineskins. The cutting edge of the Church has been moved forward into a new dimension where even the most forward-thinking and progressive churches will need to rethink their strategies for this new season of Holy Spirit activity.

Whatever we think we know, understand, and have experienced about church has probably not prepared us for all that God will be doing in this next phase. He is doing a new thing! We must therefore position ourselves where we can hear and bear all that the Lord wants to make known. Even Jesus said to His disciples at one point, "I still have many things to say to you, but you cannot bear them now" (Jn. 16:12).

Revelation is not just centered on our ability to hear the Lord properly and receive progressive truth. It is also about our capacity to carry that truth and to be built into the new thing the Lord is creating. Revelation challenges our capacity to become what God is making. It is about bearing the weight of new responsibility, fresh anointing, and significant change. A prototype church must bear the weight of new revelation, new expectations, and new opposition if it is to become the prophetic model to fulfill God's end-time purpose.

To create this model, God has to speak "deep unto deep" in our spirit. This is not just about receiving some tactical information or prophetic insight into the next phase of church growth or ministry. It is about being instead of doing. It is not about the work of the ministry; it is about the image of Christ. We have gone as far as we can go regarding revelation about the work of the church, strategies for reaching the harvest, and the development of gifts and personnel. We have hit the ceiling of revelatory insight and cannot press through without a radical change of heart.

The weight of revelation and Holy Spirit formation for this next phase will fall only on humble hearts who have a passion for Jesus Himself. We are poised to enter a whole new spiritual dimension, a climate so thick with the presence of God that it will affect our ability to stand, let alone walk. We must bear a new imprint of the likeness of Christ. Jesus came to put a face on God. He said, "He who has seen Me has seen the Father" (Jn. 14:9)! The Church is here to put a face on Christ. Renewal has given the Church something of a makeover in our spiritual personality. God is intent on giving us a face-lift to change our image.

In recent times, we have measured our success in church by numbers, budget increases, staff members, overseas missions, and the size and scope of varying projects. The only measure that will be acceptable in the next time frame is how much of the glory of God is contained in our meetings. God is restoring His manifest presence among us.

God Obeys His Own Word

When the Lord says, "new," He means exactly that: new! When He declares an end to one thing and the beginning of a new order, He is deadly serious. To reinforce the concept, He orders His people to not be concerned or even think about the old thing ever again because He wants their attention to be on what He will do next! "I am doing a new thing! Will you not be aware of it?" (see Is. 43:19) Here we have a proclamation and question joined together, signifying intent. "I'm doing this, do you want to see?" The implication is that we must let go of the old in order to even see the new. There has to be a transformation in our thinking.

The Lord has drawn a line in Heaven. On one side are the former things—strategies, programs, ideas, and structures that once worked but are being discarded. They may still be effective, but now they are not required. The biggest danger to a new move of God is the last move that is still working!

God wants to do a new thing. On the other side of the line will come revelation, anointing, and a fresh impetus of the Word and Spirit. His plans are set into a new dimension of activity within Heaven. He has new purpose. His hand is holding out new things to us.

At that precise point, God obeys His own word. He turns His back on the old things and begins to look and speak into the new thing. The three most maligned people groups in the Church—prophetic people, intercessors, and worshipers—will immediately cross that line to stand under the smile of God. They have to be where God is looking at and speaking into. They move their feet in obedience to the heart of God.

Ongoing revelation is positional. We have to move in obedience to the word of God. As we move, we progress into a place where we can hear and understand the next thing that God is communicating. If we fail to move, then our capacity to understand what God is saying and doing is diminished. Staying on the side of the line with the "former" things will put us at a disadvantage in receiving the new things that God is releasing.

> *Jesus came to put a face on God.*

When we stay on the former side, words that come to us from the new side often do not compute with our thinking. Conceptually we can agree that change is needed and even desired. However, if we fail to reposition ourselves before the Lord, we will water down the challenge of the new word to make it compatible with what we have already received in times past. We will own more allegiance to the former thing than commitment to the new process of God.

We need a willingness to move in obedience and a desire to be in the presence of God that is greater than our need for personal or corporate security.

As we know, most problems in churches occur because people will not move, rather than because they do. People crossing the line come into revelation and a new level of anointing to implement truth. People who have stayed in place—which is now on the wrong side of God—cannot understand the new thing. It's like friends telling you a funny story about something that happened, but for it to be funny, you had to be there!

It's the same with progressive truth. You have to be in the place where it fits, where it can be worked out, to understand it. Renewal, when it hit various churches, did not fit in with what they were doing. Many leaders did not understand how to respond. "Where does it fit with what we already have?" was their question.

It didn't fit. It was not supposed to fit. It was given to reengineer the church into a new place in God. The very idea that God should do only what fits with what He has already done is ludicrous. He has seldom worked that way. Much of Jesus' message was prefaced with, "You have heard it said, but now I say to you...." His words brought a change to people's perception of God and His workings.

He warned people in Luke 5:36-39 that new wine needs a new wineskin. It seems fairly amazing that the new wine of renewal should be rejected because it did not mix well with the old form of meetings that we were used to. Of course it meant change. God will not fit in with us. He helps us to adjust to Him.

Is the church for people or is it for God? Of course it is for both, but who has priority? Are the meetings too man-centered, revolving around ministering to people? Do we even know how to corporately minister to the Lord? Has our church become so far removed from God's presence that His glory never falls? Sadly, our current experience of God seems more centered on His *omnipresence* than His *manifest* presence.

Radical Renewal or Business as Usual?

What has happened from the early days of the charismatic movement has continued till the present day in many places. Then as now, new wineskins had to form, many of them through splits of varying kinds.

A new piece of cloth cannot be attached to an old garment without stretching it and causing it to tear. New moves play havoc with old moves unless we trade in what we have for what God wants to give us. Transition is about trading in church, new for old.

Many leaders do not cross the line to be where God is looking and speaking; therefore, their revelation becomes secondhand. Often, people on one side of the line criticize the new thing. We always criticize what we don't understand. They reject it, neglect it, misinterpret it, and criticize it—until they see that it is working.

Then they take hold of a hybrid form; that is, they grab on to something that is a cut-down version that will fit their current model, and they bolt it on to what they already have. Home groups, electronic music equipment, deliverance, the prophetic, contemporary worship, team ministry, youth church—these are merely a few. These all began life in criticism and dire warnings. We bolt new things onto our existing structure of church, but the basic model remains the same.

Our meetings are still the same style—just slightly longer, perhaps. They are just as boring and noncreative, with the same people participating. Many people seek a radical expression of church as an antidote to their current meetings. They push for a radical demonstration but do not achieve anything because the heart of their cry is not locked into a deep-seated dependency upon God Himself.

The pursuit of cultural relevance and trendy ways of exhibiting the gospel will be just as impotent and people-consuming as any other methodology. We want the fullness of God. Only His presence is relevant to every issue. Only He can touch people and bring radical change.

If, through you, God can heal sick bodies, renew people's minds, restore dignity through salvation, deliver people of demons, and present the fullness of His presence, then you are culturally relevant!

We still have this unbiblical void between clergy and laity. Many believers are still treated as pew fodder every week. They are fed one-man ministry, irrelevant sermons, and little supernatural expression, experience, or expectation.

> *Is the church here for people or for the Lord?*

Many Christians do not have a personal vision to serve God, are not being discipled or empowered, and have no idea of where they fit into local church and the wider Kingdom of Heaven.

If we do not move our feet, we can only adapt to the will of God—not be changed by it. Even in the midst of God's moving today, we are trying to maintain business as usual. We talk about brokenness but seldom allow the presence of God to break in. We yearn to be radical but don't recognize the sharpening that comes from a cutting edge move of God.

Radical renewal or business as usual? It seems that both do not always connect together. If our current mind-set does not allow us to experience the will of God, then it is time to change our thinking. Are we really prepared to change our ideas about church? What are those ideas based on and shaped by?

Does God Share Your Theology?

An idea shapes the way we think, forming an ideology. This, in turn, can affect our theology, or what we see and understand in Scripture. Our theology can be made to fit our ideas of how things should be. For example, take the parable of the laborers in Matthew 20:1-16. The landowner, throughout the day, hired laborers to work in his vineyard. He paid them all the same wage, regardless of how many hours they worked. When those who worked all day saw this, they protested. The landowner replied, "I am not doing anything wrong; you agreed to work for this amount. It's my choice to be generous to the others" (see Mt. 20:13-14).

The theology in this parable is this: God has the perfect right to do whatever He wishes with His substance and His people. Because the first laborers did not understand this, they felt insulted and not blessed by the landowner's generosity. Their idea was that those who work harder and longer should receive more remuneration. This is perfectly sound, but on this occasion it does not fit with God's viewpoint or intended practice. Their theology was rooted in their own ideology about what is fair and just. Thus they were unhappy and disturbed by their own perception of how things should work. Jesus' point was that people's understanding of God should conform to who He really is and how He wants to conduct Himself!

An idea of how things should be becomes an ideology when we attempt to surround it with ethics and morality. On top of that ideology we construct a theology. We try to connect a number of Scriptures to how we feel about things. In this way the Scriptures become a proof text for what we feel ought to be the truth.

Often this is not enough for some people who take it a step further in their thinking. Drawing from a number of sources, the marriage of ideology and theology produces a philosophy that is rooted in a mental concept of God and human faith, not a spiritual context. Their thinking is rooted in an ethereal twilight zone suspended between the natural and the spiritual realms. It is soulish and full of mental and emotional terminology. Philosophy requires psychology to keep it in place. The study of human behavior is needed to enable people to express their views in acceptable form as well as to control how those views are received.

When we meet resistance, we can fashion our response according to our perception of the intellectual and educational capacity of the individual concerned. If that person has no access to primary education at the highest level, he may be deemed naive and simplistic. Should the opposite be true, we possibly surmise that *he* may have opinions and ideas not rooted in the real world of practical day-to-day living. It's a sort of "heads I win, tails you lose" viewpoint.

The point I wish to make is this: How often is this jumble of ideology, theology, philosophy, and psychology put together and used on the people of God? Examine the whole principle of one-man ministry in the church. A cursory look at the Scriptures

> *Theology and ideology do not mix.*

tells us that the term *pastor* is not a descriptive word for a local church leader. It is used only once in connection with the fivefold ministries of apostle, prophet, pastor, teacher, and evangelist (see Eph. 4:11). The correct term for local leadership is the plural of *elder* to denote a team ministry. (Read Acts 11:30; 14:23; 15:2,4,6,22; 16:4; 20:17,28; 21:18; First Timothy 3:1-7; 5:17; Titus 1:5-9; James 5:14; and First Peter 5:1-4.)

Elders are a group of dedicated people working together in love and friendship to produce men and women with anointed lifestyles and ministries to empower the work of God in the locality and further afield. In all the New Testament churches established under apostolic and prophetic input we read of elders (plural) being appointed in every city (see Acts 14:23). The apostolic team working through and in support of local teams of elders would train, equip, empower, and release the people to do the work of the ministry. The fivefold ministries are consultant gifts to church leaders (and often are leaders in churches themselves) to enable them to be built wisely into the place of anointed significance that God desires for them in that locality. What we have in thousands of churches today is a one-man ministry approach that cannot be defended in Scripture.

The premise for this philosophy was set several hundreds of years ago and follows this thought process: Only learned and intelligent people can rule in the church because most of the people are uneducated and illiterate. This ideology was supported by the fact that Paul studied at the feet of Gamaliel and was an obviously bright, intelligent, and well-read individual. These individuals were then paid to begin training seminaries to further increase the number of men who were trained to a high standard in theology, philosophy, and human psychology.

> **Is your church an audience or an army?**

In those days people prized intelligence and education above all else, especially spiritual experience. Leaders were taught to do the work of the minister. There is obviously a place for intelligent and intellectual ability within the church. Most of charismatic Christianity has kissed its brains good-bye in the search for spiritual experience. Much of what passes for evangelical Christianity is dry, ritualistic, and cerebral. Fundamentalists are no fun and mainly mental in their approach to radical Christianity and the presence of God. In actual fact, the early Church fathers were a fascinating mix of the intelligentsia and the illiterate.

In Acts 26:24 Festus shouted that Paul's great learning had driven him (Paul) insane. Prior to this, Peter and John had been arrested by the religious leaders of their day because, after the lame beggar had been healed, more than 5,000 people had come to believe in Jesus. After the religious leaders had questioned them and listened closely to Peter and John's answers, they made several observations (see Acts 4:1-14):

1. Peter and John were extremely confident in God and what they were doing.
2. They were unlearned and ignorant (which is a polite way of saying they were functionally illiterate!).
3. Peter and John had spent time with Jesus.

The early apostles, then, were a team of extremes—educated and refined like Paul and Luke but also illiterate fishermen like Peter, James, and John—and probably several shades in-between. In today's church culture, Peter and John's lack of formal training would make them eligible only for the laity, yet they were apostles!

Real theology does not come from books or schools. It arises out of penitent hearts, submissive spirits, and renewed minds. Real theology is spoken in the language of slaves and ignorant fishermen. It is based on time spent with Jesus and the confidence that His presence engenders in human hearts. It has learning and experience. It is both taught by men and distilled in relationship with the Holy Spirit. Real theology is not meant only for arguing points but also for creatively demonstrating the nature and character of God through both His words and His works. Theology and experience combine to train the people of God to do the ministry. So much of what is learned in Bible college and seminary is useless in the process of building the church to fulfill the dreams of God.

The two most powerful questions we can ask today are "What?" and "Why?" "What are we doing, and why are we doing it?" We must have a mind-set and a theology that proves the will of God and helps us to build the Kingdom. "Is what we are doing still working? Is it effective? Can it work better? How do we change it? What is God saying to us this year?"

Many leaderships do not build in time for review, prayer, and corporate examination of the vision, anointing, and ministry of their church. Are we merely bolting what works on to our existing structures that don't work? Is the life of the church serving the structure and the program, or is the program and structure producing life and faith in relationship and service to the Lord?

A revolution in leadership is required to bring us back into alignment with the early Church. With all of our post-modern style of leadership we have created a church that consumes rather than a church that produces. We have generated an audience, not an army...people who hear but who do not live out the word.

Cross the Line Into a New Paradigm

We need a paradigm shift in our thinking. A *paradigm* is a new level of thinking. Most paradigm shifts begin in the prophetic, because its roots are in the heart of God. A paradigm shift occurs when our new minds radically affect our behavior and the way that we operate. The problem is people are thinking about new paradigms, or new concepts, but their behavior still hasn't changed. They are still trying to bolt the new things onto the old things that they have always done.

We have to turn our back on what the Lord deems to be old and cross the line into what He is opening up before us. Former things and new things almost always relate to structure, methodology, operation of church, and practice of ministry. The Bible does not say too much about meetings. Half the revelation is contained in the injunction, "Do not forget to meet" (see Heb. 10:25). The other half simply talks about creativity and the possibility that our meetings, when led by the Spirit, have the capacity to be different on every occasion (see 1 Cor. 14:6). Yet this is seldom the case.

God does not give specific details on how, when, or how often to meet. He knows that if He gave us specific details, we would use them to set the whole thing in concrete forever! We have developed a style full of rigidity and stereotype even with the bare information He gave us. Just think of the mess we would have created with more detailed instructions.

If God is vague or indefinite about anything, it is always for a specific reason. In this case, His lack of definition was intended to keep us as close to Him as possible. He wants us to move by every word that comes out of His mouth. Lack of definition is intended to create a dependency upon God in us so that we will be led by Him as He desires.

Structure and operation are also concerned with:

1. How we conduct the ministry of the church outside our own meetings.

2. How we disciple and prepare people for works of service.

3. Our mission to the nation and the nations.

4. The vision and calling of the church.

5. The development and release of the next generation of leaders and ministries.

6. How we conduct ourselves in worship, prayer, spiritual warfare, financial giving, and work amongst the poor.

7. Our relationship and unity with other churches in the area.

8. Our understanding and practice of the gospel of the Kingdom.

All of these things can be touched, changed, and redirected by the Lord as He sees fit. When He speaks into those things, His words create a paradigm shift in our hearts. The word *paradigm* is derived from the Greek word *paradeigma*, meaning "pattern."

> *Lack of definition from God is meant to create dependency in Him.*

A pattern is a model or a guide used for making something. A paradigm relates to the set of beliefs usually concealed in the code of behavior with which we interpret events surrounding our life. We have paradigms that govern how we see ourselves, our church, and our country in relation to the world around us.

When the earth was discovered to be round and not flat, people had to rethink their understanding of almost everything. Everyone said it would be impossible for iron ships to float until someone suspended those ideas and did something different. The concepts governing flight, radio waves, television, telephones, computers, and space travel all involved a paradigm shift. When a paradigm shifts, we see and understand new information, but the very way we see and understand is also changed.

When we experience a true paradigm shift, everything goes back to zero. God doesn't build the next thing out of the old thing. The old passes away; the new thing arrives. We need a revelation to know what the new thing is and how it works. We must go back to the drawing board and be prepared to lay everything down. This is the zero perspective. Everything belongs to God, so lay it on the altar. The promise and vision of all that God has, is, and will give us, must always be submitted to a potential death. It is His, not ours. Like Abraham, we take to our hearts that which is God-given and precious beyond the telling, and we offer it up to the Lord. Is this a pretend offering because we expect God to refuse it? No. We raise the knife with only an expectancy that He will still provide for us—if not this son, then another one (see Gen. 22:1-12). If the Lord returns it to you, it may be taken up and used. It may return reshaped and different.

The period between the old being laid down and the new being put into place is called *transition*. Some of the old things will change and be reshaped, and new things will be added. The principal idea is that we should be unrecognizable in operation and methodology whilst retaining our integrity and character.

The nature of the church remains the same, but the operational model of the church is rebuilt as we learn to occupy a new level of revelation and practice. God never changes in personality, but everything around Him changes in practice. We are constantly being made over in the image of Christ whilst God has His perfect will in our ministry. Transition, therefore, is about the church maintaining the nature and character of God as He redevelops its role and operation to suit the next dimension of power He is bestowing upon us.

Transition is about tension, change, uncertainty, fear, disturbance, redirection, remodeling, mess, excitement, re-envisioning, new call, fresh faith, unpredictability, frustration, disagreement, adventure, moving on, uprooting, and the unknown!

All these things will test our capacity to express the nature of God in the fruit of the Spirit. Spirit versus carnality is a major part of transition. Basically, if the Spirit wins, we move on successfully in a remodeled church with a new anointing, fresh faith, and a new sense of mission and destiny. If the flesh wins, our carnality will split the church.

Only Servant Leaders Can Succeed

In times of transition, the scope of anointing and vision in our leadership changes dramatically. Some are marked for new vision and a fresh leadership empowerment. Others are set aside by God's decree or because of personal difficulties that sideline them from continuing in that function. Moses and Joshua; Saul and David; Elijah and Elisha; and Barnabas and Paul are several examples of transitional leadership styles.

The problem comes when we think of leadership as a title, status, or position. It is none of these things. Leadership is a function. The particular term used to define it relates to the job description of the activity involved.

To put the title of Apostle, Prophet, Pastor, Bishop, etc. in front of our name is ludicrous and silly. Jesus never did. The apostles all called themselves apostles *and* bond slaves, signifying that both were equal terms that defined their role and job description. As such, if they were meant to be used as titles, they would rightly cancel each other out. Paul referred to apostles as the scum of the earth (see 1 Cor. 4:9-13). He referred to apostles as men condemned to death; a spectacle; an exhibit no one wants to see; fools; weak; without honor; destitute; reviled; persecuted; scum;

and the dregs of all things. Which of those things is a title? They all belong to his apostleship and bond slavery.

If we view these things as titles, as markers of status and position, we will tend to cling to the office that we feel is ours. This creates rival factions if people are defending their position. There is nothing more unwholesome and ungodly in a church than to see people in positions of leadership holding on to power and position at any cost. Paul said, "Imitate me, just as I also imitate Christ" (1 Cor. 11:1), and "Brethren, join in following my example, and note those who so walk, as you have us for a pattern" (Phil. 3:17). (See also First Corinthians 4:16; Philippians 4:9; First Thessalonians 1:6; and Second Thessalonians 3:9.)

> *There is no status in the Body of Christ.*

Paul constantly talked about the power of example and the need for good leadership models for the church to follow. Jesus Himself also talked about how those who desire to become leaders must be servants (see Mk. 10:42-45).

There is an example in leadership that is grounded in servanthood, stewardship, and slavery—not in title, status, or position. There is no status in the Body of Christ. We are building church with Kingdom values, not with those of a hierarchical world system. Leaders are to be the best examples of servanthood and slavery in the church. It was the model set by Jesus and maintained by the apostles and leaders of the early Church. It is enshrined in these words of Paul:

> *Let nothing be done through selfish ambition or conceit, but in lowliness of mind let each esteem others better than himself. Let each of you look out not only for his own interests, but also for the interests of others. Let this mind be in you which was also in Christ Jesus, who, being in the form of God, did not consider it robbery to be equal with God, but made Himself of no reputation, taking the form of a bondservant, and coming in the likeness of men. And being found in appearance as a man, He humbled Himself and became obedient to the point of death, even the death of the cross (Philippians 2:3-8).*

If we are unable or unwilling to follow the model of our Lord and the apostle Paul, we should consider the image we are creating around ourselves. If it is not one of humility and servanthood, then we need to surrender ourselves. We need to be released from title, position, and status into servanthood, stewardship, and slavery. Alternatively, we must be released from the ministry into secular employment where our poor attitude cannot have a negative impact on the church.

If we hold on to our position and status in times of tension and difficulty, we are liable to create a faction within the church. Paul said that the purpose of such factions would be to reveal who are the real leaders and who are the false. In times of tension and difficulty, those whom God approves become evident! (See First Corinthians 11:18-19.)

The church needs to become mature in identifying Christlike behavior. Never be impressed by anointing. Only be joined to people who practice the fruit of the Spirit and not just the gifts. People can destroy with their character what they have built with their gift. Be rightly impressed by the nature, character, and image of Christ that is evident in people's lives. The Lord can add gifting relatively quickly, but character takes years of making righteous decisions in order to develop integrity.

Chapter 3

Conditions for Revival

*T*he Church is on a pilgrimage, a journey with the Lord, to discover its centrality in the purposes of God. The investment of God in the Church does not include a provision for a Plan B. Plan A is still very much on God's heart—and it is to produce a dwelling place in which God lives by His Spirit (see Eph. 2:22). Visitation should produce habitation.

Reconciliation at all levels is the goal of God for the Church. The Holy Spirit is given to enhance and sustain long-term relationship with God on His terms. On top of that relational foundation with God, we must build friendship and harmony within the Church itself.

Revival is a profound encounter with God that requires disciplined preparation, placement, and prayer. Revival is what God does *to* the Church. It occurs when we allow Him to build us alongside other people. We are living stones being built together to reveal the manifest presence of God as He responds to our unity.

Currently God's problem is not the sinfulness of the nations but the intransigence of the Church. He has locked Himself into something that He does not want to get out of, which is His commitment to produce a Bride. Unfortunately, the Church has a monastic context for her life and mission. She has created a bastion of safety in a fallen world. In this place she practices all the things that the world finds irrelevant. She demonstrates constantly that she has no mercy or compassion for people who are not like her and not with her!

We cry out for an open heaven but we do not create the conditions and the climate for Heaven to come down. Heaven responds to our unity, to our togetherness, and to the love in our relationships. If we express a real covenant on earth, then Heaven will not be a shock to our system, and we will not offend the Holy Spirit who has come to bring Heaven to us on earth.

The norm for the Church is what we call revival. What we have now is totally abnormal, and no one is crying! I'm not living for what I have seen and known of success in God. I repent of everything I have ever known of success and failure. I don't want my knowledge or experience to prevent me from realizing the dream that God has put within me.

The fact is, I'm living for a Church *beyond* revival! Revival is not a panacea that cures all ills. If we are not ready when revival breaks, it will break us. We must find people who are on the same journey to provide God with a habitation. Only like-minded people can give us the same buoyancy when the storm hits. To release the fullness of God, we must repent of one-dimensional Christianity where everything revolves around meetings. We must get God out of the sanctuary and into people's hearts and homes.

> *Visitation should produce habitation.*

Our meetings are often the laughingstock of devils. We must know that our current experience of church is something less than what God wants to give us. There is something in me that is not what it will be. The seed inside me wants to be a different plant. Can't you feel it in you? If you are frustrated with current models of church, it is because something else is growing up within you. You need to connect with people in a different way to release the new thing. It involves a breaking and a releasing because what God has placed within you is bursting out of its shell.

That is what causes frustration. It is the process of germination. There is an irritation inside that will not go away. It provokes us, hopefully, to personal change and prayer. This is great and necessary. The real tragedy comes when we stop at the personal level and do not graduate to corporate change and intercession. If we want the power of Pentecost, we must return to the Christianity that released it. (See Acts 1:14; 2:42-47; 4:31-37.)

Happily there is the sense of a move of the Spirit across the earth that is bringing with it a transformation into something new. Water the seeds within your church. Nurture them wherever you find them, no matter what group is sprouting a revival plant.

Divine Interruption

Transformation comes by divine interruption. The Lord is interfering with His Church. Renewal was a holy intrusion into our way of doing things. God was taking back control of His Church, except in the places where He was resisted. Tribal securities are being shaken at this time. Networks that are incestuous and exclusive will find themselves under the hammer of God as the Holy Spirit breaks them wide open to a greater revelation and practice of Kingdom.

The Church and the Kingdom are distinct yet related. The Kingdom is the universal reign of God over all creation and the universe of worlds, including angels and men. It is eternal and unlimited. It is all-encompassing.

The Church is God's eternal purpose manifested in time. It is limited to the redeemed people of God. The Church is the instrument for the full demonstration of the Kingdom. God's Kingdom— "His rule and reign"—is to be established in the Church. The Church is in the Kingdom and the Kingdom is in the Church. The Church is not the totality but only a part of the Kingdom. The Kingdom is far more inclusive than the Church. This distinction yet relationship between Church and Kingdom needs to be understood and recognized to avoid confusing the real issues involved in both.

We do not pray, "Your Church come"; the Church prays, "Your kingdom come. Your will be done on earth as it is in heaven" (Mt. 6:10). The Church does not preach the gospel of the fellowship of believers. The Church preaches the gospel of the

Kingdom (see Mt. 24:14). The word *church* is used 115 times in Scripture, and the word *kingdom* 160 times. That should tell us something!

It is seen clearly in Acts and the Gospels that the Church is a channel, an instrument; it is a vehicle and a vessel for the expression of the Kingdom of God. It is through the Church that God will extend His Kingdom into people's hearts.

If we are building a church or a network with little or no desire for the Kingdom, then we are building our own empire, however small. Anyone who puts his ministry, church, or network ahead of the need to build Kingdom will suffer a divine interruption to his plans. I can guarantee that God will break your work wide open in order to include His desire for the whole Body of Christ. Outside of marriage, all exclusive relationships will suffer divine interruption.

Many years ago, around 1980 or 1981, I shared the following as part of a prophetic word that the Lord gave me for Peter Stott, a personal friend: "In times past, God has poured out His Spirit in grief, knowing it would be dissipated because of the greed and character of men. But in a time to come, He will pour out His Spirit because men have come together in Kingdom purpose."

God will inhabit only what is compatible with His purpose. Many churches have become a memorial to what God has done. We need to see churches full of vision about what God is doing and will complete before the day of the Lord comes.

We must find ways to keep our wineskin soft before God so that He can continue to pour out His Spirit. What is your attitude to other groups around you? Do you pray for other churches? Are you willing to help them to grow? Do you have real friendships in other networks? If they get in trouble, do you stand with them, or are you pleased at the prospect of a few of their people coming your way?

A Kingdom heart is prepared to pay a price for unity. If you are truly Kingdom-minded, the anointing and favor of God will keep your work fresh and supple in the purposes of God. Kingdom people have greater favor because they are living for a higher calling and purpose of God than just their own work.

The Kingdom provides us with a new way of looking at the ministry and the eternal purpose of God. It gives us a new framework for walking and working in line with God's heart. It provides a new dimension of being and living before the Lord. We realize that God is not coming to do what we want; rather, He is coming to fulfill His desire to express the Kingdom and become our Bridegroom. We must therefore give ourselves to pursuing the whole heart of God.

> *God will inhabit only what is compatible with His purpose.*

The Lord only lives with what is pure, holy, and consecrated. He is testing our motives and our fitness to be in the next move of God. Can He trust us? Will He release us or discipline us so that we come back into line with His desire for Kingdom? Many ministries, churches, and networks are suffering decline (rather, divine interruption to bring them to their senses) because of their exclusive mind-sets that have ignored God's Kingdom desires.

This is a season of grace when God covers us to give us time to repent. How will God come to you? In mercy because of your desire for Him, or in judgment because of His desire for you? Many people are abusing the Holy Spirit, using Him as a tool for ministry...building their own thing in the name of the Lord, of course. When we marginalize our relationship with God to maximize our ministry, we put ourselves on the wrong side of God. Likewise, when we build without recognizing the Kingdom, we deserve the chastisement that follows.

God is always compatible with human brokenness and humility. He gives grace to the humble. Brokenness and humility are the crucible that releases God's empowering presence. There is a brokenness and a humility coming between leaders of churches, denominations, and ministries to bring them together in divine purpose. God will interrupt our ministry agenda to introduce us to Kingdom.

This will slow us down in our vision, which is probably a good thing. The Kingdom can be hard, slow work if we give ourselves to it in only small doses. However, it will provide us with a compatible experience in knowing God at a deeper level. What is a compatible experience? It is crucifixion, humility, servanthood, obedience, suffering, no reputation, rejection, being despised. "Let this mind be in you which was also in Christ Jesus" (Phil. 2:5; read verses 1-8). He was compatible with His Father's will. Compatibility is the essence of good relationships! Building your church into a dwelling place of God by the Spirit is the height of compatibility.

Compare the following two prayers. Which one would you answer?

"Father, pour out Your Spirit upon us, so that Your revival can come to this area and result in thousands of people coming into Your Kingdom...."

"Father, pour out Your Spirit upon us so that we may become a habitation for Your manifest presence to come down into our midst...."

Both prayers are deliberately incomplete, to help you write a better one. Why not write one now and pray it hourly until an answer comes! The great unanswered prayer of Jesus in John 17 must be fulfilled: "That they may be one just as We are one" (verse 22). The transformation of Church and society together has the following three stages, which we need to understand and practice, and for which we must throw ourselves onto the mercy of God to see their expression.

Renewal, Revival, and Reformation

In recent years there has been a great outpouring of God's Spirit around the earth. We are witnessing some incredible sights and sounds as the Lord releases fresh waves of power and anointing on His beloved people.

Whatever people think about the recent *renewal*, it has had a dramatic effect on the Body of Christ. It has brought a fresh passion for Jesus, a new desire for intimacy. It has left a higher watermark of expectancy for God's loving nature. People have been restored to God. They have been filled with a new desire for holiness and purity. Heartfelt intercession has increased in men and women grown cold in prayer. New worship of a greater depth and caliber has sprung up in our midst.

I agree that renewal also splits churches. Whenever the Spirit moves, the flesh rises. These two are locked together in powerful animosity. The flesh of man rails at the Spirit life with venom and destructive behavior. The Spirit antagonizes the flesh, exposing carnality of thought, word, and deed. It is a wonderful thing to behold and does my heart glad to see it.

We should smile and worship God when sin is exposed and dealt with by the church. Exposing the presence of sin and secret lifestyles proves the presence and the work of the Holy Spirit. Better out than in!

Carnality splits churches. Jesus said that He came to bring not peace but a sword (see Mt. 10:34). The word of God divides attitudes, intentions, and ambitions (see Heb. 4:12-13), and no one is spared. When renewal came, there was such a profound increase of love, purity, desire, and intimacy with God that the Holy Spirit unearthed everything that did not belong to the nature of God.

When rain falls on a field ready for sowing, all the stones come to the surface. All that is hidden and hard will emerge as the Spirit falls upon the church.

The big issue after greater intimacy with God is the one of "Who is in control?" Sadly, I watched some leaders shut down renewal meetings because of this concern. Many felt unable to preside over something they could not direct. "The wind blows where it wishes..." (Jn. 3:8).

> *The muddiest part of the bank is the place where we step into the river.*

I watched other leaders adopt a "sons of Sceva" approach to renewal (see Acts 19:13-17). They did not want to serve what God was doing; rather, they wanted to use the outpouring to grow their own church and ministry. God visited briefly but did not stay, and all they could do was pretend that something very powerful happened. Most people failed to realize that renewal was a test as well as a blessing. The Lord was looking to see whom He could trust in the next phase of anointing and growth.

Who would use the outpouring for their own ends? Who would control and channel it rather than release it? Who would be willing to pay the price for the presence of God? Who would humble themselves and surrender the church back to God? Who would criticize the move because it did not fit their experience and theology? Who would help other churches to be released into what God was doing?

The Lord was testing our hearts to see what we would do (see Deut. 8:2-3). Now, I believe that He knows the men and women He can trust with revival! He knows the churches that He can begin to use to evangelize the unsaved. He knows where His Holy Spirit will be welcomed and not abused.

> *Renewal was a test as well as a blessing!*

Revival is here, present among the Church. However we must be careful here of our terminology. One of the continued offenses of the Church against the Lord has been that she has desired His power more than His presence. We have majored on events, functions, and outpourings of God for a purpose. Our emphasis has been on doing and not being. Renewal changed all that for those who were impacted by it. Renewal of our first love is the foundation for God to reclaim the hearts of His people.

We have now moved into that second phase of the move of God: *revival*. It is here, though, that we must adjust our terminology. There is no obvious phraseology in Scripture that would connect revival with our aspirations to see huge numbers of people coming into the Kingdom of God. In all definitions, *revival* is synonymous with restoring, renewing, rekindling, and recovering. The prefix *re* denotes: a) action in a backward direction, i.e., recede; return; revert; b) action intended to undo a situation, i.e., respond; restock; remove; c) action intended to demonstrate that an original act was impermanent or inadequate; and d) that the performance of the new action brings back to an earlier state of affairs.

Revival means to restore to life and use, to take up and make valid again. The Greek word in the New Testament is *anathallo*, meaning to flourish anew. Clearly, it is not talking about non-believers, but Christians. We cannot revive something that has never been alive; it is dead and needs to be reborn. Revival is for people who have become lukewarm and who are not walking with God fully.

This is currently happening now in many places in the world. People are getting right with God, and His holiness is developing again in the hearts of the Church.

Revival is the revelation and demonstration of the manifest presence of God within the Church to release the corporate man of Christ to impact society.

Revival is not an event; it is a Person revealed. Revival is not a demonstration of God's power; it is an outbreak of His presence. Revival is not an exhibition; it is a revelation of occupation by a Person who is bigger than you! Revival that breaches the world is connected with the manifest presence of God. When our churches are full of His presence, then Heaven will come to earth. The manifest presence of God will be contested violently by the enemy and by any religious spirits inhabiting the church.

Revival occurs when we have the same kind of spiritual atmosphere outside the church as we have within it. Revival is about releasing God's people into God's presence. Many people are praying for revival, wanting to see souls saved and demonstrations of power in the church. We should not set our sights so low. We do not want another visitation that can be abused and peter out like the rest.

We must have the manifest presence of God *stay* among us. We do not need a visitation; we need to make for God a habitation, a dwelling place. (Read John 15:4-8; Ephesians 2:19-22; 3:17; First Corinthians 3:9,16; Second Corinthians 6:16-18; and First Peter 2:4-10.)

The dream of God has always been to live in the hearts of His people—not just in individual hearts, but in the corporate heart. The early Church had a unity, a oneness of heart and purpose.

> *Revival is not an event; it is a Person revealed.*

They had one voice; they were devoted in a corporate sense to prayer, fellowship, teaching, and communion (see Acts 1–5).

If we are merely praying for a visitation and not actively working to make our church a dwelling place for God's presence, we deserve not to have our prayers answered. The Scriptures say that we are living stones connected together with relationship and love for God and one another. Who are you connected with? Like bricks in a wall we are living stones. Who is under you, supporting your life and ministry? Who are you resting on and accountable to? Who is alongside you in service and ministry? What is your relationship like with your coworkers? Who is above you, whom are you supporting? Who is resting on you and accountable to your integrity, love, and ministry? We are living stones in friendship being built together into a habitation for God. He lives in our friendships and our unity. Is He welcome among us?

Are there strifes, envyings, criticism, grudges, negative fellowship, and backbiting among us? Is there a lack of vision, purpose, destiny, and cohesion? Are we devoted corporately to all that the early Church felt was important?

Revival is about a corporate fear of the Lord descending on the church (see Acts 2:43; 5:11; 9:31). Revival is about stewardship and sacrifice, having all things in common (see Acts 2:44-45; 4:32,34,37). In revival, there are no personal possessions and no needs across the church. Only the manifest presence of God can free us from ownership to total stewardship. Still want revival?

Revival is about a preoccupation with the Person and the presence of Jesus. It is about the corporate grace of God being on everyone at the same time. Corporate grace is the glue that holds us together, giving us favor everywhere (see Acts 2:47; 4:33).

The effect of revival is *reformation*. This is the third stage of the transformation process that equips the Church to reach the world.

Reformation is the effect caused by a united body of people flowing together in Kingdom purpose and power, within God's presence. It is a deliberate and disciplined unity focused on the person of Jesus. Reformation occurs when the revival of God's dream is fulfilled in the Church. The dream of God is for a people who are fulfilling the first and second commandments, which are to love the Lord your God with all your heart, soul, mind, and strength, and to love your neighbor as you love yourself. Jesus said that in these two commands depend the whole law and the prophets (see Mt. 22:37-40).

Everything could be cut down to fit these two commands. If you ever wanted to simplify your life and ask for a word from God that would cover most eventualities of life, church, and ministry, this would be the word.

With everything in you, love God. With His love reciprocating in and through you, love the people around you, wherever you happen to be. The dream of God is to have a habitation among His people. It is not to visit occasionally when circumstances permit and conditions are fulfilled. His dream is a place to live in a Church that has done everything in her power to attract her beloved.

When God comes to live, His manifest presence breaks out into the community. Demons fall, strongholds are cast down, and the hard-hearted cry out for salvation. Three thousand souls are saved in one day. Faith is alive on the streets because the sick are being healed and the dead raised. Heaven comes to earth in reformation. Laws are changed, unemployment is reduced, and the crime rate falls. Marriages are restored and the divorce rate drops. Domestic violence decreases. Miracles of every description occur as society is turned upside down.

The windows of Heaven are flung open and God displays His majesty. People share all they possess because the presence of the King generates such confidence and love. No one withholds anything, thus adding to the quality of life.

The Church attacks the enemy without mercy. Every cult, coven, and occult organization is stripped of its power and key people, as salvation rips through the ranks of the ungodly. Every secret organization of powerful men is torn apart by truth and righteousness. Reformation is Kingdom mayhem on the ungodly streets of the world. People do not dare to join the Church, yet multitudes are added (see Acts 5:13-14). The Church is an enigma, a huge talking point. The world does not want to associate itself with them, but everyone holds them in high esteem. To gain a reformation, we have to give the Lord what He wants in revival.

> *When God comes to live, His manifest presence breaks out into the community.*

If your church missed renewal because it never knew it was happening, the grace of God will bring you up to speed in the revival of your people and your corporate destiny. If you messed up renewal because of your own pride and greed, you need to repent of your misconduct and bow the knee to God's fresh purpose for you. You need to serve others in the flow of revival and regain a place of trust before God. It may be that He will grace your life with a new vision and authority as you demonstrate your humility and servanthood. If you try to pull the same stunt you did in renewal, this time they may carry you out of the church permanently!

Revival is no place for pushing and jockeying for position. Put away that hierarchical nonsense and serve the Lord. Remove the worldly value system from your heart. This is a people's revival. A nameless, faceless generation is being raised up to do the work of the ministry. Only those people who actually raised up people in discipleship will have any place in leadership. But, do you know what? Most of those men and women will not care about status, position, or recognition. They won't notice that God has elevated them to any recognized place. Just like the apostles, they will be doing menial jobs in the church and will only change as occasion demands it (see Acts 6:1-4). To be eligible for ordinary tasks, such as waiting on tables, you will have to demonstrate a good servant reputation, be full of the Holy Spirit, and possess qualities of wisdom! May God help us to be so humble and such excellent servants!

Chapter 4

Understanding Church

The English word *church* has various meanings, such as a constructed building, a denomination, or a group of Christians. The Greek word, however, translates church in the Bible as a group of people called together for a specific purpose. So that we may understand what He means, God has given us several definitions, pictures, and analogies in Scripture. Notably, the Church is a building and a body. It is the house of God and the Body of Christ.

A Forceful Revelation of Lordship

Before we delve into the intricacies of what the Church is, we must ensure that we understand the very foundations of this glorious institution. The Church is a paradox, two extremes founded on an exposition of the Person of Christ.

When Jesus asked His disciples, "Who do men say that I am?" they offered the various names that the crowds were using. When He asked the disciples for their answer, Simon Peter answered that Jesus was the Christ, the Son of the living God. Jesus then replied, "And I also say to you that you are Peter, and on this rock I will build My church, and the gates of Hades shall not prevail against it" (see Mt. 16:13-19).

The foundation of the Church is built primarily upon a forceful revelation of Jesus Christ as Lord. Every believer will be asked of God, "Whom do you say that I am?" The answer we give will dictate who and what we become in God's Kingdom purpose. There must be a personal declaration, "You are the Christ," arising in our hearts. It is not enough, though, for us to be merely verbal in our affirmation of Christ. We must become a living testimony of His Lordship by word, thought, and deed. The very way we make life decisions must demonstrate His power to live in and through us to His own satisfaction and joy.

Repentance is a continual submission to the revelation of the Lordship of Christ. How other people see Jesus will be reflected in how the Church views and represents Him. Jesus knew that people's opinions of Him would differ greatly for a wide variety of reasons. He wanted His own disciples to be totally confident in His real identity. He knew that His own work would be jeopardized by a multiplicity of viewpoints regarding His essential nature. He also knew that revelation of this kind could not come by mere observation or thought. It had to be directly communicated by the Father, who alone fully represents His Son to mankind.

> *The Church is only as strong as her concept of God.*

At this point, the unequivocal blessing of God is in direct proportion to the importance of the revelation being revealed. So important is this truth to the Father that Simon Peter is singled out for specific approval and favor as a direct result of his confession.

How we see Jesus individually is critical to the nature of our ongoing relationship with Him. What we see and confess must be lived out in our lives. It can only be lived, however, if the revelation came from God Himself.

Jesus warned His disciples not to tell anyone that He was the Christ. They had not at this stage been given the power to witness specifically in His name. This would happen later at the appropriate time (see Acts 1:8; 2:1-41), when revelation would be released by the Holy Spirit and firmly backed up by signs and wonders.

Today many people call Jesus "Lord." They may even confess Him as Lord to others. However, the way they live their lives often presents a less than convincing picture. Many Christians are not governed by God. They are not led by the Spirit. They only submit to the Lord when in trouble and return to fleshly and selfish living as soon as their problem is resolved.

Many churches do not jointly own the revelation of Christ as Lord over their corporate activities. If they did, churches might not split in acrimony; our impact on the community would be more profound; and our capacity for sacrifice would attract the Holy Spirit to us in greater power and anointing.

Our priority as individuals must be to regain the revelation of the supremacy and Lordship of Jesus. To do that, we must seek God with *all* of our heart since this powerful truth can only come directly from Him. Our next priority is to blend these individual revelations into a corporate declaration and confession that radically affects our vision and ministry as the Church in the community.

Failure to do so will cause us to remain victims of our own inconsistency. The prize of our high calling will be out of our reach. Revelation is positional; it places us in the way of God's power as we confess His Word. Without this revelation, the enemy can prevail over us and the keys of the Kingdom will not work. It is not mental assent to His Lordship that is required, but a declaration lodged in our spirit by divine disclosure.

When we live it, breathe it, and continually confess it, then hell has to fall. Binding and loosing become commonplace activities as we revel in the majesty and supremacy of the Lord Jesus Christ.

Upon this revelatory rock the Church is built, and through this particular truth the intentions of God in warfare are made known to rulers and authorities in the spiritual realm by the Church herself, moving in His eternal wisdom (see Eph. 3:10). The very gates of hell will not prevail or stay closed against the onslaught of a church moving corporately in the Lordship of Jesus. Powers must fall and salvation released to a church with a "Lordship" vision, identity, and purpose.

Such a church will receive power and the specific keys to unlock their area for the sake of the gospel. Windows in Heaven will open to churches that display a corporate vision and revelation of Jesus' Kingship over their lives and through their ministries. The enemy is rendered powerless by such a display of belief and behavior synchronizing into service and submission.

The Acid Test of Real Church

At one point in his travels we are told that Abram pitched his tent midway between two points (see Gen. 12:8). These were Bethel in the west and Ai in the east. *Bethel* means the house of God. *Ai* signifies a heap of stones. No matter where Abram went on his journeying, he would return to that point where he had first built an altar to the Lord (see Gen. 13:3-4).

Our very place of submission and sacrifice where we call out to God must have definition attached to it in terms of what is being constructed for God's glory.

As the church we stand midway between two destinies. Will we be a Bethel or an Ai church? An Ai church is a loose collection of people coming together once or twice a week to do something spiritual and go home again. These are meeting-oriented churches whose only experience of God is in a sanctuary setting. There may be very little interaction between members of the same congregation on a friendship or function level outside the meetings. Deeper levels of relationship within a discipling context would be unlikely in such churches.

Bethel churches are those who recognize that the Kingdom of God is primarily relational, not simply functional. They have realized that the Lord wants to be involved in our lives through the friendship and fellowship of other believers. The New Testament breathes commitment. Each of us is a living stone whom God is shaping to fit alongside someone else in the house of the Lord. Together in our friendships we can become a dwelling place of God by the Spirit. The Lord is not shaping us in isolation from one another. How we allow ourselves to be fitted together is the acid test of how much God can trust us with His power and anointing.

There are three levels of relationships that each of us must aspire to in order to be totally fulfilled in the life of the church.

Real friendship runs strongly through each of these levels, producing a depth of relationship that will frustrate the purpose of the devil while bringing great glory to God.

> *Only the corporate man of the Church can rise up and police the heavens.*

If we were to focus on one particular brick in the middle of a wall, we would notice that it has a significant relationship with other bricks in the surrounding area. Firstly, that brick is built upon two others and draws its support from other sources. We all need *accountable* relationships in the church. These are friendships in which we are supported and helped by others. This support would include confession; the sharing of life and pressures; open and honest relationships; mutual integrity; and the development of character, gifting, and ministry. We all need people we can depend upon to uphold us, strengthen our morality, and champion our calling and destiny.

Secondly, that brick is alongside others on the same level. We all should have peer-level relationships with whom we share a common vision and anointing. In ministry we need significant *partnerships* as we develop a team ethos across the church. We need working functional relationships that carry a strong friendship base. When we know the people whom we will specifically labor with, we must build a solid friendship that can take the pressure of warfare, tension, and action.

Thirdly, that brick is situated underneath others, providing a base of support. This speaks of the *discipling* relationship that all key ministries and faithful people must develop in order to build church and reach the lost. Making disciples is a major part of our warfare against the enemy and our zeal to fulfill the Great Commission. Each of us needs to think of the people around us whom we are consciously shaping and developing.

This threefold aspect of friendship is our model in relationships for producing the house of the Lord and the Body of Christ. Developing our relationships in these key areas will ensure that not only our own lives but also those of the people around us will be cultivated by the Holy Spirit.

The Church Is Two Extremes

Ai churches are full of people who do not know each other in the way that I have outlined above. Many such churches are full of strangers on nodding acquaintance with one another. In lots of churches where there is a greater degree of familiarity, there still are not any friendships of real depth, true spiritual significance, or the power to accomplish divine purpose.

Paul spoke about the need for the church to be fellow citizens and members of God's household in the following passage:

Now, therefore, you are no longer strangers and foreigners, but fellow citizens with the saints and members of the household of God, having been built on the foundation of the apostles and prophets, Jesus Christ Himself being the chief cornerstone, in whom the whole building, being fitted together, grows into a holy temple in the Lord, in whom you also are being built together for a dwelling place of God in the Spirit (Ephesians 2:19-22).

A church with apostolic and prophetic foundations, and with Jesus as the essential integral part to uphold the vision and the work, has the capacity to rise up to become immensely more significant to God's Kingdom rule.

These foundations, plus the ability to be joined together like bricks in a wall, is what enables a church to rise to great heights of spiritual power. To be a temple and a dwelling for God is a single honor that releases all kinds of anointing and power.

Peter also spoke about the Church as a building in the following passage:

Coming to Him as to a living stone, rejected indeed by men, but chosen by God and precious, you also, as living stones, are being built up a spiritual house, a holy priesthood, to offer up spiritual sacrifices acceptable to God through Jesus Christ (1 Peter 2:4-5).

Do the people in our churches really view themselves as spiritual stones being fitted together as a house for the Spirit of

God to inhabit? Is what we have as church now totally acceptable to God?

Paul also views the Church as a body, not just as a building. Colossians 1:15-20 contains an amazing declaration of who Jesus really is; it says that He is the Head of the Body, the Church. This is further established in Paul's letter to the church in Ephesus (see Eph. 1:22-23).

Bodies are living, growing things. This growth in the Body comes from Jesus (see Eph. 4:15-16). Growth can occur only when each member of the Body plays his or her part. The growth of the Body and the rise of the building are to be promoted through love, so it is evident that relationships play a major part in the ongoing development of church.

Paul writes two immense passages of Scripture about body life in Romans 12:4-8 and First Corinthians 12:12-27. In Romans, he talks about how each member has a different part to play according to the gift given him or her. In First Corinthians, he talks about how each body part needs the other for the whole to be complete.

These passages emphasize our personal uniqueness as well as our corporate togetherness. They highlight the many differences of gifting, administration, and capacity whilst insisting that we all belong to one another. They tell us how to become members of the Body and the varieties of different functions and responsibilities that we will encounter as we work together. Scripture underscores the indispensable nature of all Body members

> *Identify and cultivate the living stones that God has placed around you!*

and emphasizes the constant need for unity and love. We are related to one another and are therefore obliged to function in our different giftings with appropriate respect, honor, and love.

The Church is therefore two extremes that need to be looked at together and held in tension through the grace of God. The Church is a building that is rigid, unmovable, and inflexible. At the same time the Church is also a Body that is fluid, constantly changing, moving, and totally flexible.

How can the Church be both extremes at the same time? How can the Church be rigid yet fluid; unmovable but constantly moving; inflexible yet totally flexible? It is a paradox.

These extremes relate to totally separate characteristics. The Church as a building relates to our "being" aspect of building friendship and mutual love for one another. The Church as a body relates to our "doing" aspects of gift, function, and ministry.

The Church as a Building

This view relates to our attitudes and character toward one another. It speaks of how we are to treat one another and live together in a manner that honors the Lord. There are so many things that we can disagree about, so many differences of gifting ability, vision, and ministry. This is quite apart from our personalities, pressures of life, tensions, warfare from the enemy, and perspectives of the church. The list of potential disagreements is huge. How can we avoid giving up on one another and splitting the church?

The solution is to have solid relationships grounded in a love that is rigid, unmovable, and inflexible. No matter what the provocation, we simply will not be moved away from expressing the love of Jesus for one another.

If we examine all the "one anothers" in the New Testament, we will have a whole range of positive choices to make during times of difficulty.

We are told to love, help, and be kind to one another; to bless, pray for, and bear one another's burdens. We are to encourage and lift one another up in the Lord; to be at peace with each other, doing good, and exhorting each other continually. We bless God immensely when we prefer one another, express forgiveness, and edify each other. Believing the best of one another in times of potential disharmony encourages us to stay close to the heartbeat of the Lord.

These are all nonnegotiable attitudes that truly reflect the personality of God. They lead us into places in God's heart that will cement us together into a dwelling place for His presence. Mistakes occur in church when we forget that what we *are* together is far more important to God than what we *do* together.

The Church as a Body

This view relates to our ministry and to all the things we do together as church in the service of God. The church should be full of movement, vision, and challenge. We walk in power but through suffering. We need to be working hard on the burden that God has given us. The church has action, aims, and goals. There is warfare, healing, and ministry. We learn to fight, overcome our weaknesses, and conquer the enemy. We have plans in ministry. We build structures and groups and take on projects and initiatives.

Each of these has immense power to bring a sword to our friendship, creating disunity in our partnership and dividing us in fellowship.

There is a call to action that requires a certain level of drive and initiative. It is vital that we pursue the call of God by understanding that the vision and destiny of the church must produce people who are living on the battlefield.

Everything given to us by God must eventually take us out onto the battlefield in the Spirit. We must live with a sense of destiny and purpose.

> *Divine order in friendships attracts the Holy Spirit.*

Mistakes occur when we relate to the body before the house. They are both important, but we need to determine which has priority in times of tension and difficulty.

We simply cannot relate successfully and consistently on the basis of what we do together. There are too many differences, probably legitimate, because of gift, ministry, vision, and perspective. We are too prone to disillusionment and frustration. The foundation for ministry and function must be our friendship and what we mean to each other. We can only relate consistently and successfully on the basis of mutual love and care.

Wrong Order Produces Disorder

We are learning the art of nonnegotiable love, being built together as a house and joined together as a body. Unless the revelation of Church as the house of God is uppermost in our thinking, whenever we move forward in God's purpose we will always lose people from what we are doing!

No movement will ever reach its maximum fulfillment because we cannot settle for activity instead of belonging. We pay a price on both sides, both to be and to do. We must make sure that we are paying the correct price at the appropriate time. The good is always the enemy of the best. We always settle for less when we major on function instead of fellowship. We need relationships with an agenda, not merely purpose-driven fellowship. We are the house of God being fitted together. This is nonnegotiable.

If we are forced to the place of having to do deals to accommodate one another's perspective or attitude, then we have missed the point entirely.

At that point, we are out of divine order and have failed the test of real love and grace. We will have proved again that gift and ministry are more important than the heart of God. Such disorder will eventually split the church or render us impotent and unable to rise above our self-imposed ceiling.

Functional relationships can only be seasonal. They are not enduring; their basis is a gifting that is not enough.

Nonnegotiable Love

We can build friendships only on appreciation. We cannot build them on disapproval or dissatisfaction. We must actively look for signs of appreciation in one another and learn to enjoy the people around us. Paul had a great philosophy in Philippians 4:8-9:

Finally, brethren, whatever things are true, whatever things are noble, whatever things are just, whatever things are pure, whatever things are lovely, whatever things are of good report, if there is any virtue and if there is anything praiseworthy—meditate on these things. The things which you learned and received and heard and saw in me, these do, and the God of peace will be with you.

This attitude holds us together in disillusionment. The world has Kleenex relationships that are used and then thrown away. Differences are not wrong, but how we tackle them may be!

Tension and Friction

We are all like blocks of undressed stone—we have many lumps, bumps, and abrasions that need squaring off and smoothing out. This happens in the context of our life and ministry as we work together. Difficult people and circumstances are a gift of God to us to shape our lives in the character of Jesus. We all will have people and situations that cause tension in our hearts and minds. These people and situations are "grace-growers," because of the unique opportunity they provide for us to grow up in the Lord.

Tension does not mean that something is going wrong; it means something is happening. Whenever we relate in depth, tension is always one of the ingredients. We must learn to live with and appreciate the tension of other people's being different to ourselves. There is no movement without tension. It is a normal part of our functioning together.

This is where we learn how to practice the grace of God and the fruit of the Spirit in one another's lives. Normally grace is not an issue as we enjoy our friendship and fellowship. However, the Lord has arranged the people around us and engineered many of our situations so that He can develop the fruit of His character in the soil of our circumstances.

The fruit of the Spirit only grows in bad soil. When someone has just said or done something really unkind, we have a choice to make regarding what action to take. We can be unkind in return, or we can speak and act with great mercy and kindness. The fruit of kindness grows in an unkind situation when we make the right choice. It is moving in the opposite spirit to what is coming against us.

It is easy to be joyful when things are going well for us. However, real joy does not depend on what is happening in a positive way. Real joy comes from the Lord and is a source of great strength to us in times of trial and difficulty. The fruit of joy grows in poor circumstances in which we need to rejoice in the presence of God and His eternal promises.

> *Bad ground produces good fruit...as we submit.*

The fruit of patience grows in troublesome situations in which we want to strive to take shortcuts or avoid difficult things instead of allowing the Lord to teach us to persevere in trust. God uses people and events to develop His character as well as His gifting in us.

We must learn how to enable the oil of the Holy Spirit to come between us and prevent the tension from becoming a friction. We get overheated through lack of oil, lack of grace, and lack of the fruit of God's nature in our hearts. Be challenged about this aspect of our walk with God. Learn to see other people through the eyes of God. When encountering difficult people, practice the grace of God. Develop the fruit of His nature. As you do, opportunities will open up for you in the nature of God.

There is always a tangible success for us in these situations. Nothing may change in the circumstances, but something may change in us. Alternatively, our circumstances may change in many ways as the favor of God is poured through our chosen behavior. We must learn to respond to God and not react to circumstances.

We can respond to the Lord when we really understand that in these times God is doing something either in us or through us. In trying times within the church and ministry, the Lord often uses our differences to bind us together in greater love and friendship. Sometimes our differences can be so acute that we have to put the issues on one side and deliberately renew or strengthen our friendship. If we really understand the divine order of the house before the body, we can do this in the grace of God and win a significant victory together over the enemy. The devil seeks to penetrate, divide, and rule in our relationships. When we let go of one another in favor of gifting, vision, and ministry, we only entrench our relational immaturity, which in turn makes it difficult for the Lord to trust us with new people, especially new converts. Spiritual babies cannot be brought up in the faith by spiritual babies. Carnality reinforces immaturity.

As our friendships grow and the nature of God is established within us, we can pick up the issues and realize that they have no more power to divide us. The devil has no patience; therefore, it is vital to know that as we wait on the Lord, it is the devil who gets frustrated. He likes quick gains and easy targets. Make it hard for him by growing in grace and fruit. If we make it a point to move in the opposite spirit, then everything the devil throws at us only makes us stronger. In this way we make him frustrated and confused. We demoralize the devil when we choose the Spirit life.

In these good choices the rough edges in our lives get smoothed out and we learn how to fit together better in our relationships. We have great opportunities in adversity to become like Jesus. Always know who are the grace-growers. Usually the very thing we find awkward and abrasive in them is what God is trying to correct in us. Grace-growers are a gift of God. Differences and tensions between people are often the work of God to grow good fruit and help us to become like the Lord Jesus.

Disillusionment and Reality

It is a valuable part of team development to become disillusioned with one another. It is the precursor to real growth in friendship. Disillusionment is the breaking of our illusions about one another. The Father never gets disillusioned because He has no illusions about us (see Ps. 103:14). He has compassion upon us because He knows us so well.

Most of us go through life initially presenting a certain image. We hide behind masks to cover our weaknesses, insecurities, and inadequacies. At certain times our faith-walk can be a mixture of hope, hype, and pretense, rather that trust and confidence in the Lord.

There is a tension between the ideal of what we want to be and the actual of who we really are at this moment! Disillusionment is the stage in-between. We all have a veneer of polished behavior that we show the rest of the world. Behind this veneer is usually an inferior quality of life. We know the difference between real oak and chipboard with a veneer coating. The real is heavy and solid. It can take a beating. It is tough. The scars and abrasions do not detract from its appearance. With veneer-coated furniture it is the opposite. Every knock and scratch only highlights the inferior grade and lack of quality. It does not last long in difficult circumstances. Lack of quality is revealed in abrasive situations.

It is important to have our illusions broken, because then we can enter reality in our love and appreciation of one another. We can choose to respect the qualities and love and represent one another in the areas that need to be covered by real friends. We all have low spots in the wall of our life.

The enemy seeks to invade these low areas because this is where he infiltrates the work of God to destroy it and kill relationships. We see a perfect example of this in Nehemiah 4:1-17. Here Sanballat, Tobiah, and others opposed the rebuilding of the wall of Jerusalem, even conspiring to attack the Israelites. Because the walls were in such bad shape and full of rubbish, they believed that they could attack undetected at whatever point the builders left the wall, which was only half-built. But Nehemiah thwarted them by having half his people work on the wall while the other half kept watch. In fact, even those who worked on the wall still kept one hand available to grab a weapon if needed!

> *All true friendships can handle rubbish.*

The enemy detests what God is building. Whether it is the walls of Jerusalem, the Church of Jesus Christ, or friendship in the Body of Christ, he has a passionate desire to attack and destroy.

Those people who deride relational church have the spirit of Sanballat and Tobiah. They ridicule relationships because they do not understand the real process of friendship.

Intimacy with God is about getting the rubbish out of our lives so that the love of God can get in. All true relationships deal with rubbish. All real building creates a mess that must be cleared away. As Nehemiah did, we must set up a guard in our friendships over one another. The strength of the builders can fail because of the rubbish if we do not understand that the rubble in our lives exists because God is dismantling the old nature and constructing a new one.

The rubbish is the disillusionment we sometimes feel about one another as our illusions are shattered. It is a healthy thing, then, this breaking of images! Our strategy to develop our friendships is the same as Nehemiah's in rebuilding the walls of Jerusalem. We must station people in the low spaces of our lives.

We all are aware that the enemy seeks to exploit the low places in our lives. Putting a guard there is the only sensible thing to do. However, if the enemy already has penetrated parts of our life, then mounting a guard there ourselves may not be fruitful or effective. We may need particular ministry to dislodge an enemy who already has commandeered that particular place in our lives. We may need our friends to help us regain control and evict the enemy who has made it a stronghold. Having friends around us in church to help us is part of the rich heritage and culture of a vibrant New Testament church. We station people in the low places of our lifestyle and in the exposed places of our ministry. Working for God makes us a target. Friends give us cover in love. We do not want to be deficient in our character; otherwise we will be exposed to the enemy on the battlefield of service.

The best kind of support is through family-life first, then cell friendships, and finally corporate relationships in the wider Body of Christ. We are here specifically to fight for one another, not against each other. Discovery of sin and weaknesses should lead us to provide compassionate and gracious support. We need to know how to speak the truth in love. It is one of the aspects that adequately checks our maturity in Christ (see Eph. 4:15-16).

As we develop an internal church strategy for friendship, we will maximize our potential to frustrate the devil. Friendship warfare is critical. Going into battle on behalf of our brothers and sisters is a key part of building relationships in Christ. Once we have it up and running, it becomes a key part of our continuous strategy to help one another grow in morality, holiness, and right living.

We need workers and builders in place within the church to foil the schemes of the devil. I have numerous prayer partners, intercessors, and supporters of my ministry who consistently go into battle on my behalf. I have prayer coordinators in several countries who are part of a strategy to network prayer support for the ministry both generally and in times of principal need and demonic attack.

In Nehemiah's time, half his workers held defensive and offensive weapons whilst the other half worked. I consider my intercessors to be a critical part of the ministry. Many times their prayers have brought breakthrough, an increase of anointing, particular favor and support, as well as healing, health, and strength under attack.

Our friends are there to keep the enemy at bay and prevent him from getting too close. We are here to defend and protect one another. An important part of our relationship with people we love is that we be open and honest about areas of struggle that we have in our lives. Ironically, once we confess our need, our friend's support removes the struggle and creates a place of strength where once before there had been only glaring weakness. That is victory over the devil! We work alongside coworkers who can do the work but who also have a hand in protecting us as we in turn enable them to be effective because they are protected. In disillusionment, we either opt out of our difficulties or work out our differences.

The Key to God's Heart

The principle for church relationships is that God dwells in the house and moves in the Body. We can act together as the Body of Christ, but unless we are built together as the house of God, we will always be erratic and ineffective. It is the house of God that provides the solidity we need in church to love one another and fight off an implacable enemy.

We must pay as much attention to *being* something together as we put into *doing* something together. The corporate order in Ephesians is house first (chapter 2) and body second (chapter 4). Currently we are all at the doing stage of preparing for revival, with all its tensions and difficulties. We must understand that God's presence depends upon the house being built. Then the effect of God's presence is seen throughout the body.

> *The oil of the Holy Spirit prevents legitimate tension from becoming an unworkable friction.*

Much of today's revival terminology centers around "body" language. We are praying for a move of God. We are training, equipping, and praying for God to prepare us with active faith. We pray for the manifest presence of God but do not consider the conditions God requires for Him to come. We must build Him a habitation. Does God feel at home with us? Do we really care? Are we prepared to put work into our relationships in the church in order to allow people around us to shape and discipline us as a living stone? Who is the Holy Spirit cementing us to in the church in His Kingdom purpose? When we come together as friends and church, are there any chinks in the armor of our relationships? Is anyone indulging in negative fellowship in our church and so holding open a door to enemy activity? Is the work of the ministry causing us difficulties in disagreement and tension? Has our tension now become a friction? Do we sense that the love of God is growing so profoundly amongst us that our worship anointing has increased? Questions, questions, questions. Without honest examination and open-minded reflection, we cannot grow.

We can tell a lot about a church by the quality of its worship. Worship is the key to God's heart and therefore the key to real growth. The love of God is shed abroad in our hearts for the Lord and one another. A natural consequence of loving the Lord is that we love one another. We lay down our lives for God and one another (see 1 Jn. 4:16). As the love of God and one another grows, we are brought together in Him, and there is a powerful release of the Spirit. Worship is the natural outcome of such a release.

Whenever a church continuously struggles in worship, it is usually because of a relational issue within the church. We need breakthrough worship that flows out of anointed hearts joined together by what every joint supplies. Even the ordinary stones must cry out to the glory of God. How much more should we, as living stones being built together in love, become a temple of praise.

Among churches today we have two kinds of worship: synagogue and temple. Synagogue worship occurs when people come to church to hear the word of God, receive ministry, and be entertained. It represents the doing aspect of body worship. Often, because the main reason for meeting is actually people-centered rather than God-focused, this worship is usually reduced or restricted when time is pressing.

In temple worship, people come to praise God, to pray, and to make an offering. Their sole concern is for God Himself. This is home-building worship and requires a high level of adoration of God and mutual cooperation amongst people to be effective and glorious.

God seeks people to worship Him in spirit and truth (see Jn. 4:23). Worship releases the presence of God into our midst. That is why it is the key to God's heart. In worship we are completely taken up with Him.

Do our worship leaders spend more time motivating people to worship than acclaiming Christ? What type of worship songs do we sing the most? A true worship song is completely Christ-centered. Its sole focus is the total adoration and glorification of Christ. Many current songs are worship prayers dealing with our need or desire to worship Jesus rather than actually doing it.

Worship, then, is a major indicator of the church moving into a new wineskin, a different paradigm. If we have to spend a high proportion of our allocated worship time motivating people to get to a place of adoration that they should have been in when they first entered the meeting, we are in trouble spiritually.

In the new wineskin, people come ready to worship. The worship bands are Levites with an anointing to take us into the high places of God's manifest presence. From the moment the first note is struck we are at 35,000 feet and soaring in the Spirit. We are meant to be eagles, dining on snakes and riding the thermals of high praise. Anything else is for chickens!

It is possible to tell which churches have a strong revelation of the Lordship and majesty of Jesus by the strength, passion, and stamina of their worship. Many churches have good worship, but it is not enough. We must train our people how to corporately minister to the Lord. Currently many of our worship times consist of individuals opting in or out of worship depending on how they feel, on their current capacity to rise above their circumstances, or whether or not they like the songs or the music. Our worship can be a triumph of style over substance rather than a profound focus on the Person of Jesus by group consent.

Churches that are moving into a new place in God are seriously upgrading their worship anointing. They understand the house of God priority. They are teaching their people how to minister to the Lord through deliberate, corporate focus of attention on Jesus.

> *Temple worship is a key to breakthrough.*

Chapter 5

Revitalizing Your Church

Local Team Leadership

*L*eadership is a team effort. The New Testament always relates to a core group of leaders working together in dynamic purpose. There is a plurality of ownership, servanthood, and government worked out in a team environment. The most common biblical name for leadership at the local church level is a group of elders (core leadership team) being served and helped by a group of deacons (wider leadership team). The definitions in parentheses are contemporary job designations.

As we understand it, the role of pastor does not solely relate to local church government; it is a consultant gift belonging to the fivefold ministries (see Eph. 4:11-13). Scripture is clear in its outline that elders have a close working relationship with apostolic ministry (see Acts 15; 16:4; 20:17; 21:18). They are appointed by apostles (see Acts 14:23; Tit. 1:5-11) who lay down guidelines for behavior in ministry and who express certain qualities required to hold this particular office in the local church (see 1 Thess. 5:12-13; 1 Tim. 3:1-7; 5:17-20; Tit. 1:5-11; Jas. 5:14-15; 1 Pet. 5:1-4).

From these definitions we can glean the fact that there are different types of elders who may serve at different levels in the church. The early Church seemed to have a much freer and unsophisticated approach to theology than our modern-day counterparts who have to explain everything to the last degree. The language of the early Church was suited to the hearts and minds of slaves and ignorant fishermen and was spoken to many people who did not have the benefits of full-time education. Early Church approach to truth was practical, deeply spiritual, grounded in the supernatural, and very reasonable.

I am quite sure that the early Christians did not suddenly whip out a Greek lexicon from their back pocket to give us the actual Greek meaning of what Paul said at that evening's Bible study! They took his words at face value and simply went out and did it. They practiced the truth and walked in the word in a way that we should aspire to do in our generation. Many of the words written about the Christian faith then were the letters that we have collected today in the form of Scripture.

It is probable that many of those early believers never saw or heard about the other letters. In their town city or village region they may have lived their whole Christian life on a fragment of the truth remembered or written down during certain apostolic visits. These truths would have been reinforced constantly by local elders, who used mainly simple phrases and expressions. No doubt there were more civilized places where more intense intellectual discussion and dialogue was prominent. Truth, however, was backed up by the supernatural revelation of God. There were demonstrations of power through anointed people who walked with God personally at a level of deep humility and suffering.

> *God's Word and God's power can never be separated.*

Paul's testimony was declared in the early part of First Corinthians, a letter to the church that reinforced things he had spoken to them on his previous visit (see 1 Cor. 2:1-5).

Paul went with a simple, uncomplicated message regarding the cross of Jesus and the demonstration of God's power. It was not the persuasive nature of the teaching that was meant to reach out and touch people. It was simple truth expressed well and backed up with supernatural power.

Christianity is an affair of the heart, supported by a renewed mind, and held in tension by glimpses of Heaven as the Lord moves in power. Early believers were told to expect power in their relationship with God (see Acts 1:8). The true gospel is the word and the power of God combining with irresistible force (see Rom. 1:16).

It seems that all our sophisticated understanding of Scripture has produced millions of books and tapes but has not reached our city streets with the gospel. We can take apart every verse of Scripture and explain it away with several different options of understanding. We have multiple-choice definitions of truth, different versions of Scripture, a variety of theological perspectives, and no power. Hospitals are filling up and churches are closing down. Penal institutions are being built with astonishing rapidity all over the globe to house the sinners we are not reaching.

Our churches are filled with people who have a cerebral relationship with God and do not change in their lifestyle. Theology is meant to help us discover God and live in the abundance of Christ and His resurrection power. Primitive Christianity means a return to the original roots of supernatural Christianity, practiced in simple, uncomplicated ways.

When it came to choosing leadership, the early Church had certain criteria for character and gifting. People had to be decent, loving, caring individuals, practicing the truth in their own home life. Added to those character qualifications were certain attributes required for working amongst a group of people who come together for a common purpose.

The three main areas seemed to involve the following: the government of the church; the teaching of the people; and the care and attention required in shepherding. Leadership was probably more experimental in those days with many people appointed during the evangelistic enterprise of church planting. There was more hands-on discipling and mentoring. The point is, they would not have been as stereotyped and complex as we have become today. They were involved in building prototype churches that had to be robust enough to be left for certain periods of time until regular visits could be made.

Their leadership was more rugged than ours, though their lifestyles were probably no more difficult. Tension and stress abound whether in a survival-need culture or the more industrial business centers of our modern world. Those of us who have the privilege of conducting our ministry across such different frontiers of faith in this age will understand what I mean.

The early Church seemed to have different types of elders. In spiritual gifts there is a variety of gifts, a variety of ministries, and a variety of effects. Each person receives a certain manifestation of the Spirit within the variety of gifts and expression (see 1 Cor. 12:4-11). The gifts mentioned here—word of wisdom, word of knowledge, faith, gifts of healing, working of miracles, prophecy, discerning of spirits, tongues, and interpretation of tongues—are distributed at the discretion of the Holy Spirit. But the point is that all the varieties are not mentioned! We see the variety of gifts available but are not made aware of how they will be ministered or the effects that each level of ministry gift will produce.

For example, take the ministry gift of the prophet. In 25 years of ministry, I have personally encountered 16 different types of prophet. I know of several other designations that I have heard about in conversation but that I have not met at this point. Each of these particular expressions of prophetic ministry will have a variety of effects within the Body of Christ. I know prophets who have well-defined ministries with certain fields of endeavor. There are prophets who move only in personal prophecy to individuals; they are a blessing ministry. Others are more strategic in building alongside apostolic anointing. Some move only in healing; others solely in pastoral situations, bringing comfort and encouragement. Others minister on a visionary level, bringing direction to the corporate life of the church. Some are evangelistic and will mainly minister to the unsaved while others prophesy within a holiness context for the Body of Christ.

> *When the old wineskin is dying, the new wineskin is created by people who are not afraid to be vulnerable.*

Some prophets come alive in warfare situations; others have an anointing in the business community. Some move powerfully in deliverance and inner healing; others are excellent with children only. There are those who are brilliant in youth situations and those who are excellent in a prophetic teaching context. There are others who are quite wonderful in discipling and mentoring situations and still others excellent in a missions/sending-out context. Then there are those who have a certain anointing to prophetically inspire people in key jobs in society. There are reformation prophets who want to see missionaries in the legal community, police force, local government, education system, and medical field.

At times, we can move across the range of ministry and effects as circumstances dictate. Many people may operate at a deep level in one or several areas but have a much shallower expression in other designations. Sometimes prophets can spend whole seasons in one type of ministry area, then move into another designation at the same level of depth. When they move into another area of ministry and effect, they may retain or lose their previous anointing as the Holy Spirit dictates.

Several years ago, I went through a pastoral season with my prophetic anointing. The Holy Spirit could enter a person's pain and distress, do keyhole surgery with my prophetic gift, and bring a release from years of bondage in a matter of moments. When He moved me into a prophetic context of working in training, equipping, and discipling within the church, the previous anointing dried up. Then I spent several years ministering prophetically to people regarding their destiny, ministry, and future call of God. I prophesied to thousands of people in that context before I was moved into my current role of church rebuilding. Now my main prophetic function is in regards to church transition. I can help churches discover where they are going, where they have been, and where they are now! I understand some things regarding process and the nature of transition.

I believe in the same context that there are different types of elders with particular ministries. Some elders will be governmental—excellent teachers and caring shepherds. Others may be good at ruling and teaching but may not have the personal skills to be pastoral in counseling or visitation. Others may be lovely people-oriented leaders and great at pastoral work, but not particularly gifted at teaching or strategy. Some may be good at pastoral work with a greater or lesser capacity to teach.

Some elders clearly have a public leadership gift whilst others leave the church squirming with embarrassment and horror when they get behind a microphone. Constancy and communication are vital. We expect all leaders to have the former, but only a proportion may effectively demonstrate the latter.

It would seem from Scripture that there are those who rule well and others who have lesser ability. Similarly, there are those elders who are better at teaching and preaching than others (see 1 Tim. 5:17-18). Not all elders have to be ruling and involved in the government of the church unless it relates to their particular sphere of ministry. We all do not have to attend every meeting together while we talk over situations that have no bearing on our area of ministry. Finance meetings used to make me want to manifest! I would sit there, bored out of my tree, whilst we talked about buying curtains, carpet, or office equipment. I am not especially pastoral, though I have my odd moments of anointing. So for me to discuss the warts behind Sister Blenkinsop's left knee and how to deal with them is not a riotous blessing. I come out of such blessed gatherings wanting to do spiritual warfare and praying for a demon to appear so I can exercise authority and work it out of my system.

We can have elders' meetings involving ruling elders and shepherds to discuss and pray over pastoral needs. We can have leaders' meetings involving teaching, training, and discipling initiatives with those involved. We can have finance and administration meetings with appropriate people.

We need to be all together when we are being friends together rather than just enjoying our working relationship. We must be all together when discussing major areas of prophetic direction, envisioning, and financial or material decision-making.

Some of our elders may not rise above overseeing a few cell groups or a particular area or department of activity. Some may be on staff; others may be temporary or voluntary, depending on the requirements of the work. Some may oversee other elders and departments in a greater oversight capacity. They may interact specifically with apostolic ministry and may be apostolic also, as Peter expressed: "I who am a fellow elder..." (1 Pet. 5:1).

Consider too that the terms *elder* and *deacon* are probably cultural terms in the Bible rather than biblical terms that are meant to fit every culture, situation, and country.

In our culture in the United Kingdom, these terms are not particularly helpful to people of varying generations. I believe it is okay with the Lord if we change the terminology as long as we keep the criteria and the concept of leadership intact. I prefer *core leaders* to describe elders and *wider leaders* to describe deacons. It may be just peculiar to us, so don't lose your shirt over it!

Much of Scripture was written in a fairly tight geographic location where these cultural terms would have been normal and easily understood. If the Bible is to be a global book that radically affects our behavior in all cultures, then we may want to adjust some matters of terminology as our conscience dictates.

The terms for the fivefold ministries are interchangeable across cultures, customs, and nations, so we can use them appropriately. It is not worth anyone blowing a gasket over (allow me my English idiosyncrasy). I just thought it may be helpful. Do what seems good to you and the Holy Spirit.

Around this team of leaders/ministries who oversee the extensive work of the church, we will have a much wider group of workers and supporters under the broad heading of deacons (see 1 Tim. 3:8-13). These support personnel are made up of potential elders, developing ministries, apprentice leaders, and other quality people. The diaconate forms a major part of the training and

> *Part of the law of the Spirit of life is to love people and use things... not love things and use people.*

proving ground for the ongoing development of people into places of power and significance. It is accepted that all deacons will be tested for faithfulness, anointing and ministry capacity, people skills, character under stress, team focus, obedience, leadership, and personal accountability. As they prove out and develop the deeper characteristics required for a wider spiritual anointing and position, we can gradually make room for them as the Holy Spirit designates. One of the significant aspects of this group of people is whether they are ready to endure pressure and function consistently at a higher level of calling. Many people are willing to move into a recognized place of function. Few, however, are ready for the squeezing that comes with new position. Things are formed under pressure.

If, in our stress, we turn to the Lord and learn to live in His peace, rest, and provision, then that which is formed in us will be precious, like a diamond. A diamond is infinitely precious, but it also has a powerful cutting-edge capacity to cause breakthrough. However, if we fail to walk with God more closely, then our hearts could become hardened. Instead of a diamond, we will have a lump of granite without the capacity to bring glory to God and the penetrating capacity to overcome.

There are many leadership books and programs that do not help new people in leadership cultivate their personal relationship with God as part of their development plan. Every new level of responsibility must be accompanied (if not preceded) by a renewal of love and desire for the Lord Jesus. If we do not deliberately provision our people to love God at a deeper level, they will not enjoy the pressure situations that we expose them to in the continuance of their ministry. This will lead to eventual burnout at worst, or general ongoing tiredness where they are prone to lethargy and potential resistance.

It is the love of Jesus that upholds our lives. His presence creates a rest and peace that renew our mind, heart, and bodily strength. In Him we perfect the art of bouncing back in a time of crisis. In Him we have an energy, a renewable life source each day, that enables us to keep short accounts and shrug off the cares of yesterday. We learn in Jesus how to live in day-tight compartments, meaning that one day at a time, we experience the God of now, not yesterday or tomorrow. We learn how not to let the sun go down on our anger and how to close our day with thanksgiving. His presence helps us to dream appropriately as sleep refreshes our bodies. We begin each morning with gratitude and fresh expectation. New manna comes daily in the form of revelation, power, and His presence. Double portions of God come on a weekly basis as we face the issues of a life at war.

We need to produce people who are up for the fight, who can relish the battle, but who also know how to bring their mind and heart to peace. We need people who can live from within, in the secret place of the Spirit. This must be part of our training and development of people before we put them into positions of power, where they will be exposed to a new level of warfare and personal attack.

Delegated Authority

Leadership is tough. It affects our lives in very adverse ways if we do not do it God's way. Moses was constantly living on the edge of stress and breakdown because of the sheer volume of ministry required. His father-in-law Jethro saw the toll it was taking on him physically and questioned, in a sincere manner, the methodology of his son-in-law. Moses' methodology of doing everything himself was clearly exhausting him. Jethro's advice to delegate the responsibility was the wisdom of the Lord, and it came to Moses in a highly practical manner from a source close to his heart and family life.

The principle of delegated authority runs throughout Scripture. First determine who are the key people in the work. Who can work under pressure and be faithful and reliable when the going is rough? As leaders, we want people who are battle-scarred but by no means battle-weary. Tried and tested people can take the strain and will not buckle under the weight of the work. We need people with substance faith who can inspire others on difficult days.

> *Those who cannot adapt to change are living in a museum.*

The work of God is too much for one person. The Lord sets us in teams. The goal of good leadership is to facilitate the development of key people in the work. These people can then inspire and cultivate other people so that the broader work of the church may become effective. This is the principle under which the five-fold ministries operate in the New Testament Church: training, equipping, empowering, and releasing others to do the work of the ministry (see Eph. 4:11-12). Leadership must have an action plan to select, train, and release people into leadership with appropriate mentoring and oversight. We need people at different levels of capacity. We need people who can take the pressure of leading 1,000, 100, 50, or 10 people. We must teach burden-bearing, establish the right criteria for productive leadership, and understand the balance of how a team is put together.

Do not just choose people only on the basis of gift or anointing. Look at the character and personality of new people. Examine their basic temperament. Look for steadiness and continuity in their personal life. It is easier to add than retract. It is better to increase a person's responsibilities than claw back delegated authority that has gone wrong. A team should be a blending of temperaments, skills, abilities, and capacity to endure pressure and stress. People should be teachable, humble, open, and honest. We must create a climate of love and affection based on real core values of honor and commitment.

With the exceptions of relationship with the Lord Jesus and marriage, no other covenants can reasonably be expected to last for a lifetime. God does move people on to other places and into other realms of ministry. We must allow people the freedom to follow the leading of the Holy Spirit. It is inevitable that we will both disappoint others and be disappointed ourselves. If our ability to release other people to the Lord is pure, then we need not be offended.

If people move on unwisely or prematurely, we can love them enough to keep a candle burning in the window to help them relocate back to the church family. If that is not possible, we can lose them graciously, knowing that the Lord will resupply in His time. Do not express disappointment in people by staining their character. People have a right to make mistakes. Only the Lord is perfect. If we put question marks over the heads of people, we will reap the same demerit in our own lives. I have been stupid in this area, so I know its truth.

For my part, I am learning that if I bless and honor what I can in people who have left, however difficult the circumstances, I will reap people who will have the same attitude of love and grace that I display in Christ.

Blocking the Vision

When we begin a new work, we receive a pioneering vision. A work can begin in the heart of a single individual who acts as a catalyst to launch into a new area of activity. His or her foresight, planning, focus, determination, and faithfulness make the vision a reality.

At this stage, the whole vision may be bound up in the life of this individual. The person sacrifices, works, sheds tears, and is misunderstood and written off by some as he or she faithfully pursues the call. Vision at this gut level is highly personal. As the work grows, other people come into it who did not pay the price of those early years. We have to own the vision in order to make it a reality. However, we also can embrace it so fully that we cannot give it up, not even to the Lord.

The vision we start with is never the vision with which we finish. Most vision only lasts approximately seven years before it goes through a cycle of necessary change. Pioneering vision must give way to empowering vision. The Lord never gives us the whole vision at the beginning. Part of His vision for our work is that there will be people He will give us whom He wants to influence the ministry. God tells us enough to get us started and to keep moving. He does not give large visions at the beginning of new enterprises. Vision grows with the work. It is complemented and added to by the commitment and faithfulness of those whom God joins to the work.

The Lord always seeks to enfranchise His people within the work of the ministry. Vision must flow out of relationships with a common agenda and purpose. Vision that is set in concrete from the beginning will break people's hearts by its unworkable nature. One man's vision must be released

> *Experience enables us to recognize a mistake when we make it again.*

into the core vision of the team that grows up within it. All vision changes in some way.

As the vision touches, releases, and builds people up in Christ, He will release vision within them that is real and personal. We do not need the clash between corporate vision and personal destiny. People must not be forced to choose. Corporate vision must breathe and be flexible enough to be inclusive, not exclusive, of people's calls. This means that reasonable dialogue regarding the individual destiny and calling of people and the corporate vision of the work must occur at regular intervals in the calendar of the ministry.

If the church is running on one man's vision, we are going to have real problems with divisiveness. If people have to leave the ministry on a regular basis, it is probably because the vision of the founder is consistently disenfranchising their lives. This is the dilemma for founding visionaries. In order to beat the odds, fight the circumstances, and press into God's purpose, we had to own the vision with the Lord.

Later on, though, the Lord will bring in people who also must own the vision with Him. At this point, the main blockage is usually the founder of the ministry. We must pass from ownership with God personally to stewardship with other people corporately. If we fail this subtle and elegant test, we will insist that people are present to serve our vision. Yet, vision is given by the Lord. Ownership rests entirely with Him. He has enfranchised us with His vision and now He seeks to include others in the same arrangement. This is where vision must change.

The whole nature of the ongoing vision within the work must rest on the fact that sooner or later we have to find out what God is doing in the lives of people He has brought into the work. Leadership is really about facilitating the development of people whom God has given us. Understanding and cultivating their personal destiny is a core aspect of the growth and fulfillment of the wider vision.

As personal vision grows, God adds people to it. This causes an expansion of the work. In the process of that expansion, the vision changes from the personal foresight of one individual to the corporate activity of a group whom God has brought together.

Corporate vision cannot be founded on one man's destiny. To develop corporate vision the founder must die to personal ownership and become a steward for a loving God who seeks to include others. This does not happen overnight. There is a process to follow. We must make time to talk with members of the church to begin to discover their identity in the Lord. What do they feel strongly about? What is the burden on their heart? What are they praying for in terms of working with the Lord?

Our role as leaders is to understand the vision that the Lord is actually building into the lives of individuals, and then make room to see that vision flourish. Individual vision must be heard, understood, and accepted by the leadership of the church. We need to enable people to actually understand where their personal identity can fit in and complement the corporate vision of the church. The corporate vision will be expanded by various contributions. The detail of the vision will grow and be enhanced by the additions.

If people are being anointed with a personal call and destiny by the Holy Spirit but the leadership does not cooperate with Him, then we create double vision or di-vision. Many church splits have occurred over the issue of disagreement in vision. If people cannot see where their own calling fits in with the corporate concept, they will be insecure.

It needs high levels of love and commitment to negotiate this particular situation. Neither side can hold the other to ransom. Both must be willing to believe the best of one another. Clearly some negotiation will take place. Neither side will be 100 percent right. Leadership may be too set in their ways. The individual may have delusions of grandeur about his or her role and function. Agreement will release covenant. If both sides are willing to die to self, the cross will make brothers of us all.

Individuals cannot insist on their rights. Leaders must become aware that members of the body are not present merely to serve the vision of the leadership.

Leaders model how a servant spirit should behave. Members follow that example. The result will be a partnership that enables us to look forward together, a partnership where leaders understand personal vision and where it fits in to the work of the church. The individual understands the corporate vision and knows where he can fit in to serve the church. In a true partnership, both serve one another.

Division occurs because we don't actually take into account God's call on the individual. The corporate vision may be too inflexible to allow individuals to shape it effectively. People become disillusioned and disempowered by such high-handedness. We cannot push people into a mold that we have created; otherwise, they may legitimately look elsewhere to fulfill God's call upon their life.

By the same token, the church cannot be put over a barrel by unscrupulous people who will serve only if given a position of power. We earn the right to serve other people. If our personal vision cannot be endorsed by the leadership, then we must ask certain questions of ourselves: "Have I presented my vision in an acceptable manner? Have I gained a good enough track record as a serving member of the church? Can I be trusted? Have I proven faithfulness? Do I really want the best for others or do I want everything on my terms? Is the timing right for my ministry to emerge or am I being premature? Do I require more development before I can turn my aspirations into achievement? Am I preoccupied with myself or do I have the best interests of all the group at heart?"

> *Mentors do not manage disciples; they facilitate them.*

God opens doors for us that no man can close. He is full of plans and purpose to facilitate our growth into His wider vision of Kingdom. If a door is not opening, it may be that the Lord does not trust us as fully as He would like. If a door closes, it will probably be an issue of trust between ourselves and the Lord.

In order to create partnerships that are mature and responsible, both sides must bend to the will of the Holy Spirit. Leaders must grow into fathers who release their sons into fruitfulness and not castrate them. I have seen many eunuchs in the house of the Lord and very few fruitful sons.

Pioneering leadership must allow others to become radical alongside them. We must create a team where we all can be influenced and supported. This will not strip the main leader of authority and power; rather, as Moses discovered, it will enhance his capability to move forward decisively in the plans of God. Delegated authority combining with enfranchised vision creates a groundswell of significance and power that will produce breakthrough.

Moses changed his priorities from overseeing the whole work by himself to seeking a greater level of power through enfranchising others. He selected people and worked with them for a period to develop their role in the work. His ability to facilitate people into a deeper anointing actually eased his own burden considerably and helped him to specialize in the ministry. Leadership that cannot delegate cannot rise to heights of significance. It may penetrate the high places of anointing, but it will not be able to sustain momentum. It will become too general. It will lose key people too often, forcing it to be continually trying to make up ground it has forfeited.

People Are Our Main Resource

Jesus operated in the same principle as Moses. He had a core group of people—Peter, James, and John—who shared His heart. He surrounded these with the remainder of the original group. He taught them extensively. He discipled them and sent them out on assignment. He tested them to determine their faith level (see Mk. 4).

Around that group there were 70 others who were committed to the vision of His Father. These were no doubt assisted in their development by the original 12. The church is grown from the inside to the outside as we resource the people under our care.

We begin with a relatively small number of people whom we can trust. We look for the people like Gideon's 300 who were ready, not just willing. As the relationship grows, so does the vision partnership. Around this core group of people we develop a wider group of people who have the potential to move on further.

Despite all Gideon's reservations and problems, God saw that he had potential to become mighty! God nurtured that potential and Gideon grew into a place of stature in the nation. He also learned how to recognize the potential and readiness in other people. With 70 receiving training and empowerment, the group has the potential to grow into 120. Such a number was in the upper room on the Day of Pentecost.

The power of the covenant within the group grows exponentially with their anointing, creating an environment of love, trust, and passion. Power is released in abundance as we commit to God and one another. Once we begin to cultivate people, their own anointing will grow to cover others. Thus we are constantly growing the church out to progressive levels of significant power and faith.

Finally, when we are getting the bulk of the congregation actually working, living in faith, and expressing their hearts together before God, then He will trust us with something of much greater importance. We will have a much more powerful impact on our own group and also on unchurched people.

To turn a church around, we really have to begin to identify certain groups of people. We will find that there are normally three types of people in church: those who make things happen, those who help to make things happen, and those who are always asking the question, "What on earth is happening?" We define them as being initiators, enablers, and resisters. Every church has those three types of people in it: people who can multiply something, people who add something to the work, and people who are divisive or who are just taking away as much as they can but not giving anything back. We always find those three attitudes somewhere in church life.

Initiators

Initiators are breakthrough people. They are the people who are not afraid of change or a challenge; they are people who want to get on and serve God. They may have lots of raw qualities around them, and they may be frustrated.

The Value of Difficult People

Frustrated people are probably our best chance of building church. I would rather have 50 frustrated people than 500 apathetic ones. Most people are frustrated only because they care about something. Many leaders turn their backs on frustrated people because they are difficult to accommodate. It is a pain that I want to have in church. There are some pains that we want to have because they can be catalysts to improve the dynamic of the work.

Frustrated people are a good pain. They are good because they do a number of things. For one thing, they force us into thinking about the future, about what God is doing. They make us run ahead of the pack ourselves to anticipate events. If we do not have frustrated people, we all will tend to sit on our laurels. If no one is making any waves, we will assume everything is fine. So we settle for what we have got. Frustrated people never allow us to settle for anything. They are always pushing us. We know that the good is the enemy of the best, and frustrated people always push us into doing something better. Frustrated people also may be a provocation to our tendency to procrastinate.

There is a dynamic involved where they are pushing us all the time. I can look back over years of training and leadership and see that frustration was often a necessary catalyst. Most of the material I have developed in the realm of the prophetic has come because people I was discipling in prophetic gifting and ministry kept pushing me out of my comfort zone. They continued pushing me and raising questions about the prophetic ministry. I had to keep running to stay ahead of this bunch of people. So gradually all our material went through a refining process. It was refined at least six times. Their questions helped to

> *History dictates that often real progress is determined by people who will not merely accept the status quo.*

shape the direction of our School of Prophecy on several occasions, making the training more relevant to the ongoing supernatural development of the church.

The future of any church will rest in part with how we handle our frustrations and our questioning people. We all are stakeholders in the church that we love. We need a leadership who understands about the key role frustration can play in building the church. Frustration and the answers it will generate are a precursor to real growth and change. To get right answers, though, we must ask appropriate questions.

Many times we only perceive the "hassle factor" that provokes us in the faces of frustrated people. God's Spirit often broods over the work of God, agitating us and stimulating us into new places of understanding and practice.

Initiators are breakthrough people. They want to pioneer and are prepared to pay a price. There are lots of good things that we can harness in frustrated people. They want to do something, they want real involvement, and they do not want to be fobbed off with anything less. That is what makes it awkward for us at times. There is no doubt that they are awkward customers, but awkward customers are better than no customers. They are people who are more forward-thinking and who can make things happen. At the same time, their character may leave a lot to be desired. We can simply look at those people and see things in their lives that would make it easy for us to count them out rather than take the time or trouble to include them in.

We have potential champions in our midst, and we need to realize who they are. These are the people who can make a difference. They have got something of faith in them as well as a dimension of anointing and power. They also may have areas in their lives that still need working on.

These are people in our church who may irritate us. I hope they do. They may frustrate us. They are bored and can express themselves wrongly. Some of that is because they have never been taken seriously before. They have something in them—an edge—and sometimes the edge cuts for us and sometimes against us.

They need to be befriended because these are the people who, if we get hold of them, will be breakthrough people. If we get hold of them and bring direction into their lives, if we love and care for them, if we will become their friend and father them, they will run through a wall for us, because they are breakthrough people. They will punch through opposition. When the enemy is active, these are the people we need to encourage into significant warfare.

The problem is, some of these people have a difficult personality. Possibly that is because of how they have been dealt with in the past. We know that one of the important things we as leaders need to have is an anointing to allow people to outgrow their history.

It is impossible to continue in fellowship with people who hold back in relationship and trust because of events in the past. When true repentance has been established and the lifestyles of people have been radically altered, we must allow people to grow out of that part of their life.

Several years ago when praying for a number of people after a meeting, I encountered a man whom I had known in the early part of my ministry. He made it quite clear that he would receive prayer but would not accept any prophetic input. I was intrigued enough to ask him his reason. His reply was that he had not liked some of the things I had done in 1979 and felt that he could not trust my current level of gifting within the prophetic ministry. Trying to keep my voice even and mild, I calmly mentioned the possibility that a lot may have changed in my life over the intervening 15 years since we had met! I could not remember the situation he was no doubt remembering as though it was yesterday. This is unusual for me; normally I can call to mind all my past cringe-factor situations. For the uninitiated, a "cringe-factor situation" is a memory of certain past circumstances that still have the capacity to embarrass us today. Ten is the highest cringe-factor; one is the mildest.

I had no embarrassing memory of this man personally. I did feel sorry for him that he had not grown out of his own past. Fellowship and function are impossible in these situations. Where there is no trust we have a breakdown of fellowship. I am not referring to recent events where scars are still fresh and we need to reestablish trust. The power of the cross to overcome our history and give us the power of new life must never be underestimated or go unused.

As leaders we encourage people to take advantage of the grace of God. People must be taught how to boldly approach the throne of grace knowing that they will find grace and mercy to help in their time of need (see Heb. 4:16).

It is somewhat easier to police people than it is to mentor them. I have met hundreds of people who have been controlled rather than coached. The only answer to misuse is not non-use but proper use. Where people have abused their gifting or position in the past, they must be helped to overcome these areas with proper training and discipling.

Many current initiators may have elements in their history that were not good. Mostly we learn by our mistakes. When we do things for the first time, we often learn how not to do them, primarily. Retrospective revelation includes the ability to learn from the past and move on into a new practice and pattern of behavior.

Learn to take a second look at people. Get beyond the surface level. The least we can do is to ask the Lord to show us the people as He sees them. It is a human condition to want mercy for ourselves and judgment for others when reviewing past behavior. We need mercy. The mercy that God gives us to be able to lead others must be extended to them as they allow themselves to be developed.

> *At what point is a person allowed to outgrow his history?*

I am not saying that we must overlook certain behavior and make light of the past, especially if current conduct is unwholesome. People grow by appreciation. People are worth persevering with, even if they are finding change hard to accept. It is good practice in godliness for us to hold fast to God's kindness and persist with things we do not like in order to establish the qualities that we believe exist in embryonic form within the individual.

Every two or three years everyone needs a fresh start, the opportunity to put away the past, to outgrow events. God is changing people quickly in these days. It is a powerful expression of love and kindness when we can affirm people even though we may have some difficulties with them. It is good to be honest yet loving, to talk to people openly about areas where they cause us difficulty, yet at the same time declare the things we appreciate about them.

Personality and Character

It is good to see people exploring ways in which they can take their relationship to a new level, especially when those relationships have gone through times of difficulty. Talking about how we can overcome the mistakes of the past, to make our relationships more meaningful, will truly glorify the Lord Jesus. As He hung dying on a tree, He became a role model of forgiveness both to His disciples and to His persecutors.

None of us has any ambition to repeat our poor history. Sometimes the best gift we can give someone is a clean start, a new page. God understands this only too well! I wonder sometimes how many Christians are courting judgment in their own lives by their refusal to let go of the history of another.

The grace of God is renewable each day. Life in the Spirit is rejuvenated on a daily basis, as we renew our mind. While the outward man perishes, the inward man is being refreshed by the Lord (see 2 Cor. 4:16). Throughout the day as we commune with the Lord we can be refreshed by His presence. We want people around us to be set free to live in the present moment with the Lord. To release vision and anointing for the present and future, we must put a guard on one another's past.

There is a difference between character and personality. Character relates to our morality, integrity, lifestyle practices, how we deal with our sexuality, and how we behave under pressure. Personality is more concerned with our temperament, how we face issues in terms of self-confidence or low self-esteem. The gray area between the two is our learned behavior from poor role models, bad early life experiences, and harmful authority encounters, all of which have had a negative influence on our personality.

When examining personality, we look at how people do things, how they communicate, how they feel about themselves. We are all the product of our yesterdays until God changes us. It is too easy to make a character issue out of a personality trait. I am an introvert; that is my personality. I like who I am. I am pleased with how God made me. I am quiet, shy, and can be difficult to get to know on a personal level. I do confide in people, but I have to know them really well. I have been accused of being secretive and evasive about my private life. Some of that was due to lack of rapport and trust. Mostly it was because people expected self-disclosure from me in the manner that an extrovert would share.

Introverts share differently. We perceive, speak, and act quite differently from outgoing, expressive people. Extroverts may talk very freely when they are comfortable with people. They can share their life story in an hour. Introverts will drop clues that need following up. They need to see ongoing evidence of love, concern, and affirmation as they disclose themselves.

My friend, Andreas Herrmann, says that introverts have a very colorful inner life. It requires a big effort to allow someone into that inner world, particularly the painful parts. I usually share among a group of friends and am delighted if they talk to one another about me.

I have a friend who has a very sweet spirit but is very analytical in his thinking. He always asks lots of questions, seeking more and more detail in information. If I talk to him for too long on a subject, he will tie me up in knots. Sometimes I want to turn the volume down or switch his brain off. There is nothing wrong with his character. I would trust him with my life, my wife, my children, my possessions. At times he frustrates me; mostly he is a delight to be with. Sometimes he can be in a certain frame of mind that will aggravate people around him as he questions. If they answer him badly, he pursues the issues like a cat after a mouse. It is just the way his mind works. I like him. I respect his morality. His personality gets on top of him and his friends, at times. He is worth knowing and having as a friend. We all aggravate people; most of us are just too thick-skinned to know how we do it.

Try to separate character and personality with the people around you. Understand the personality of God-given friends. Learn to put up with people for the sake of what God is producing in them. The grace of God winks at us because He can tell a personality trait from a character issue. He brings both together in our lives so that we see and understand ourselves. It is part of His loving us and teaching us how to love ourselves.

One of the key things I look for in initiators is a willingness to sacrifice. The price they are willing to pay will tell me a lot about them as coworkers. People will make sacrifices for the sake of a vision or for their gifting. We need to enable people to sacrifice for the development of their character. We do not want people to pull down with their character what they have built with their gifting.

Initiators will form part of the core team of leaders and ministries within the church. As we identify our key players, we can begin to develop our strategy around their gifting and disposition. We need people we can build with and build upon. When we are considering who these core builders are in the church, give particular thought to including youth and children's workers in that grouping.

> *God's grace can tell the difference between character and personality.*

Apart from the fact that we believe the youth are the church of today, not tomorrow, we also want to make a statement that our children matter. In ten years' time, our current youth will be mainline leaders and our children will be the dynamic youthful voice of a generation having grown up in the Kingdom, not the world. We are people-shapers at all levels.

Make a list of the current key players in the church. Who are the initiators, the catalysts, the potential pioneers? Who are the breakthrough people of today? Who will be the breakthrough people of tomorrow? Who, among this broad group, are those with whom we can share our heart and vision? Can they form a cell around the calling, vision, and destiny of the church? What development will they personally require in the area of relationship, vision, and training in ministry? What "on the job" training can we supply as they come alongside us in the work? What type of model of leadership are we using as an example for them to follow? We get the people and attitudes that we model in ourselves. Leaders are fathers and examples for the flock.

We want to ensure that our people are going to be around serving the Lord for the long term. This means we will need to determine their training needs fairly quickly. They will also need effective monitoring as they pursue their gifting in a place of function and responsibility. This is where the partnership is developed between leaders and core personnel. Their sphere of influence within the church will develop through the influence of senior leadership on their own lives.

Ultimately that development must open a roadway for key people to advance to peer level anointing alongside us as we cultivate their gift and ministry.

Enablers

These are the second grouping of people whom we must identify and develop after our initiators. Enablers are good support people. They have proven faithfulness, understand the vision of the church, and have a will to work. They may have the potential to develop further in time, or maybe they are that sort of wonderful people who form the backbone of any enterprise. They help to make the vision a reality. If the initiators are the head of the spear, then the enablers are the shaft. It is their solid weight of loyal, faithful support behind our projects and initiatives that provide us with the resources to achieve a breakthrough.

Many times this grouping can be overlooked and their faithfulness taken for granted, simply because they do not make waves and do not draw attention to themselves. They are good-hearted, constant, and dependable. Enablers are often a mixture of people who understand where their calling fits in with the corporate vision and people who have no dynamic sense of calling but are willing to serve where the need is greatest. They can be charismatic or conservative in their gifting and approach to team ministry.

When we begin to develop people in ministry, it is important that we teach them about general service. "Whatever your hand finds to do, do it with your might" (Eccles. 9:10a), and "Whatever you do, do it heartily, as to the Lord and not to men" (Col. 3:23) are two vital ground rules for basic servanthood in the church. Firstly, we must teach people to look for things to do in the church rather than simply be asked to do something. The best servants are proactive as well as hardworking. They learn how to anticipate.

Secondly, it is vital that they learn about stewardship. Everything we do is for an audience of one, the Lord Jesus. If people do not learn this important lesson, they may become owners of their ministry instead of stewards. Owners have a vested interest in themselves. Stewards always think about the benefits for other people. (See Colossians 1:25; Ephesians 3:2; First Corinthians 4:2; 9:7; and First Peter 4:8-10.) We must develop people who do not differentiate between what is overtly spiritual and what is completely natural at this level of servanthood. Everything is the same to them at this level. Service is service. Later on, as their anointing in spiritual things begins to increase, we will make necessary adjustments in their stewardship to accommodate what the Lord is doing through them, according to Paul's experience (see 1 Tim. 1:12).

As people begin to serve generally, the ground of their heart is plowed up by the Spirit. In the process of gaining humility, we must lose our proud ambitions for power, place, and recognition. As we gain a reputation for quality servanthood at the "whatsoever" level of anointing, God begins to mark us for further development. He plants a seed in the ground that has been dug over by the Holy Spirit. Good mentors look for such seeds of grace in people they are discipling. These seeds contain the beginnings of a personal call and vision.

Something begins to change in the heart of individuals as they serve generally. God begins to get hold of them, opening them up for an increase of anointing. If they are left too long at this level, frustration will set in. The joy in leadership and mentoring is to be able to recognize that change in people and to nurture it. Seeing new shoots of growth emerging in people is a delight. Influencing, nurturing, and watering those seeds with deliberate movements will enable leaders to produce another crop of enablers. Some of these enablers will grow on again to become initiators and pioneers. Many will stay at this level. They will not move onward but will grow outward to become a strong influence at the helping, supporting level. Their input supplies the genuine strength of the presence of God in the work.

I am looking for shoots and I am looking for roots in people. Maybe it is the prophetic in me, but I always want to look beneath the surface of someone's life and see what is growing in God. I want to know where this shoot is going to appear when it comes through the surface. I want to be the first one to put a drop of water on it and nurture it, cause it to grow. It is helpful to let that person stand in my shade so that when the heat of pressure of circumstances is on his life, I want him to find shelter in God near me. I want to make sure that I stand in the sun so that he does not get fried. There is something to nurture in people's heart. It is all part of the fathering and the serving that we need to see in leadership. People are the best asset we have.

> *The servant spirit in the church will be of the same quality as the servant heart of the leadership.*

I am often totally amazed at the quality of people that God produces in our churches, people who work without complaint or remuneration because it is their loving sacrifice to a heavenly King. We can feel the passion of God through such people. It is good to appreciate them and honor their work, which is done in private and often may go unnoticed in the public setting. No matter how large the church conference, how powerful the worship, or how anointed the speakers, the most significant people there will be the cleaning team. If the toilets are blocked or not cleaned, if the church is full of trash or smells, it will hugely detract from all that is happening around the platform! Apostles and janitors are equally as vital.

Conviction and Availability

It is vital that we know who our support people are by name and, if possible, by function. Some people enable out of a sense of conviction. They feel a kinship with a particular call and vision. It finds an echo in their heart. Left to themselves they may not have pursued anything. They are not initiators; they are support people. They may not have the personality or anointing to be catalysts. However, when someone emerges who wants to move out in a particular area, we always will find willing supporters who want to serve out of the conviction that God has called them to that project or initiative.

There are those people who have no defined conviction about a particular role or ministry but who genuinely make themselves available to serve. Always ask people personally. Do not just give altar calls for volunteer help; do it by personal invitation. Some people have low self-esteem and others are not confident in putting themselves forward at public meetings. Good leaders inspire the confidence in people to become available for service.

People with no conviction about ministry often do not mind helping out, if others define their objectives at that level. As they work, the Holy Spirit inspires them, and definition in the shape of ministry and further usefulness begin to emerge. It is so exciting to watch people develop from those first faltering steps into a stronger walk in servanthood.

People are willing to be trained, shaped, and told what to do in that first phase of availability. Later on as they grow, the way we disciple them changes to allow their convictions to grow and be expressed. Then they share with us what they want to do for the Lord. We can help to shape that by acceptance and further training as we develop them from servants to stewards in the work. Stewards have more responsibility and must display a different attitude and approach to the work.

The transition from servant to steward must have the seal of leadership approval. We need to agree with the call that is being defined in the servant and then help to disciple that call into a stewardship role of anointing.

Putting people into a working environment will cause them to be stretched. Vision grows in hearts learning to be vulnerable in self and dependent on God. As people grow in faith and service, the counsel of God begins to impregnate them with vision. God builds them layer by layer in their life, so that faith, service, and opportunity begin to combine and vision begins to grow in seed form.

The principle of general service, which is "whatever your hand finds to do, do it with your might" will eventually, in most people, give way to specific stewardship. Stewardship contains a defined call and vision. It carries with it specific responsibility. Stewardship is always about other people, never ourselves.

A good steward always looks to see how he can live for and benefit other people. It is a characteristic that we must never lose no matter how anointed and significant our leadership and ministry become in church and Kingdom circles. Stewardship is a state of mind as well as heart. Read Philippians 2:5-8, first for you yourself, then practice it before others. The goals of real stewardship as well as the character that pleases God is laid out in this passage:

- Do nothing from selfishness or conceit.
- Have proper humility of mind.
- Regard others as more important than yourself.
- Look out for the interests of others, not just for yours.
- Have the same servant mind as Jesus.
- Do not grasp at the place and function God bestows on you.
- Become a bond slave (the highest form of ministry and status).
- Humble yourself through cross-driven obedience to God.

Sadly, many leaders and ministries do not continue to practice these characteristics when they are put into exalted positions. Stewards require defined discipleship relationships to enable them to progress in pleasing the Lord. Their life must be built upon principle and example rather than just training and opportunity. Some general servers may have an identity problem that must be resolved before they can progress to stewardship and calling by conviction. Making a list of the enablers may help us to determine training and discipling needs in this next echelon of people. Turning soldiers into mighty men and women of God is a privilege that requires a strategic approach to people development.

If all that our leadership anointing does is enable us to have good meetings, we are not going to get very far in building people. With the best will in the world, we will simply bless people rather than establish them

> *Good mentors bring definition to the lives of people they are discipling.*

in God. To build something into people requires a relational context outside of a meeting environment.

Involvement and Commitment

There is a difference between involvement and commitment. People may have the capacity to be involved at 30 percent, 60 percent, or 100 percent, plus all the shades in between those arbitrary figures. That is not indicative of their covenant or commitment; merely of the time and energy at their disposal. Busy career people, those who own their own businesses, or those with young families have limited time to express their spirituality in a group/church context.

We need to define the level of commitment to the proportionate amount of involvement we can realistically generate. So, if a family can be only 30 percent involved with church initiatives, we want them to try to be 100 percent committed to that level of involvement.

We have to be realistic in understanding that the present structure of our church may not fit the resources we actually possess. Which comes first, the type of people we actually have or the kind of church we want to build? Is it our ambition for a certain type of church that is driving us in our leadership? Are we trying to fit people into a structure, or are we allowing the structure to be defined by the people and resources that God has given to us? I know plenty of church leaders who have a vision for a resource church, but their resource base is insufficient for that type of church community. They have too much aspiration for their people to achieve.

Apostolic wisdom always will match vision with resources either through development of the existing base or realignment of personnel elsewhere in the network. The structure of the church is meant to serve the life of the people. So often, it is the opposite that occurs. The lives of the people are bound up in serving a structure that is non-releasing, non-equipping, or non-empowering.

Are we building with the people we actually have or with the people we wish they were? Possibly, we may need to dismantle our current structures, meeting methodologies, and ministry practices to build a living, breathing organism rather than a rigid inflexible wineskin. A covenantal church founded on genuine love and relationship has far more appeal to the Holy Spirit than a functional church merely based on gifting and ministry. Obviously, we need both together; however, it is the foundation that determines the building. A foundation meant for a single-story dwelling will not sustain the weight of additional floors. Enlargement is preceded by greater depth; otherwise, catastrophe occurs. Similar growth in ministry requires a greater depth of covenant relationship.

Real friendships are the base line foundational to the requirements of God in relational church. We want relationships with an agenda, so we add gift and ministry to the friendship mix. We build layer upon layer into our foundations. On top of friendship and function, we build a servant heart and a stewardship mind-set, so that our power is not corrupted by ambition.

If we recognize that our foundations do not contain the three elements of friendship, function, and sacrifice, then we must take steps to rectify the problem. Clearly, we cannot simply abandon function for a social relationship agenda that will enable us to love one another at friendship level. We must make room for friendship in an agreed way to allow our relationships to breathe new life into our vision, structure, and work.

We want to return to a first-love relationship with the Lord Jesus, out of which grows covenant love with one another. The alternative is an excellent serving and working relationship with the Lord but a poor friendship at sonship level. We have become ministers in the work who do not see one another as real friends with whom we can share real life.

We need to step back from the current insanity of meetings and programs, full of teaching but non-discipleship, which produce limited fruit but mountains of activity. Jesus did not come that we might have meetings and have them more abundantly! He came to give us *life*. It is relationship that gives and sustains life. Meetings are an excellent means of inspiration and communication, but relationships create transformation.

Meetings allow us to receive and process information through teaching and instruction. Discipleship enables us to change and make the adjustment from one level to another. Low self-esteem and a poor self-image will not be corrected in a meeting. Many, many people view themselves in a small way because there is no role model personally attached to their life. This cannot be changed from the platform. It comes through viable contact between people.

People who feel insignificant remain ineffective and small. They become grasshoppers in their own sight and may never inherit all that Jesus died to give them. Good leaders take what is small and enable it to grow. Starting where people are at, they take them through progressive levels of encouragement, appreciation, and development to a place of effectiveness and personal significance.

Discipling others is a relational undertaking. Real covenant love seeks to maintain an ongoing moving balance between being and doing. At intervals we create space for friendship; in other periods we make time for gift and function to cement our relationship into Kingdom purpose. The desire to look out for one another's interest and serve each other is the oil that keeps our necessary tensions from becoming the friction that divides.

Stepping back from the brink of mere function to produce a different model of church—one that will endear us to the Holy Spirit—will provide us with a greater anointing for real spiritual breakthrough.

These two groupings of initiators and enablers form the core group of the church, and we cannot afford to lose anyone from that core company. The function of part of the leadership has got to be involvement with that core of people. I want to suggest that the function certainly of the main leader has to be almost total involvement with that grouping of people. Within our leadership team, we must have people who can specialize across all the relevant groupings in the church. Otherwise, we spread ourselves too thin in a one-dimensional way across the whole span of the church. In that case, we will probably not achieve very much, and may end up mostly fire fighting.

> *If you think*
> *you are too small*
> *to be effective...*
> *you have obviously*
> *never been in bed*
> *with a mosquito!*

Most current leadership energy tends to minister to the lowest common denominator. With this mind-set, if we have 120 people in church with approximately 20 percent of them as a core group of initiators and enablers, then most of what we are doing will have a maintenance pastoral approach. We will be looking at the bigger bunch of people and trying to do something with them because we unconsciously believe that quality comes through quantity. Our core group of workers are not causing us a problem, so we do not do much with them. We try and enlist their help to enable us to work with the resisters and the strugglers, but we do not give serious thought to their development beyond some basic training to do their job.

All our messages will be aimed at the resisters; all our output as leadership will be aimed at the strugglers. The people who are not causing us any problems get very little input and very little support, and eventually they suffer from burnout through overwork with no development. So we have a system that makes victims of our heroes in church life. I believe that the function of the main leader is to look after that core group of people, to train, equip, monitor their development, mentor them, and add to that number as often as possible. We cannot afford to lose anyone from that core group because the faith level in the work and the capacity to do the work will actually diminish greatly as a result. More pressure is going to come to us, and eventually, we become disillusioned as leaders who threaten to quit because of exhaustion and burnout, which is what Jethro noted to Moses.

He said, "Not only are you not able to do this, but you are wearing the people out as well" (see Ex. 18:18). Leadership not grounded in team creates a bottleneck that prevents building and spiritual breakthrough. The end result is a leadership that bleats at the people when no one is helping because the leaders have not created the environment for discipleship and mentoring. We simply give people jobs with no ongoing development, bar troubleshooting, if it goes wrong. It is a sure recipe for mediocrity. Low-level discipling produces low-level anointing. Lack of strategic care produces poor fruit in ministry. People will not offer themselves to serve when all they see is exhausted, burned-out people who have become tired of the work through lack of friendship and mentoring.

Resisters

Every church has resisters. Sometimes they are disillusioned and dissatisfied people; sometimes they are people who have a nomadic church lifestyle. They come to the church, and everything is wonderful until they discover that we really do have feet of clay. Then they are off searching for the perfect anointed minister and the most anointed church. Of course, the rule in these things is if you ever find the perfect church, don't join it because you will spoil it! Resisters are often people who have excess baggage from their past in their life that they have never dealt with. The past is always coming into their present to disturb them and prevent them from enjoying the future.

Sometimes they are people who are just taking a free ride; they have not learned the spiritual principle that you get more if you give more. Church is not a place where we come only to receive; church is a place where we come to express. If we express what is in our heart from God, we will get something. It amazes me when people criticize the events in a meeting. My response is to ask, "What did you contribute to it?" Often the reply is that "God did not give me anything," which, of course, is nonsense. Did the Holy Spirit not give them any worship to contribute? Did He not give them faith and energy to release into the atmosphere? Our spirit-man is linked to our vocal cords. It finds expression through worship, prayer, expressions of faith, praise, gifting, encouragement, song, confession, and blessing.

Most people are unconscious resisters simply because they do not think through their contribution. They come to church waiting for something to happen, rather than specifically to add what they have, to create the environment of faith for God to move. The result of such unbelief is that we create a negative environment that prevents the Holy Spirit from moving through people. Our attitude either gives the Holy Spirit pleasure or is a source of grief to Him (see Eph. 4:30a).

Is it really possible to worship God week after week with our mouths closed? Worship is a drama that involves heart, mind, mouth, arms, and legs. It is very physical. It has to be acted out in the body. When people observe others in full acts of worship, it inspires them to join in. Unless, of course, there is sin. Then condemnation usually makes us cynical and critical, like Michal over her husband David (see 2 Sam. 6:16). If people come with the attitude of Peter at the Gate Beautiful, then our meetings enter a more significant dynamic of anointing (see Acts 3:6).

Resisters are people who can be taking a free ride. They have not learned to rise above their circumstances. They are people who are wounded but as yet unhealed. Some of that is because they have not fully forgiven others or called upon the name of the Lord. There are those who have made a career out of being wounded and rejected by others. We all know that due to the grace of God and the sacrifice of Jesus, healing is possible and desirable at all times.

We do not have a right to be wounded constantly over the same issue, in the face of such a profound love. We do not want to tread underfoot the cross of Jesus. Healing begins when we want to be healed. In those times of pain and difficulty when it is hard to make right choices, we must remember that "it is God who works in you both to will and to do..." (Phil. 2:13).

In our desire for God, we learn how to let the Lord direct our will. My wife puts it this way: "I am willing to be willing." In other words, it means, "This is hard for me, Father, but I open myself

(I am willing) to the direction of Your will (to be willing)." God is faithful. Many people use their poor past as a cloak to hide themselves from present responsibility. They want to be pastored with someone else carrying the weight and the burden. This, of course, is absolutely fine in genuine circumstances. However, the goal of pastoral ministry is to release people into the all-sufficiency of Christ so that people can learn to police their own lives well. The only acceptable form of control in church life is self-control. Resisters are people who are led by their feelings and not by faith. They live in a vacuum. If we do not fill our lives with Christ, all kinds of things rush in to fill the gap. Unbelief, fears, anger, low self-esteem, and rejection are all classic profiles of victimhood.

Resisters want people to be responsible for them but will not give them the authority to change anything. Resisters remind us of why we are working for the Kingdom of Heaven. We all have been resisters at least once in our life. Sometimes it is deliberately through pride, arrogance, and stubbornness; other times it is because of sin, ignorance, poor self-image, and damaged history. On other occasions, we may

> *To enjoy freedom we must exercise self-control.*

have been the victims of poor church structures, domineering and untrustworthy leadership, or an unbelieving church family.

Many situations can bring us to a point of inertia, but only the life of Christ can offer complete internal deliverance. Many resisters simply have stopped making positive decisions about their lives and have ceased to trust the Lord for their growth and spiritual development.

We are not talking of new or recent converts who have not yet heard all the truth and who are still working and walking out their deliverance from an abusive past. New believers do have excess baggage that requires sensitive handling. There is a necessary dependency on others to provide them with the impetus to believe God and break free.

Many resisters have made Jesus their Savior but not their Lord. Often that does not occur at the moment of conversion because of poor preaching of the gospel. If our aim is to get people to make decisions for Christ rather than to be convicted of sin and repent, then we birth people into a wrong concept of Christianity. The gospel is not "come to Jesus and get your needs met," but "Jesus Christ is Lord—what are you going to do about it?"

There must be a presentation of the saving grace of Jesus together with His absolute Lordship over our lives. Rebellion will not be tolerated by the Holy Spirit. People must lose their own life for the gospel in order to find it again in Christ.

Historically throughout Scripture, we see a people caught between two minds. When in trouble, they give themselves to God; when things are going well, they take their lives back again into their own hands. Israel was a prime example of this throughout the Book of Judges.

Some people are resistant to change because there is no active faith at work in their own lives. Some people have been caught up in a flow of negativity due to bad fellowship with cynical people.

We cannot build on our resisters; we can only bless them. They are a sponge that cannot take weight. If we are preaching the gospel successfully, we will always have a steady flow of new believers accessing our resources. They will be a drain on the work initially until we bring them to a place of discipleship. Resisters do benefit the church indirectly by teaching us grace. People have to put on Christ as we seek to move forward in God's purpose.

Two Functions of Leadership

We have mainly two people groups to deal with in church life. First, we have the people whom we are building upon, and secondly, we have those whom we are blessing. Our leadership team needs to reflect that joint capacity. We need to love *all* the people whom the Lord has given us. Some of our people need to be loved into submitting to the Lord, until they come to a place of discipleship and function. Then, as we build upon them, the scope of our love needs to change to reflect the different tensions and requirements that arise out of a ministry function.

We must know who we are building with and who we are blessing. I am not advocating a first- and second-class believer system.

We would love to build on everyone, but that would not be fair to those who need special help with their history and identity. These people need milk, not solid food that would be inappropriate and indigestible.

Those who have walked out their identity and are free of the past are concerned with the future in a wholly positive way. They want to do something; they want to make their lives count for the Lord. They need meat for strength. They require shaping, training, and development. They want to serve. They are concerned with calling and vision. They do not want to drift along in their life and need a sense of direction—otherwise frustration will set in.

Operating a model of blessing and building will mean making changes in our corporate structure. We need both building and blessing models in our leadership: the building model to develop the initiators and enablers into a defined and functional core team of ministries and new leaders, and the blessing model to address the development required to take new believers and resisters through to a place of breakthrough into servanthood.

Discipleship is a major issue in today's church. It has to be at the top of our core criteria for leadership development. It is the function of the core builders in the work to lay down an action plan for individuals. This should contain a statement of their calling and vision, an endorsement from the leadership, core criteria of that calling confirmed through prophetic input, plus details of their training needs and servant opportunities to develop alongside others "on the job."

This will enable us to partner with them in faith vision, power, and gifting. We have a set of agreed goals and defined time periods in which we are working together in cooperative friendship.

We start with what we have in terms of people resources. If we have 120 people in the church with perhaps 15 people who are deemed as buildable material, we must bless God for what we have and not bemoan the 105 who are not ready for real discipling. Actually, in a positive way, it is better to begin with a smaller number. It will become more relational rather than program-driven.

> *When we practice our beliefs, we can turn the world upside down.*

We will probably make some mistakes, so it is better to make them with fewer people involved. New ventures in obedience always contain special and particular grace and mercy. Use up all that is available! As we develop the 15 potential disciples, we have a team working with and blessing the remainder of the people. Discipleship is best initiated by request from the one being discipled, or by invitation from the mentor, rather than by a broad public appeal.

Initially there is an imbalance: 15 people for building against 105 we are blessing. This is fine. The main thing is that we know what we are doing with both sets of people. We put both leadership anointings to work as we develop people in different ways to obtain breakthrough.

When the 15 people have been trained and equipped to a certain level, the next phase of their development can occur. They become mentors in training as we oversee them discipling others. We choose the next echelon of people to be built upon, and we assign them to our premier group for mentoring with our support. Some people can mentor two or three people; others only one. Have no hard and fast rules here. It flows with people's personal capacity in God, time constraints, and life issues such as family, career, and health.

Within a certain time period, those first two groups may build our raw materials to between 30 to 40 people. Our third group can now be an additional 30 to 40 people who are under construction in the Spirit. Suddenly, the balance of power and anointing has shifted in the church. We now have between 60 and 80 people under faith construction, receiving impartation and specific, targeted development. The water level will rise in the church quite rapidly as we pass the 50 percent marker.

Continue to look for people who are approaching breakthrough on the blessing as well as the building side of the work. Leadership teams need to operate with a high degree of anointed cooperation. The blessing team is always looking for people to pass on to the building people. The mentors are looking to release more people into the blessing team as coworkers. We resource and rejoice in one another. Mutual love, trust, destiny, and partnership that is grounded in real friendship is anathema to the devil and utterly attractive to the Holy Spirit.

We become stronger in faith as we specifically target people for growth. What is wonderful and outrageous is this truth: The more people we build into, the more we grow in faith and power, then the more people meet God and become believers. The more we gain new believers, the stronger our blessing team needs to be. The stronger the blessing team is, the quicker their anointing works on getting people free, and therefore, the more discipling we need to offer to people who are released to serve in the house.

It may be slow initially, but if we stick with the principle, we enter a spiritual dynamic that is exciting, powerful, and profound. We come into a place where the level of faith, expectation, and significance has risen to such a point that divine acceleration is released to us to make rapid strides forward.

God begins to add as we are faithful. He begins to multiply as we persevere into breakthrough. As we persist in the anointing, it cuts a channel of power that everyone begins to flow down as the Holy Spirit pours Himself out upon us.

People with specific anointings in teaching, equipping, and mentoring either will be added externally or will begin to grow up fast within the church.

If we are continually in maintenance-mode, we will never grow out of the grouping that we have. We will burn out and become tired of the work as opposed to just tired in the work. People with energy and passion will get frustrated and move on because of lack of development. Once we lose our core resources, we are potentially doomed to mediocrity because we have no people who can develop others.

Churches need that dual capacity of building and blessing. I like to see large pastoral teams in churches capable of moving across a whole range of truth and freedom initiatives. A large number enables us to give pastoral people a break for a few months to recharge their batteries and discover a different aspect of the Lord for themselves. Times of such refreshing will lead to greater fruitfulness in the ministry. Two-thirds of the team working with one-third refreshing themselves is a good ratio to work with, irrespective of how hectic the ministry or urgent the needs. Jesus went away to pray when thousands were following Him. He knew how to say "No!" to ministry and to open Himself to the Father's love in a specific way. Rotating people keeps them fresh in heart, renewed in mind, and strong in faith.

It is hard to continually wade through the morass of sin, deception, selfishness, abuse, sickness of mind and heart, rebellion, anger, mistrust, cynicism, suspicion, rejection, hurts, wounds, hatred, and unforgiveness. Pastoral people become weary of the dark side of human nature and demonic oppression. They need some joy, gladness, and laughter to refresh their souls.

Take a look at the front end of the church where the door to the sanctuary meets the entrance to the world. New people enter our pastoral system first to be loved, refreshed, taught, and released. Our prime objective is to establish the Lordship of Christ, lay proper foundations of truth in doctrine, eliminate any excess baggage from the past, and bring them to a place of making healthy decisions before the Lord. We teach them how to live in Christ. We help to sort out their personal belief system, knowing that as we do, their behavior will change.

> *Discipling others creates a momentum in the church that encourages God to give us a divine acceleration.*

In many churches we merely try to control or change people's behavior, often using coercive peer pressure involving hard challenge, shame tactics, or expressed disappointments and value judgments against people. What many churches do not have is an effective partnership between teachers and pastoral people. We try to control behavior without helping them to establish a belief system.

I am always interested in why people do things. Establishing the pattern in people's behavior will determine what it is that they actually believe about themselves. Why does the same problem keep occurring? The problem is not just their behavior, it is the belief behind it! Behavior is the result of belief, whether good or bad. Prophetic people also can play a significant part in working with pastoral people to address this issue. Teachers present truth in the form of principle and doctrine, which resisters are encouraged to believe and practice as part of their rehabilitation and renewal. Prophetic people speak words of life, vision, and destiny over them, and these words are woven into their development plan as they establish their new identity in Christ.

We always will have resisters with us, simply because we will continually lead people to Christ and because we will get transfers from other churches as well as spiritual nomads coming for a drink of the Holy Spirit, who don't put down any roots.

There are unconscious resisters as well. These normally are deeply wounded people or new converts who draw life from us legitimately and are unable to contribute in meaningful ways, though there will be notable exceptions. There are also conscious resisters, people on the take, people who play the system to manipulate care and support without taking personal responsibility for their actions and lifestyle.

The second phase of activity normally starts when we begin to talk to people seriously about their future. We want to establish their identity in the Lord and begin to work within mutually agreed parameters. Hopefully, this can be contained in a simple action plan for people's development. It must contain details of training requirements, character development, serving opportunities, fruit of the Spirit, potential for leadership, relationship building, accountability, and self-disclosure. We can determine the levels of input through training, monitoring of "on-the-job" resources and ministry capacity, and the necessary amount of impartation required to equip, empower, and release people.

We are looking at producing people with a servant spirit, monitoring their development, empowering them in service, and seeing real spiritual growth that can be an asset in the work. Some of these people will move into other fields of ministry, both local and itinerant. Some of them perhaps will be rooted back into the pastoral side of church, whilst others may be engaged in the evangelistic side of church life. Where the crossover comes from the blessing side to the building side is where we talk about membership.

We do not talk about membership while they are being healed; we talk about membership when we actually have done something in them. At the point when they want to cross over the line into something on the building side, where they want to start talking about ministry, identity, and service, then the final part of our pastoral development program is to talk about covenant to the house.

We need to build in them a sense of covenant to the house of God we represent. We will talk about tithing and giving, identity and service, and partnership with accountability as people become stewards of their lives and not owners. We want them to play a vital part in what we represent. So when we bring somebody into membership, it is because we recognize that we have something that we can build on in his or her life.

Sonship is perhaps a more powerful expression of belonging and commitment in the church than the more customary description of membership. It depicts a people moving into increased levels of responsibility through the various stages of stewardship. People are growing up from immature children driven by needs and inexperience to a mature place of development and participation, where they cultivate a covenant relationship to the house of the Lord. As this is worked through into a place of reality, we will witness an acceleration of growth in these people.

So the criteria for moving people from the pastoral blessing element of church to the discipling and building side of the work is as follows:

- People prove by behavior and belief that they are set free from past issues to serve the Lord.
- They have completed the introductory assignment regarding their identity and areas of serving and gifting, which will form the basis for their discipleship and training.

- They have developed relationships in the church and are serious about their sense of covenant to the house.

- They are willing to be serving/giving members of the church and realize that initially this will be expressed in giving of time, money, and energy.

This is neither a set of rules nor a hard and fast criteria. Church is not a conveyor belt where we push people through some production schedule to make clones of everyone!

As people develop through this phase of discipleship and mentoring, we will be adding people to the work of the ministry. Here in Southampton we have over 30 schools of training in a wide variety of subjects. We continually seek to update our development program into a radical framework of discipling with opportunities to serve at all levels of the church. Marrying the internal training and serving opportunities with church planting and missions is a common goal across the broad spectrum of the eldership working in partnership with the apostolic team in the network.

As people develop through stage two of their mentoring and training, they will take on board specific levels of ministry and responsibility. Some may join the full- or part-time teams; others may stay as voluntary workers. The point is, we are creating partnerships across the church that allow people freedom to pursue God and develop appropriate serving options in line with their calling and destiny as individuals before the Lord.

As those partnerships expand in faith and anointing, we will expect that their relationship with the leadership will demonstrate a similar growth in favor and appreciation. We want them to cultivate a vision beyond the church and network into a Kingdom perception. As we release them into an itinerant role across the streams, we will promote them because of proven faithfulness, reliability, friendship, and anointing. They will have proved out in their testing ground because they will have been mentored by a succession of people who have similar characteristics.

> *God inhabits what we build into people.*

The next stage is creating a wider global team of able ministers who have demonstrated their consistency and maturity. They will have a servant leadership anointing and can be trusted with people and situations. They will have exhibited their ability to operate in teams and partnerships with a wide variety of significant others.

They will have an external Kingdom focus to their life and ministry, not merely being network-oriented or parochial in nature. Through opportunities to travel and serve they will have had the access to churches to cultivate wider relationships and extra local partnerships. They will have displayed their team building skills at a wide level and will be able to relate and fit in to most places with joy, patience, and enthusiasm.

We will have discovered together where they each fit specifically into the work and how best we can use them. All ministries will need to provide evidence that they can suborn their calling to the corporate call of God in times of high pressure when we need all hands to the pump. They will need to exhibit their capacity to disciple and mentor others. All leaders and ministries need to have disciples, trainees, or apprentice personnel into whom they are inputting on a personal basis. That relationship, along with the training program and serving opportunities, forms the backbone of all people-development in the work.

Finally, before their release into a broader band of itinerant national or international ministry, all partners must have demonstrated their accountability in terms of home, lifestyle, team, and ministry within the leadership of the church. This is a prerequisite for release of gifted people to a wider sphere of ministry beyond local church parameters.

We want people to be a credit to the Lord and to represent the church well. As this occurs, the church will plant more often. New teams with an external dimension will be pushed out of the church to function as helps to other churches. Our own internal capacity to minister to an increased number of people is enhanced by fresh teams of people assisting in the work, which causes renewed expansion. We also are able to rotate people from the busiest and most difficult places of church activity into meaningful times of refreshing and renewal.

The resource church grows as we give serious time, thought, and energy to making disciples who can move through all the phases of development into places of high calling. We will see the church grow numerically, spiritually, and influentially as our people expand across the battlefield bringing breakthrough across society at all levels.

Antioch, Ephesus, Jerusalem, and Corinth were churches that majored on the development of people. They grew to be regional centers continuously releasing a steady stream of people who affected entire geographic locations in mission.

We cannot change everyone's world everywhere, but we can change someone's world somewhere. This process begins as we get hold of the people resources the Lord has given us and begin to shape them. Out of that initial development will arise a strategy that will enable us to cultivate people for the purpose that God has ordained. From individual development springs our corporate anointing and destiny through the creation of partnerships in the love and call of Christ.

Chapter 6

Implementing Change

I was somewhere on the earth, in a country I had never previously visited. The attack had started days before I left home. All my bones ached, I could not eat, and my stomach was as hard as a rock. My head pounded viciously and I felt gray and listless. It ached to sit or to stand, and I could lie down only for a short while. My sleep pattern was nonexistent. My wife was ill, and I wanted to stay home. The thought of two days on a plane filled me with foreboding.

I had choices to make. Everything in me wanted to rearrange the visit. Numerous justifications flitted through my mind. God was silent. Carole Shiers, my personal assistant, quietly put my prayer partners on emergency alert. I stopped prevaricating and started packing. In the process of gearing up for the trip, I stepped back as far as I was able into my spirit man.

As I dragged my body around the house lifting and folding clothes, I put on my bond-slave outfit. A slave has no rights. He is the property of another. I am being sent; I can only obey. The first act of resistance to the enemy is to submit to the Lordship of Jesus (see Jas. 4:7). People came and prayed for healing—I felt worse. There are times when God delivers us from or in various situations. There are other times when He keeps us through our circumstances (see 1 Pet. 1:5). This was a keeper.

It is great to be delivered...to feel the love and the power of God fizzing through your body...to feel the gradual draining away of sickness and the in-filling of health and wholeness...to go to sleep sick and wake up well. However it happens, I love it. It's the goodness of God in operation.

Being kept means moving to a different rhythm. It requires an alternate discipline. Always the answer is in the internal presence of God. He is the internal changeless core of our lives. By submitting to Him and stepping into Him, we give up our physical state to His care. I had planned the praise of my journey: first the worship in the cab to London, and then the praise songs in the airport. I also wrote down a few positive confessions that I would enjoy repeating.

Every positive word I speak to the Lord is also thrown in the face of the enemy regardless of the physical battle. The secret place, the refuge, the fortress, the high tower, the inner man of the Spirit, the changeless core which is the essence of the presence of God within—I wonder briefly what things I will learn about this inner place of the Spirit on this trip.

> *Internal perspective relieves external pressure.*

The soulish part of me is grumbling, wanting to learn these things at home. The battleground is an excellent classroom. We learn things about God we simply could not learn at any other time. The fight provokes the revelation. In choosing to obey I am aligning myself to His purposes, whatever they may be. I have no clue as to what to expect, no prior intelligence. God will not explain Himself yet. "Turn the dial and set your heart to trust"—this is all that can be done at this point.

I went, God worked, we won, and I came back. Just another day at the office—no big deal. I cannot remember the day I got healed. I noticed it on Wednesday, but the Lord told me it was Tuesday morning. I believe Him. In the secret place, Jesus is our preoccupation. The battle was fierce and physically threatening. However, in the secret place we are not intimidated; we are fascinated by the Lord and what He is planning to do.

This internal development is a core part of the work of the Holy Spirit in our lives. There are many things that will upset us if we let them. Choosing where to live is as important a decision in the spirit realm as it is in the natural. Making that place habitable, turning it into a place of rest and beauty, will refresh us as much in spiritual terms as our natural home does at the physical level. Comfort is comfort. The Comforter enables us to make a home in the secret place.

I set the opening of this chapter in a warfare context to remind us that we are caught up in a global battle. How we face everything really matters. Each person has a contribution to make in the Body of Christ. The simplest and easiest form of attack is for the enemy to convince us that our contribution is insignificant. Passivity gives the devil an easy victory. He gets a walkover because we fail to show. If our contribution is not wholehearted for God, our divided heart provides the enemy with hope. The carnal part of us always provides opportunities for the enemy to move in and occupy. In change we often go to a place of self-preservation rather than submission to the purposes of God.

In change we discover who are the servants and who are the selfish. The process of change is often longer than it needs to be, because we are having to change hearts from selfish preoccupation to mind-sets of servant and steward. People simply must settle the issue of Lordship and then live there.

In Gideon's time (see Judg. 6–7) he had 32,000 men. He was outnumbered at least by 4 to 1. We know that because 120,000 of the enemy were killed on the battlefield (see Judg. 8:10).

Approximately 69 percent of Gideon's army were intent only on self-preservation. Too afraid to commit themselves, 22,000 men took the soft option and left. Outnumbered by 12 to 1 (at least), the Lord examined the hearts of the remainder of His people. He brought them to the river and watched them drink. Ten thousand men were willing to fight, but only 300 were ready. They were watchful, alert, and clearly up for the fight. This company stayed and the remainder were allowed to leave. Willing is good, but ready is better. Somehow we have to work with the fainthearted who have no internal place of relationship with God. Carnal Christians are the bane of a church preparing for war.

Gideon now had less than 1 percent of his original army, but the atmosphere had changed considerably for the better. He was outnumbered by 400 to 1. However, that one could potentially slay a thousand. Better to have one in your midst who can kill a thousand men than to have a thousand who cannot slay one!

If we want to change a situation, we first have to change ourselves. To change our attitude and outlook effectively, we first have to change our perceptions. Real change comes from the inside out. The prime issue is the place where we live in God. If we are preoccupied with the natural realm, then we will only want to avoid the pain and hassle of warfare. We would rather pay and let someone else do it. Such people will have a grim surprise on the day of judgment.

If we are preoccupied at the soulish level, we may be willing, but we cannot be risked. Such people need warfare training and gradual introduction to warfare situations. This is not "made for TV warfare specials" where only the bad guys get hurt and the good guys get a flesh wound. (Actually, a lot of Christians could do with a flesh wound, but that is a matter for the cross!)

It is amazing how few plans and strategies churches make to prepare their people for battle. Change is an integral part of growing up in God. The ability to adjust to God's ongoing purpose depends solely on the submission to His Lordship. God has a divine "Yes!" in His heart toward us in Christ (see 2 Cor. 1:20). This same "yes" has to strike a similar chord in us. God gets what He wants. It is our joy to submit.

The ability to change is a vital ingredient in a church's place before God in the community it represents on behalf of the Kingdom. A static, one-dimensional church cannot break through. It is the people who live from their spirit who are a provocation to force the breakthrough. Only they have the capacity to do the unreasonable thing. Gideon's company did the unthinkable. They went out against an enemy at least 400 times larger and prevailed, because they believed the Lord.

Our current levels of spirituality do not yet breed this type of people in our midst. Real change is internal. It does not come from hacking at the leaves of attitude and behavior with quick-fix ideas or techniques. It comes from striking at the root, at the fundamental paradigms of our thinking and our believing. What we believe controls our behavior. The Church cannot rise higher than her concept of God. This is what gives definition to our character and creates the lens by which we view our circumstances.

We can decide within ourselves how circumstances will affect us. Between our reaction to events and our response to God lies the power to choose what we will do and how we will do it. God has a changeless core within His own heart. Many believers do not possess this reality and are not looking for it. It is part of the Christ-life, but it can be established only through our Spirit-led choices.

> *We cannot effect change unless we have experienced it.*

Constant change in our life situations is here to stay. True Christians are people of transition, moving from one degree of glory to another, reflecting the nature of God. It is therefore essential that we develop the same changeless core in the Spirit.

The key to our ability to change is a changeless sense of who we are in Christ, what we value in spiritual terms, and what we are about in the purposes of God. It is always about our identity, the nature of God, and the vision for the Kingdom.

Plan of Campaign

The main problem in change is, "How can we sow for tomorrow when we are still reaping today from things we did in the past?" We are the product of all we did wrong or right in previous times. How were our current mind-sets, structures, attitudes, and behavior set? There has to be a releasing, an undoing, a dismantling before there can be an empowering, a building, and a tying together of the new things God is bringing us into. We will need to get closure on the past, which was spoken of in previous chapters.

When I was the business development manager for a busy training and recruitment company, part of my role was to anticipate change and enable smooth transition to follow. Part of that anticipating was gauging the effect that potential change would have on the mood and morale of our people and also to examine our capacity to be stretched by the new initiatives we were planning. Part of that analysis was to conduct a S.W.O.T. (Strengths, Weaknesses, Opportunities, and Threats) experiment within that part of the company. This would be an examination of our current strengths to determine our response to innovation; an appraisal of our weaknesses to see what would prevent us from achieving any new goals; an exploration of the opportunities that could be open for development by the team; and an analysis of the threats against our stability and effectiveness during the process of change.

We must always work to our *strengths* in the church. We must start with what we actually have, not with what we should have or would like to have. It is important to continually profile our current giftings and the faith level in the church. Churches need a register of what gifts and ministries are available in the body and at what level of anointing they function (i.e., general, specific, significant, or breakthrough capacity).

We need to determine our language and terminology in such a survey so that people do not become upset or confused by various categorizations. We do not merely want to preach change to the church; we must be able to grow it. Change comes in three ways. Firstly, it comes from the top down, from leadership by example to and through the church. Secondly, it comes from the bottom up via inspiration in our hands-on involvement with our people. Thirdly, it occurs from the inside out as we impart truth and anointing into the inner man of the Spirit through training and effective discipling.

Change is hard on people. We need strong leadership with a mercy center. However, do not let mercy get the upper hand, or we will back down when the going gets tough. People need to see purposeful leadership with kindheartedness. If we remain calm and encouraging, our people will take their cue from what we are modeling. Look at what the people can do and believe the Lord for the rest, whilst planning how to actively increase the capacity of the church to move up in the Spirit.

It is important also not to be blind to our *weaknesses*. There is no point in complaining about our deficiencies. Rather, we must mount a guard over them and prioritize how to deal with them effectively. Distinguish the urgent from the important. That which shouts the loudest is often not the most critical issue.

Always go to the root causes where belief determines behavior. Examine the faith level and self-esteem of the church as well as the people's concept of God. The Lord will always ask us to do the impossible, so being overwhelmed by the vision or task ahead is merely a normal occurrence in church life. Confidence in the Lord must always be high on our agenda as we train and equip our people for works of service.

Feeling vulnerable and inadequate is part of our calling. We need a theology of our weakness and God's strength, or we will make trouble for ourselves. There are few things more disheartening than to see people trying to overcome their weakness by trying to be strong for God. Real power is perfected in weakness as the power of Christ rests upon us (see 2 Cor. 12:7-10). We are not adequate to the task that God has set for us, but His all-sufficient grace enables us to overcome as we joyfully embrace our weaknesses. When we are weak, we are strong. This is the paradox that we learn to inhabit for Christ's sake.

As we go through transition we must determine the pace of the journey and how we can encourage certain people to speed up. We initially may have to go at the pace of the slowest as we pray for quickening. Patience and perseverance are always required with significant movements in the life of the church. We may need to bless people with prayer, prophetic input, and personal ministry as a part of our mobilization.

> *To build a church, first build a relationship with a builder.*

We have to strike the fine balance between not allowing any distractions to prevent progress yet slowing down enough to get as many people on board as we can. It is important to show value and appreciation to all our people at both ends of the faith spectrum. We have to give key people their head in moving forward,

knowing that the stretching will be good for all of us as we monitor our progress properly. Expansion is always followed by contractions where those who are stretched catch up with one another.
The tail completes the journey and catches up with the head as
things slow down a little and we explore fully the new place God
has drawn us into.

It is important in such times of expansion and contraction
that we have an external voice we can rely upon to impart wisdom
and strength. Access to an apostolic ministry that really understands process and the ways of God is an important part of our
journeying into new territories. As we analyze our weaknesses, we
must determine honestly how to deal with them through training,
development, and discipleship. External involvement with significant ministries may be crucial to our planning. Supplied with a
brief from the leadership, they can come with a building block or
an external perspective that will be listened to far more attentively by the flock.

It is not that the church disrespects their leadership; it is just
that at certain times significant truths should not come only by
familiar voices. We need the words of non-family members both to
initiate and confirm all that God wants to speak into the local body.

In order for us not to become despondent over our weaknesses, we must examine the *opportunities* that the Lord is presenting to the church. These are the reasons why we are having to gear
up to a new level. What is God giving us? What are the positive
indicators of growth amongst our people? How can we harness the
excitement, potential, and personal vision of our people into a corporate context? Good leaders are in touch with what God is doing
in the hearts of individuals. They want to cooperate with the Holy
Spirit to facilitate all that is growing up in the Body of Christ.

Identify who are the main warriors, the key people who make
things happen. Who are the captains of 100, 50, or 10 people?
Who has the potential to rise up to a new level? Who needs to
continue adjusting to their current level? Like a commander evaluating the fighting capacity, mood, or morale of his troops, we
must determine who we can commit to the next level or whether

we need more time to get ready for a stronger, harder push to breakthrough.

We must learn to prioritize strategically in our building of people. Knowing the initiators, enablers, and resisters is part of the requirement of change. Being able to gauge the current capacity of our people is crucial. We must build on our key people and give them quality input. This is where the partnership between teachers and prophetic people can be so vital. Teachers dig deep and have insight; prophets see far and have foresight. The building and envisioning of people is exponentially greater through such partnerships.

Such alliances do not accept a little change. They will not tolerate anything merely cosmetic. They will go right to the wire to press for breakthrough. They will focus on people who are doing well and use them as a catalyst to produce growth in others. It is better to have the problem of reining people in than to have to apply the spur to get them moving! The best problems are always the positive ones of real growth, exuberance, and zeal.

Outlining the vision and examining the opportunities that are unfolding before us will enable us to begin to key in leaders, ministries, and potential servants. It will give us openings into the lives of our people to push them forward. It is helpful to match potential with proven ministries so that effective discipline can take place. People have to do it! They must be free to make mistakes. A major part of discipling people is giving them loving and effective feedback that builds their gifting, character, and self-esteem. We grow through retrospective revelation—the capacity to look back and determine what went right, what did not work, and how we would change it for the better.

The final part of our church examination is to take a critical look at the *threats* we are facing as a church in this time of transition. We must turn our thoughts both outward and inward to determine the nature of the opposition that will be against us. Firstly, we must have intelligence about any direct attack from the enemy. For this, we need to release our prophetic people and our intercessors to work together with the leadership. One of the functions of these ministries is warfare. True prophetic people are warriors with a built-in prejudice against the devil. In the time of Jehoshaphat when Judah faced potential annihilation by the warriors of Moab, Ammon, and Mount Seir (see 2 Chron. 20), the Spirit of God came upon Jahaziel and he prophesied thus:

> ...*Thus says the Lord to you: "Do not be afraid nor dismayed because of this great multitude, for the battle is not yours, but God's. Tomorrow go down against them. They will surely come up by the Ascent of Ziz, and you will find them at the end of the brook before the Wilderness of Jeruel. You will not need to fight in this battle. Position yourselves, stand still and see the salvation of the Lord, who is with you, O Judah and Jerusalem!"*... (2 Chronicles 20:15-17).

> **Opportunities create the context for change.**

Elisha would regularly get words of knowledge about the battle plans of the King of Aram against Israel (see 2 Kings 6:8-12). He would warn Israel about the specific plans of the enemy so that they were guarded and well prepared against the assault.

The whole Book of Joshua is a specific account of God revealing His word prophetically to His people, then intervening on behalf of that word to overcome the enemy in the conquest of Canaan. To a Jew, history is the sphere of God in action on behalf of His people. It is God speaking and then moving to fulfill His own word. As the Book of Joshua is to the Pentateuch (the first five books of the Bible), so the Acts of the Apostles is to the Gospels. They are both prophetic/historic accounts of the divine intervention of God on behalf of His people. God speaks and moves in concert with His children. These books are a critical part of our understanding of how the Lord wants us to live and move with regard to fulfilling the plans and purposes of the Lord in the day of trouble. The conquest of Canaan and the Great Commission are the same story. It is about the inheritance of the people of God and entering into warfare on His side.

We should loose prophetic ministry and release intercessors to pursue the heart of God. As we commit ourselves to this partnership, we will realize valuable intelligence regarding the plans of the enemy. Always put the watchman on the walls of the work and give them the ability to sound a warning.

Secondly, we must have intelligence on the work of the enemy within the church itself. When Nehemiah was rebuilding the walls of Jerusalem, he faced much opposition from an implacable enemy (see Neh. 4), who wanted to attack directly and destroy the work. When this failed, the enemy took the indirect route of suborning someone from inside the camp to intimidate Nehemiah (see Neh. 6:10-14).

The only thing the enemy can use inside the church is our unredeemed nature—what Scripture calls "carnality" and "the flesh." We must be warned about any internal move of the enemy amongst our people. Home cell leaders and pastoral people can provide invaluable assistance here as we seek to pinpoint any negative fellowship, cynical conversation, and power-broking amongst the people. When Aaron and Miriam rose up against Moses, the Lord dealt with it swiftly, with mercy and firmness (see Num. 12).

This is where prophetic people in particular need to be aware of being used by the hand of the enemy. Prophets are for God; they have no agenda but His. They are not political but spiritual. When a prophet takes sides in an issue, he has already lost the favor of the Lord. Prophets do God's bidding and none other. They enter into godly partnerships with men and women of God. However, in times of crisis and tension they are meant to be totally impartial because they represent God's heart and no one else.

We need to determine the source of fleshly violations in the church. The mouthpiece and the heartbeat of criticism and negative fellowship may not have the same host body! Track the words to the heart. Trace the bullets back to the maker, not to the one who fires the gun. In transition there are often struggles for power.

In times of change, the resisters among us dig in their heels in an attempt to slow down the process. We must learn to detect such immature behavior and deal with issues of carnality in our midst. It is a breach of fellowship for which people can lose their privilege of membership, however briefly (see Num. 12:15).

It is important as we explore change to do so in a context of releasing blessing, faith, and hope. Prior to outlining new plans and introducing change, it is helpful to create a climate of encouragement, appreciation, and blessing among the people. Make sure we have a fire-fighting team on hand to cover any potential damage.

Another potential threat is the time scale of change. People will always want to know the answers to these questions: "When will it happen? How long will it take? Why can't it wait until later?" People do not like to be pushed into change. Often it has been poor leadership or bad planning that makes change so necessary and intimidating. Constant change is here to stay. Everything changes around God except His nature. He is the only constant in the universe; everything else revolves around His will and purpose.

> *Prophetic ministry reveals the hand of God in action and makes the enemy visible.*

Evolution is a better change agent than revolution. Evolution is about constant small changes that occur far back with planning and foresight. Evolution is a continuous godly development that produces expansion and enlargement on a regular basis within the church body. We train and prepare people for increase, growth, and ongoing maturity. We enable our people to live in the grace and the favor of the Lord. We empower them to become God-conscious. We bless our people and release them at every opportunity to love the Lord, to worship Him, and to lay their lives on the altar as a simple act of adoring sacrifice. Such people are easily moved by the hand of the Lord.

In such churches, change is made easy because of the climate of love and trust in which we live together as a body of people. Even if we have to take a large step, we can do so because the people are not involved in self-preservation. They have settled the issue of Lordship in their lives.

Revolution has to occur sometimes because we have serious work to do to overcome the flesh in our midst. Civil war occurs in our hearts if the battle of spirit versus flesh has not been won by God. The Spirit will keep warring against the flesh until He wins (see Gal. 5:17). A revolution is a battle to establish supremacy. It involves taking sides, having opposition, and enduring a breakdown in relationships.

When change comes, many churches have a revolution because of past disappointments, broken promises, tension in relationships, mistrust and suspicion, and poor results in the past. This is why closure is so necessary in our churches. Closure is the capacity to declare amnesty to overcome our history; it is the ability to bury the past and begin again, with outside help and support.

Often the biggest threat is our history and the need to not repeat past failures. "How do we know this is going to work? How can we be sure it is God and not another good idea? This church has a history of launching things in a fanfare but not following through to completion." Such comments and questions are relevant and important.

Another threat to the church may be the style of leadership we employ. It is always good to check ourselves for signs of domination, manipulation, and control. Are we threatened when people speak their mind? Are our people allowed to have an opinion without being labeled subversive? Do we encourage our people to hear from the Lord? Do we have the patience to wait on the Lord as we sift through the thoughts of the people? Do we build such waiting times into our planning as necessary parts of the schedule? Do we enfranchise our people at every opportunity to influence us with godly perspective? If someone outside the eldership comes with a strategy, a plan, and a purpose for the church, are we able to take it on board with little or no relevant adjustment? Most leaders unconsciously lord it over their people because they do not deliberately enfranchise them to hear the Lord. It is rather implied than stated that leaders hear from God and followers obey. The best leaders are facilitators to enable all their people to hear and obey.

It is important for leaders to step into the shoes of the average church member. What do they see? Look at their perspective on the church, the meetings, the vision, and the ministry. Apostles, when they come, will take the temperature of the church by talking to everyone. They want to get a feel for where the church is, across its broadest front. Church surveys are wonderful instruments for gaining an accurate reading of how things are going.

When we perceive potential or actual threats against the work, it should result in a rallying call for the people to come together and close ranks. Deal with appropriate historical difficulties, tensions, and disappointments in a godly way. Leave a suitable gap between acts of reconciliation and introducing new changes so that fellowship can grow unhindered for a season by function. Remember "being" is as important as "doing." The success of our functioning together is determined by the strength of our fellowship and love for one another. Always practice the "one anothers" in the Bible.

There are certain inherent *dangers in change,* which we must be aware of if we are to negotiate these choppy waters successfully. Change for its own sake must be avoided. Change is not a recipe to ease boredom or stagnation. Change involves a process of cultivation, maturity, and progress toward advancement and expansion. It is not to be entered into on a whim; nor is it to be embarked upon unless the plan of development has real thought and strategy behind it.

Churches can become overloaded by change because too much is happening too soon. We must be careful to give our people a positive taste for change. We cannot continuously keep giving out challenges that bring our people to places of weariness in their spirit. Every church needs periods of consolidation and peace in which to be built up and increase before the Lord (see Acts 9:31).

We must be careful also that the change we are promoting is real and lasting and not just cosmetic. There must be an underlying philosophy for the changes we want to make. It is probably no good to change the church from a program-based congregation to a cell-based one if the bulk of the leadership is not going to change as a result. I do not necessarily mean a change of personnel (though obviously new people in that context are vital), but mostly a profound change of attitude and philosophy to meet the new demands.

The church may change in the way it operates, but if there is no metamorphosis in culture, style, or personnel, then all we have is the same meat but a different gravy. If our church is a one-dimensional stereotype and we are moving toward being a multifaceted prototype, then the quality of the leadership to undertake such a transition must be examined.

> *Cosmetic change is not in God's makeup.*

Leaving people in places of influence simply because they have always been there is debilitating for the generation coming through. It has a kind of "dead man's shoes" aspect to it, where people cannot get promoted unless someone dies. Sometimes it is healthy to appoint people with potential into places of authority and function. It is at least as risky to do that, as to appoint someone who has always presided over the old work. In the former, we may have reservations about their ability to stand in the pressure and faithfully serve. In the latter, we may have concerns about their ability to be radical and function on a different level. Both are a risk. How we overcome that risk will partly determine our ability to grow significantly in this new dimension. In order for a team to play football in a totally different way, a change of philosophy is required in the coaching staff. This means either replacing the ideology or the personnel or both.

Women become depressed when they are all dressed up but have nowhere to go. For our ladies, getting ready is a major part of the fun. They dress for the occasion, so knowing where they are going, who is going to be present, and what type of occasion it is, are all an important part of the preparation. Without the proper intelligence, they get worried and anxious. "Am I overdressed? Is this good enough? What will everyone be wearing?" The thought of arriving at a place and being the odd one out is mortifying to them! A good husband/boyfriend provides the right data to add to the fun and get everything off to a good start.

In a similar way with the church, we must not allow people to get fired up with the vision if the infrastructure of the church is not going to change. All we are really heading for is another rerun of our past with the same results. The people who brought us out of one thing may not be the people to take us into the next realm. If the style and culture of the work is not overhauled and changed, we will disenfranchise all the people who cannot fit within the current framework.

In a similar vein, we must try and avoid changing the infrastructure when the people are not ready for such drastic overhauls. Big changes need lots of time to work through and must be followed by a period of consolidation so that we all have the opportunity to become settled in relationships as well as in new changes. If we lose familiar people for no apparent good reason, it creates insecurity and apprehension.

Values can be lost in the process of change, so we must take time to reinforce the core value system of the church. Values determine our character and identity. If the salt loses its flavor, it is good for nothing. Our values give us the flavor and the essence of Christ. Our openness and honesty, our nonnegotiable love, our mutual trust, and our unity in diversity are all a part of how we see and relate to each other in times of stress and tension.

Obviously change may mean some people losing their status, position, power, and influence. This will mean careful handling if we are not to leave a trail of broken and disappointed people in our wake. Major changes of personnel are best handled over a lengthy period of time unless the people concerned are ready and willing to move on quickly to other things. Many choose to move aside simply because they recognize that they have fulfilled the call of God over that part of their lives. Others happily take up different roles in the work because they are such excellent servants. Some people we can use in a mentoring/discipling capacity, getting the benefit of all the years of faithful and excellent stewardship for the new generation.

There inevitably will be some people who are not able to adjust to the new paradigm at the same level as their role in the previous structure. They must either accept a different role with reduced profile or even be replaced altogether. They may have served in a salaried position for many years. It will take a serious readjustment of life and heart to search for secular work after having been in a religious (in the world's view) environment for so long. They will need a generous amount of time to retrain and find suitable employment. This will be reflected in the gracious way we handle their transition into a new way of life.

Some people will no doubt feel aggrieved at what they see as their being pushed aside. Some may fight from their corner and cause disruption and division. This could be a serious threat and must not be underestimated. We cannot go on endlessly finding jobs for the boys without ruining our church economy or polarizing all parties into a fudge of aspiration without the means of achievement.

A new prototype of church means a new design coming from the introduction of different people with new concepts and the capacity to develop them. Inevitably some of our people will be flexible and spiritually supple enough to be molded into the new style of development. Those who are not as supple will find their inflexible approach no longer practicable. They probably will feel disenfranchised, and protest is the weapon of powerless people.

We must be careful as well of who and how we enfranchise new people. There needs to be clear training and development of all people coming into leadership and key roles. In particular, we must define the levels of accountability and covenant required of such people. We need defined, not assumed, relationships where expectations on both sides are clearly communicated and understood. We do not want to be in the position of having to take back delegated authority and responsibility because of misuse. This will cause unnecessary disillusionment and will disrupt faith and trust.

When contemplating change, we must ask ourselves a whole series of questions. The most vital question to ask is, "*Why* change?" This is a philosophical question that will enable us to shape our ideology and vision in the new paradigm. The subordinate questions of "*What* must change?" and "*How* will it change?" must then be considered in sequence. This will provide a framework for us to begin to assemble our ideas and thoughts, and will enable us to pray into these design-concepts with wisdom and clarity.

> *Protest is the weapon of powerless people.*

The subsequent questions of "*Who* do we involve? Who is going to step up into this new realm?" and "*When* do these changes happen?" also will be important in their turn. Most churches focus on what, how, who, and when but fail to ask the most significant question of why. All major change needs a philosophical base. It will provide us with awareness and foresight. Awareness involves an understanding of the situations we find ourselves in, and foresight is the ability to prepare and plan because we have learned to anticipate times of transition.

Christian philosophy is always about metamorphosis—being changed from one degree of glory to another, diversification, remodeling, reformation, conversion, and exchange. A static church experience reveals a one-dimensional relationship with God. Our traditions should always embrace the ebb and flow of God's Spirit and the rhythm of diversification that exists in a multifunctional body.

Good leaders have access to a reflective, contemplative, and prophetic expression of God, which encourages such awareness and foresight. Reflection enables us to be students of history and understand the rhythm of creativity in God's heart. Contemplation enables us to consider where we are now and what we may need to adjust to stay on track with the rhythm of God. The prophetic enables us to look ahead to the future and work out a pathway of upward and ongoing progression before the Lord.

This provides us with continuity and a road map for faith and realignment. The alternative is that we merely live our lives from moment to moment, which will eventually mean our leadership will operate in a vacuum. If we abdicate our responsibility to lead with awareness and foresight, other people will fill the gap we have left, and who is to say that is wrong?

Expansion and Contraction

Initially both these extremes are involved in our time of transition. Expansion is prophesied in the form of enlargement of the vision and increase of anointing and personnel. Through prophetic contradiction, the opposite will occur first and the church may suffer a contraction and a reduction of personnel and resources.

This is a necessary contraction designed to burn up the wood, hay, and stubble and release us from fair-weather friendships that may sink the ship in the storm process. The Holy Spirit is always extracting the precious from the worthless and will inevitably reduce us to that which is precious: gold, silver, and precious stones. That does not mean to imply that those who leave us at this time are worthless. Some move on for very honorable and godly reasons. Their leaving has simply coincided with recent developments. Others are reassigned because the Lord is realigning His people throughout the Body of Christ. Still, we also will be aware that some people may leave us prematurely, and our hearts will ache for them as well as for ourselves. Inevitably, transition identifies the nomads and the uncommitted. These rootless people will go and attach themselves to someone else's fruitfulness. They only look for blessing and do not want to be built in anywhere.

There is an ongoing interaction between the finite and the Infinite; the former must decrease as the latter increases. Transition helps that process. As the personal anointing grows, so the corporate man must expand. However, this corporate enlargement only takes place on the altar of personal sacrifice and willing contraction. All that God gives me must be laid at the apostles' feet so that their anointing to develop the mature man in the stature of Christ (see Eph. 4:11-13) can be released unhindered by personal considerations.

There can be no development without the catalyst of change being present. Change must occur on both the personal and corporate levels. Therefore individuals must be helped to understand where their personal change can support the ongoing development of the corporate man of the church. I want what I have in me to be sowed into the dimension of the whole Church, or at the very least the part I am serving. For that to be effective means I have to determine my current degree of "fit" into the prevailing life of the church. When that is likely to change, either because of personal or corporate expansion or some other occurrence, then I will have to discuss my personal circumstances in the light of corporate as well as individual needs. We take both together because they overlap in reality all the time.

> *As personal anointing grows, the corporate man must expand... or a contraction will take place.*

Expansion and contraction work on a number of levels. If a part of my ministry is being expanded, then obviously another part will be suffering contraction at the same time. When I join a team, that part of my ministry is expanded because of what all the other team members bring to me. However, on another level, they also cause a necessary contraction in terms of how I operate. My personal autonomy will suffer in joint responsibility. Decision-making will also change, and thus personal responsibility will be affected. Whatever happens to me personally has an effect on the corporate man of the church for either good or ill.

Our meetings are a microcosm of this fact. If enough people come with an attitude of worship, anointing, and breakthrough, those who are leading the meeting will enjoy an increase, an expansion of faith and anointing. The worship leaders will reach for the heavens; the input and ministry of others will come in at a high level of revelation and power. The result will be a breakthrough of some kind. If, however, the opposite occurs and the majority of people come to church in a negative mind-set, then we will probably experience some kind of contraction. The worship team will spend most of their time motivating the people to worship instead of orchestrating their praise. Unbelief and apathy will deaden the atmosphere, and we will probably have a breakdown rather than a breakthrough.

Overcoming Assumptions

We were taught in school to never assume anything. My teacher used to glare at me with Scottish evangelical fervor and roar, "Never assume, Cooke laddie! Because if you assume, you make an ass out of you and me (ASS/U/ME), and you are the only donkey in this room, laddie!" Since that time, I have always asked questions. I have managed to make an ass of myself in other ways!

Never assume anything with God. There is always something else He can teach us about the same set of circumstances. God will engineer every situation so that we can never quite rely on everything we know by truth and experience. We have to consistently learn that fellowship and relationship is the goal of all God's dealings with mankind.

The Jews had a certain expectation regarding the Messiah. He was the warrior king who would deliver them from the Roman Empire. He would set up His Kingdom upon the earth and rule the Gentiles with a rod of iron. There were many assumptions of how He would come to deliver them and set them free.

Being born in a stable and learning a carpenter's trade for years was not the way they imagined the Messiah would be revealed. They assumed a glorious revealing of His power at a critical moment. They were not prepared for the Messiah to grow up in their midst in humble circumstances. Jesus came as a servant, not as a king. The manner of His coming did not compute with their thinking of the Messiah.

Jesus came for the Gentiles as well as the Jews, which further confused many of the theologians of the day. The poor people received Him gladly, but those who studied the Scriptures about the Messiah misinterpreted almost everything. He came to build a spiritual kingdom, not an earthly one. Deliverance from the enemy would be an internal overcoming of spirit over the flesh, not the military one of victory over the Romans in the physical realm. Jesus battled those assumptions all through His ministry. Even His death was misunderstood and His resurrection was not believed.

The disciples had to accept the challenge of change as they walked with Jesus. Fellowship with Him was a provocation to all their thinking about the Messiah. He stimulated their reasoning whilst overturning all their thinking about the Messiah. Christians are the salt of the earth, giving a true flavor of God's presence into humanity. Constant fellowship with God by truth and experience keeps the flavor of God high and the effect on humanity very real.

As soon as we forget that all truth must be made real in our experience so that we walk in the Word and the power of it (see 2 Jn. 4), then we make assumptions about what it means. Experience of the Word clarifies the revelation. Knowledge is made real by the experience of God. The Pharisees had a knowledge of the Messiah that did not compute with their experience of Jesus. The knowledge that they had was cerebral. It was probably sound in biblical terms and well-reasoned. On this and other occasions, their sound and well-reasoned theology was unable to receive the reality of Jesus as the Messiah. Most of His battles regarding truth and experience were with men of solid biblical reputation.

As far as they were concerned, the Messiah would not break the Sabbath law (see Jn. 5:8-16). They persecuted Jesus because He made Himself equal with the Father (see Jn. 5:17-18). In His long discourse with the Jews, Jesus made a number of telling points regarding their assumptions, including that although they searched the Scriptures, they did not see that the Scriptures testified of Him (see Jn. 5:37-47).

God had testified of Jesus not only in the Scriptures but also in the realm of experience. "You have neither *heard* nor *seen*," Jesus said. Failure to experience God leads us to certain assumptions. Truth combined with experience causes people to live and abide in the Word of God. The Bible is Scripture. Jesus is the Word of God. The Word is a person, not a book (see Jn. 1:1). The Word became a living reality in touchable form; He gave us His fullness and continuous grace (see Jn. 1:14-16). Unless we have an experience of salvation, we cannot be saved. God has to come to give us fullness of joy and the fullness of His presence, which makes us complete in all the fullness of Christ (see Jn. 15:11; Eph. 3:19; Col. 2:6-10).

As we have received Christ, so we ought to walk in Him (see Col. 2:6); that is, by experience and truth combining to produce a reality of His presence on every level of existence. The Jews searched the Scriptures, but the search did not provoke faith because the manner of their search was wrong. They had an assumption in their minds before they searched. Their searching then was often to disprove something if it did not compute with their own prejudice and expectation.

There were other Jews, however, who were more noble mind-ed. That is to say, their hearts were open to God. They received the Word and then examined it daily to see if it was true. In Acts 17:10-15 Paul and Silas went to Berea and preached to the Jews there. The Bereans had no assumptions that blinded them to truth and experience. They were openhearted and searched the Scrip-tures for proof that Paul's teaching was accurate. They were not trying to disprove it; they were trying to prove his teaching! The Pharisees sought only to conserve their own built-in assumptions, and so, many of them missed the greatest moment in their histo-ry: the coming of the Messiah.

Jesus spoke to the Jews in Jerusalem and challenged their theology:

You search the Scriptures, for in them you think you have eter-nal life; and these are they which testify of Me. But you are not willing to come to Me that you may have life (John 5:39-40).

Their assumptions denied them an experience of the reality and the fullness of God. There are Christians today who love the Lord but whose theological assumptions have led them to deny many of the core truths of spirituality and experience in Scripture. Cessationists are not complete in Christ because they deny the core truths that made the early Church walk in the fullness of God. Jesus told people to beware of the teaching of such people whose built-in prejudice led them to interpret Scripture according to their assumptions (see Mt. 16:11-12; Mk. 8:15; Lk. 12:1).

Jesus asked the questions: "Whom do the people say that I am?" and "Whom do you say that I am?" In asking those questions He was checking to see if His disciples had got rid of their built-in assumptions that they had learned from the cradle. He was meas-uring the change! He knows that the church is built on the rock of the Divine Revelation that people receive from God. All our power to wage war on the enemy would flow from the revelation of the person of Christ, the Word of God (see Mt. 16:13-20).

When the lame man was healed at the Gate Beautiful, Peter and John were preaching and testifying of the resurrection of Jesus. Various scribes, elders, and rulers took hold of them and brought them before the council of the high priest (see Acts 4:1-22).

This is an interesting clash between the rulers and theologians of one way of thinking and the apostles of another. The rulers and scribes had to acknowledge that Peter and John obviously had spent time with Jesus. The miracle could not be ignored, but they chose to threaten the disciples as they released them. The apostles were commanded not to teach or speak in the name of Jesus. Peter's words cut through years of obedience to a spiritual hierarchy that had ruled effectively over many thousands of people: "Whether it is right in the sight of God to listen to you more than to God, you judge. For we cannot but speak the things which we have seen and heard" (Acts 4:19b-20).

Again the issue was truth and experience. The truth of the council had not led them to an experience of God or the ability to recognize what God was doing. They had no prophetic edge that comes from relational communion with God—"We have to speak of what we have seen and heard." Effective teaching has testimony enshrined within it. Without experience, the Word of God cannot abide in us. This was the core message that Jesus spoke to the Pharisees (see Jn. 5:37-40).

> *The early Church was a pioneer of change; the present Church is a refuge from change!*

The early Church was a pioneer of change in its society. It turned the world upside down with its revelatory teaching and presence of God (see Acts 17:6). This Church altered the way people lived their lives, which provoked everyone around them. They were a talking point; they caused consternation in the values of people everywhere. They could not be ignored (see Acts 4:32–5:16).

The early Church was a pioneer of change; the present Church is a refuge from change. We are now in the ugly position of needing a revival to restore us to the position we never should have lost! How many churches will not experience revival because they hold an assumption of how it will come? Students of previous revivals inform us of the signs of revival. That knowledge will tell us what God did, but it may not reveal what God is doing now.

Teachers tell us what God has done, which is brilliant. Prophets tell us what God is doing, which is excellent. A partnership between the two will produce revelation with impartation, which will propel us into a move of God. If we believe that we are in the "endtimes," then possibly this coming revival may need to be viewed with an eschatological perspective rather than just a historic viewpoint. Probably we will need both.

Past revivals often have been grouped around personalities who were catalysts for the move of the Spirit. This coming move will be a "people's revival" because God is raising up a nameless, faceless generation of people with a passion for souls and a zeal to cause a reformation in society.

We cannot effect change unless we experience it. The Lord is challenging all our assumptions in these days. Jesus' walking on the water (see Jn. 6:16-21) provoked His disciples to reevaluate who He was. His appearance on the Mount of Transfiguration (see Mt. 17:1-7) demanded that the core group of His disciples enter a whole new level of spiritual experience, one completely foreign to their history.

Many of us are being radically challenged in these days of change and transition. Assumptions get in the way of truth and have a detrimental effect on our understanding of the process that God is using to restore the Church to her rightful place on the battlefield.

The Process of Change

I have already mentioned that many years ago I was the business development manager for a busy training and recruitment company. I learned a lot about leadership in that time. I learned how to motivate people and how to disciple them using effective feedback and appraisal of performance. Alpha Training was a cutting-edge company that could be relied upon to provide innovative, flexible, and effective solutions to business and management issues in industry. They were a forward-thinking and progressive bunch of strategists with a great feel for people.

The two key members of the core management team were Dorothy Shirvell, who ran the company, and Janet Scott, who ran the personnel department amongst other things. Alpha was a brilliant work experience mainly because of the skills and interaction of these two women. Dorothy was a strong, passionate, cutting-edge thinker. She drove the company forward with her demands for insight, intelligence, and hard work. She was creative and a great facilitator who brought other people into play. Any time spent with Dorothy usually left you with a buzz of creativity and expectation. She made demands on people. Everyone had to conform to a standard of excellence. Deadlines would be met!

Janet was kind, thoughtful, and sensitive with immense people skills. Many of the adjustments we had to make to preserve our radical nature demanded a level of excellence and professionalism that was outstanding. The pressure was enormous at times and the burden of expectation was huge. Yet we were all friends. The atmosphere was light, relaxed, and very fun. We enjoyed being together. It was friendly and competitive. We helped one another and supported one another. We celebrated our victories and toasted our defeats. Janet's influence on the attitude in the company was enormous. She encouraged, consoled, and stimulated people. She brought out the best in us. She made the company a family of professionals; Dorothy made us a team. Janet influenced our attitude; Dorothy inspired our ability. Janet made us smile...she eased the tension. She was sharp and insightful but had this wonderful heart for people. She helped us to live and breathe commitment and togetherness.

Dorothy and Janet epitomized the spirit of Alpha Training in terms of excellence and attitude. At that time, I was the only Christian in the company, and yet it was church to me five days and 60 hours per week. I loved the church I was attending, but it was from the company that I drew a lot of my comparisons of Kingdom and church life. The Alpha Experience, as we all called it, was a warm and inspirational challenge to walk a path of excellence and to overcome all obstacles in the pursuit of the vision that we held before us.

I loved the balance between Dorothy and Janet and how they made room for one another. They were inclusive of others and brought the best out of them. Everyone was encouraged to take part with ideas. We all were equipped to do the work and were actively encouraged to pursue training for ourselves. We all had a development plan because the leadership of the company wanted to see everyone succeed and become better.

Some people left and got jobs with more money and bigger positions. Ex-Alpha people maintained close ties with current employees. All agreed that they sorely missed the camaraderie and spirit of Alpha, which were not present in their current companies.

> *A cutting-edge vision without cutting-edge leadership will make us vulnerable in times of change.*

It was the awareness in the leadership that made the company such a joy to work for. They understood about change. They knew that "leadership" perceptions were different from "follower" perceptions in the matter of receiving and responding to change. As a member of the core management team with a department of my own, I knew the tensions and difficulties we faced in changing the dynamics of the company.

When looking ahead and focusing on new direction, leaders anticipate the road ahead. We major on reasons for change. We formulate a logical process for pursuing and promoting change. Leaders operate as the initiators of change, not the subjects of it. Leadership terminology involves words such as *challenge, opportunity, faith, excitement, benefits, new, radical, effective, productive, power, warfare, relevance, new level,* and *dimension.*

Church members have different perspectives. Change affects them emotionally. They feel that they are subject to a process that they have not helped to formulate. Change is being done *to* them! Their terminology may involve such words as *interference, threat, stress, the unknown, fear, anxiety, resistance, insecurity, energy, tiredness,* and *helplessness.* They have a fear of the unknown and of making wrong decisions.

There will be an information gap, which must be filled by trust. Church leadership must be trustworthy. Leaders discuss the changes for months in their meetings, but the church hears about it in a couple of meetings! Members may not have been involved in the process of change and have no access to communication or consultation. All changes of program, personnel, and policy will introduce fear factors whether they are expressed or hidden (which is usually the case!). Leadership must have a high trust factor to work through existing relationships.

There are implications in change. Many leaders, after months of dialogue and consultation amongst themselves, become impatient to push change through. They have lived with the process of change for a long time and now want to do something. They forget that the church also needs several months to come to terms with everything!

How will the church be affected by change? What are the best and worst case scenarios? All change will involve pain—even changing from the worst to the better. Imposed change will disempower people. The process of change must enable us to do a better job of enfranchising our people to a new level of involvement.

The process of how we change is just as important as what we are becoming as we change. The reward of change must be greater than the pain of the process, or people will not go for it. All change will impact people. Therefore, it is important to ascertain what people feel (not just think) about change.

People respond in different ways. Some response will mirror the way we feel ourselves as a leadership. People will be excited, willing, and stimulated to go for it. Do not make that response the spiritual norm and outlaw all the rest of the emotional responses. Other people may be intimidated, apprehensive, or have lots of reservations.

Change means taking time to change people, to help readjust their perceptions, their mood and morale, and their behavior patterns. Some people love the status quo; others may see the need to change and move forward. Resistance can increase with age. Youthful intolerance may produce change for its own sake due to a low threshold of boredom and an inability to relate to other cultures.

All of us have a basic human need for security and significance. Not being involved in the consultation affects our comfort zones and our self-esteem. People must deal with their insecurities because change cannot create artificial certainties just to make people feel better. At the same time, involving people empowers the church. Change affects the whole group; therefore, it needs the group's agreement and commitment. Leaders must evolve a strategy to facilitate that requirement. Change involves high levels of trust; therefore, a confident environment must be created. Existing trust levels must not be taken for granted or abused. Leaders need to develop an emotional bank account of trust that will lead people to set aside personal considerations in order to move forward into something new.

Counting the cost is a personal consideration. We all are creatures of habit who love stability. A potentially destabilizing factor makes everyone edgy and uncomfortable. We all live with varying degrees of selfishness, which are always being challenged by the Holy Spirit. The battles and blessings of the past may affect our current desire for change for good or bad. People fear loss of control. Actually, people fear loss more than change; they like to feel safe. If we are to enfranchise and empower the church, we must target the right people in the process.

Personalities in Change

In the change process, it is helpful for us to know whom we can rely on and whom we will have to nurture more carefully. There are some people who have a healthy, robust attitude to change because they have worked their way into a positive outlook on events in their relationship with God. These are the *initiators* (see Fig. 1); they are the people who want to make things happen. They are most often the catalysts for change in situations. They will probably be in the leadership of the church helping to determine the vision of what the congregation wants to produce in reality. They are the key resource people who have that break-through edge. In some churches, they may be part of the apostolic influence that undergirds that particular work. They are people shapers, prayer warriors, with a prophetic edge to their lives.

> *Imposed change will disempower people.*

The second group is the *early adopters*, the quick response people. Usually the first to respond in meetings, they have a passion to be where God is present. They have established the Lordship of Christ in their lives, and their walk with God is built on practiced obedience. Quick to see what God is doing, they are ready and willing to step into the gap. These people would have been part of Gideon's company of 300 (see Judg. 7), alert and watchful. They may be home cell leaders. They have an active prayer life and a living faith. They are ready for change.

The third and probably the largest group are known simply as the *majority*. These are the committed body of people in the church. They are the enablers in the body—the good, solid, faith-ful servants without whom the work would founder. They trust the Lord and demonstrate their steadfast spirit in their giving, attend-ing, and working within the church. Their loyalty and devotion to the Lord and the church for the most part is unwavering. Once they get behind an initiative, it will quickly gather momentum. Sometimes they may need some support and nurturing to enable them to see where everything is going. Like Gideon, they know that they are called to the fight; they simply want some assurances that things will work out (see Judg. 6:36-40) in the way that God has declared. If we come alongside with effective reassurance, the majority will lend their considerable strength to the enterprise.

The fourth group are the *laggards*. These people generally are struggling in their relationship with God. They lack passion, fire, or any conviction in their faith. Their lives are not constant, but up and down, often reflecting a soulish type of Christianity. They are easily influenced by the enemy. They often can be attenders but uncommitted to the real life and ministry of the church. Yet given the right moment and sensitivity of the Spirit, they can be moved

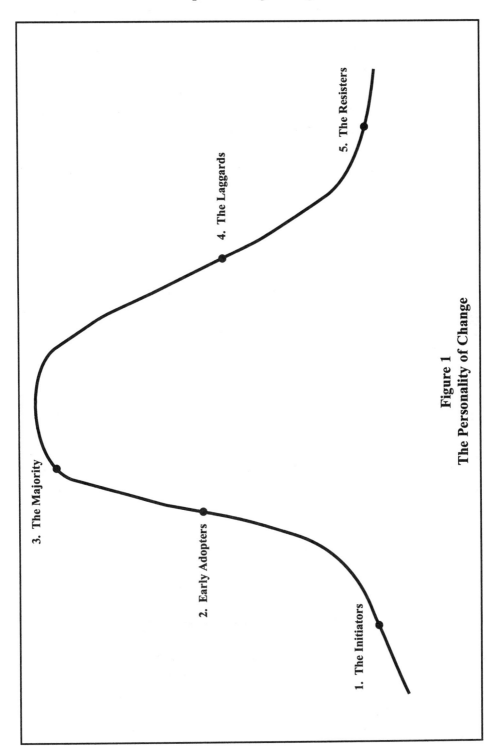

**Figure 1
The Personality of Change**

by God. When that occurs, we have a window of opportunity of which we must take full advantage.

These people have a short attention span. When the window is up and open, we must move fast to motivate them to move on into the majority. Here they can gradually be affected by the positive influence of the faithfully committed. However, if on their down days, more unscrupulous people get hold of them, they are just as liable to join the ranks of the negative and cynical.

The fifth group are the *resisters*. These people are not with us in spirit; we do not have their hearts. They may be present because they like the worship, the teaching, or the association with a good church. They have their own vision and agenda, and nothing must interfere with their call from God. They have little or no accountability and would deem any attempt to assist them with the development of integrity as control, dominion, and manipulation. Easily offended, often cynical, they hide behind a cloak of religiosity. They can be strong-minded individuals masquerading as weak people. They are not open to change and will resist it in order to keep the status quo. Sometimes they are simply one-dimensional in their understanding of church and ministry and prefer a traditional church stereotype rather than a new church prototype. Any trouble with negativity, cynicism, and rebellion is likely to come from this group of people. Note the leading lights in this bunch, and watch them to see who they are influencing.

Most of our initial energy and direction must occur with the initiators and early adopters. They need to be part of the original planning, discussion, and strategy team. They can help to iron out the bugs in the thinking and shape the concept of what God is putting into our hearts. They will be faithful to pray and will have positive contributions to make as we shape the vision for the next phase. Their excitement and faith will generate a good spirit, which is helpful for morale.

Through these initial catalysts, we can influence and stimulate the majority of people to get behind the new direction. The catalyst people through relationships, leadership contact, small group involvement, and various connections can meet, relate, and support people with friendly and positive intent to encourage faith to rise in their hearts.

The laggards and resisters, in turn, can be affected by the faith and positive attitude of the early adopters and the majority. They probably would relate to those people groups more than they would with the initiators. The initiators need to spend most of their time with people groups #2 and #3 and allow those people to impress and persuade groups #4 and #5.

There are four basic attitudes in church life, based on well-known mathematical symbols. There are those who multiply (x) faith and generate a high level of power, positive influence, and significance to the work. Their presence and involvement in anything guarantees a high quality and anointed contribution. Then there are those who always add (+) something to the work. Their faithfulness, servant heart, and patient good humor keep us in good spirits. They are a tonic to be with and contribute the generous and gracious side of the nature of God. Everyone loves them, and they are a constant reliable support in all that we do.

There are those who simply take from us (-) and have little or no capacity or compunction to give in return. They may have an expectation that the church will meet all their needs rather than their own faith in God. To be fair and decent, we know that some people are merely in that stage of their life where they need continual help for a season. It is the people who perpetually live in that place and have no intention

Change involves taking time to change people.

of developing faith or strength to rise up and cope with their own lives, that I am referring to at this level. They drain away our resources and are liable to go elsewhere to leech off someone else.

The fourth attitude is the divisive (÷) one that robs and kills the congregation. Such people are malcontents with hidden agendas and unsurrendered lives. The enemy is just as liable to speak through them as the Holy Spirit is! They have mixture in their lives and no purity of mind and heart. They may be double-minded and unstable in their walk with God. Quick to find fault and exploit other people's weaknesses, they are the bane of any church seeking to move into new dimensions of power and significance in the Lord.

The laggards and resisters may be positively affected by other people groups and tag along with us. Or it just may be that they have been unable to prevent forward movement from taking place, and they are biding their time in order to slip their poison in somewhere. In a positive way, they keep us sharp, watchful, and alert to the Holy Spirit. We must not fall into the trap of giving like for like in our contact with them. Difficult people offer us a wonderful opportunity to practice the love, grace, mercy, and kindness of God. We will have ample openings to move in the fruit of the Spirit and develop the character of Jesus. Just think of all the lovely patience, peace, gentleness, and self-control you are going to develop around these people, not to mention the sheer joy of eventually winning their hearts and lives for Jesus!

It is entirely possible that, having failed to get their own way, the resisters may leave the church and take some of the laggards with them. We simply must ensure that the damage is as limited as possible. Encourage people to have open hearts and minds toward these people and circumstances. We do not want any negative or cynical comments to emerge. Do not make value judgments on such people. Keep a light burning in the window and be ready to receive the prodigals on their return. Of course, we must ensure that they are repentant and have learned from their experience before we receive them back into fellowship.

We must target the right people in the process and be aware of proper and improper attitudes in the evolution of change. Identify the key and core personnel and enlist their support and impetus, whilst retaining a gracious approach to others less fortunate in their perspective.

The Emotion of Change

When the new vision or direction is presented to the bulk of the church, there will be a variety of emotions that must be worked through on both a corporate and, definitely, personal level. All changes impact people in their soul, which is their mind, emotions, and will. In this section, we will examine and identify the likely stages of the emotional roller coaster that some people (not all, thank goodness!) will ride before they arrive at the right perspective. Some people will hit all the stages; others will connect with a few but miss out on others.

It usually starts with an "*Oh no!*" response in some quarters (see Fig. 2). There is shock at the thought of change, or immediate denial in the sense of "I'm not doing that!" People are unable to accept change on a personal level. They feel that they have enough change to cope with as it is and are unable to take action. Lack of communication in such people's lives will cause uneasy behavior in the church. People are not sure who to talk to or what to say. They do not want to be trapped into talking with someone positive when they themselves are looking for sympathy and potential excuses for not responding.

This can then change into "*Hooray!*" as people catch the buzz of the Holy Spirit and gain a little faith. Probably, people are picking up on the anointing and positive attitude of our initiators and early adopters. People begin speaking more positively, and generally there is hope (but not actual faith) that the leadership know what they are doing and where they are going!

Some of this may simply be people catching hold of the general euphoria, or perhaps they are resigned to making the best of it. Outwardly they put on a brave face, but there is that inward sigh. It can manifest itself in the church through an uneasy bonhomie with people making jokes in black humor or restrained sarcasm. People can move from "Oh no!" to "Hooray!" and we can think we have won the day! Sometimes, with basic, fairly simple changes, that may well be the case. However, with more profound reforms, people will still go through the varying stages. The "hooray" stage may be a false dawn, so be careful and watchful.

The next stage is "*Where?*" and involves a searching and a questioning. People want more detail and are requesting information because that represents security. Some people may want to revive old ideas or return to things we used to do. Unconsciously, they are searching for familiarity in the landscape of change. Some people put forward ideas that may need to be genuinely considered. Others give suggestions and input when they really want (unconsciously for the most part) to control this new environment.

Some people may not want to move forward and will settle for the line of least resistance. Staying put is too uncomfortable, so they opt for returning to Egypt. They have forgotten (conveniently, perhaps) all that went on before and simply want what is familiar, however boring! Leaders may take some flak here, particularly if they cannot answer all the questions.

> *Change situations provide a great opportunity for rubbish removal.*

We may be like Abraham, whom God told to go but who had to move out not knowing where he was going (see Heb. 11:8). He obeyed and went in faith, knowing that this movement was connected to his inheritance. He had to bear all the inadequacy and uncertainty of a walk of faith. At such times God does not give us vision or direction but comfort! Leaders will take some criticism because they cannot give detail. We can be tempted to manufacture something to ease the pressure, but that takes us down a very rocky road of indiscretion that will have even worse repercussions. It is better to speak out your trust as powerfully and with as much humility as possible and trust the Lord. Develop a Teflon hide so that garbage thrown at you does not stick and you don't take it personally.

It is important that we allow the church to vent their emotions. This is our chance to show the church the kind of leaders we are in Christ. Demonstrate the Father's anointing by supporting the church emotionally as they discharge their feelings. Be blessed by God and be a blessing to the people!

The fourth stage is *"They should!"* and involves a fair amount of toxic waste being pushed into the church. People are looking for supporters to uphold how they feel. Everyone is a leader with a viewpoint. The real leaders are "they." Everyone has a solution. People get together and express their opinions to one another. *"They* should do this; *they* should do that." They are not part of the team at this point (otherwise it would be *we* should), but they still want to influence the situation. This is okay. At least they are thinking about solutions, which is a positive sign. There is also grumbling and complaining. A lack of openness can prevent real dialogue from taking place. People often cannot help attacking others. It is only insecurity talking for the most part, but we have to be alert to nip anything more sinister in the bud.

The fifth stage is *"guilt."* People blame themselves because they cannot be more positive. They realize they may be holding up progress but are locked into this downward spiral of negativity. They just want peace and for the situation to return to normal. They are full of self-doubt regarding whether they can really make the transition. They may have tired of the battle and want to quit. Sometimes leaders carry guilt too, particularly if their recent history in terms of decision-making is not very effective. It is hard for leaders to watch their people going through the pain of change and transition without feeling a sense of guilt for having caused the suffering. In change, the enemy uses the uncertainty to attack and try to take advantage of any potential weakness. Of course, there is going to be some real ammunition around in the lives of certain people.

It is vital here that leaders resist the urge to preach about change publicly. It may add fuel to the flames. Instead visit every household, preferably with a team of people, to pray and speak a blessing into the home. Take a gift and show appreciation for all that the people have given and done for the sake of Jesus. Impartation will release revelation into people's lives. Bring the prophetic gift and the love of God to bear on each home. Release a flow of encouragement and faith. Be calm. People will begin to listen out for God simply because the leaders have calmed them down. Some may get ideas at this point, which may or may not be useful; however, it does indicate an upward swing toward commitment. We must give people every opportunity to begin the journey toward committed behavior.

In the trial of transition, two things are happening that need development. Firstly, change is a battlefield where we are exposed to conflict and confrontation. There is a violence abroad with

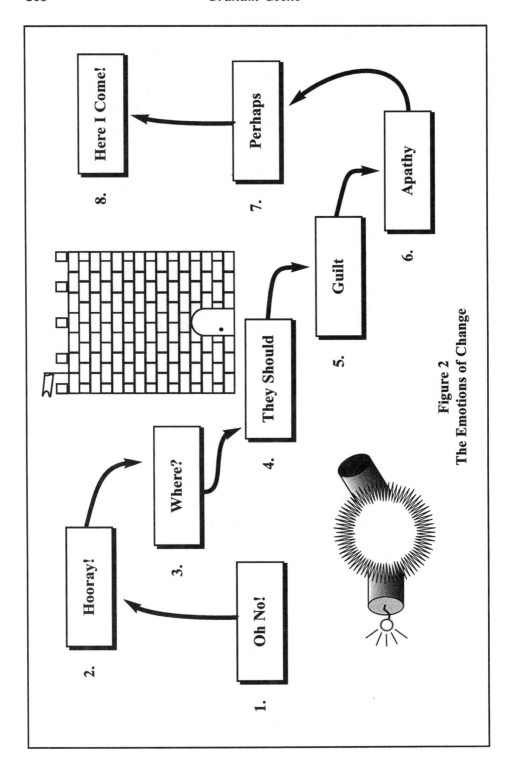

Figure 2
The Emotions of Change

many bitter comments and hurtful expressions. We will have to defuse many situations that potentially could be very explosive! People under stress are good at laying the match to the fire and retiring. Expressing some comments are like tossing live hand grenades into the midst of a crowd of people. The damage potential could be huge if we do not all demonstrate a godly restraint.

People will regurgitate their mistrust and suspicion, tying it in to past mistakes and poor leadership decisions. In stress and tension, people go over ancient history. Challenges will abound to our leadership, our patience, our character, and our integrity. Personal carnality will rise in the most surprising of people. Fear, anger, and resentment will be exasperated by enemy pressure. In the midst of that, people will have legitimate lines of inquiry or really helpful contributions, which we may miss completely or misconstrue as criticism or negativity.

Leaders need caring for as well. This is where an external perspective and support from apostolic and prophetic people is vital. On the battlefield, people may be concerned primarily with self-preservation.

Secondly, we must build a fortress on the battleground where people may receive input and strength from the leaders. We lend to others the strength, comfort, and security that God gives to us. We supply appreciation and validation for people's lives and ministry. We protect our people from the onslaught of the enemy and from the hearts of unscrupulous people. Shepherds keep guard against wolves. We enable people to make right choices by affirming and empowering their lives in Christ. We generate the love and warmth of the Father-heart of God to enable our people to stand up and be counted in the time of change.

Initially we must adopt a policy of turning key homes into fortresses. Key homes are often the houses of loved and significant people in the church, or they may simply be the places where people congregate the most. Turn those homes into places of positive impartation, comfort, and support. Eventually, our goal is to make every home

> *In times of stress, the real leaders and fathers emerge in the church.*

a fortress against the enemy and a place of power, safety, and support for God's people.

The sixth stage is *"apathy,"* which is rock bottom for many people. They are too tired and beaten up. Events in their own lives have not enabled them to feel good or to generate faith for the corporate transition. The church situation has added to their general stress, and they have no internal resources left. They may not even be able to take prayer and input because they cannot face the thought of having to respond, stand, and fight off the enemy. They have low energy and may be acutely depressed. Sometimes it is helpful to give them a sabbatical from the church scene for a few months, to maintain our friendships but have no expectations. They are suffering from shell shock or post-battle trauma and just need a break. Let us be kind and merciful to work out a strategy where we can love them and allow them to regroup in peace and join up with us later.

Be careful to whom you offer that option because some will use it as an excuse not to fight because they have low motivation in Christ anyway. Some people have a natural predisposition to do the minimum and not take up any slack or strain on behalf of others.

Some people are present physically but withdraw themselves spiritually. Often they move to the back row. They do not enter into worship and may stand there in meetings in a defensive posture, with arms folded. They have a "let's wait and see" expression. They withhold their prayers, their worship, their faith, and often their tithes and offering. They contribute to the "drop-in" resources and attempt to justify their behavior. Many others will have similar reservations but will still be faithful in attendance, giving, and personal support.

Fair-weather friends and resisters will probably leave at this stage. We must work with the undecided and continue to empower those who want to hang in there with us. Allow people to leave. This is not the army; we cannot court-martial people. Let them go with a blessing, and make sure they know that they will be welcome back. It will probably hurt us to let certain people go, whereas we may be quite relieved at the prospect of some people jumping ship!

If people do come back, for the sake of those who stayed and endured, we must make sure that there is appropriate repentance and restoration. It is a spiritual principle that those who do not fight can share in the spoils of victory, but those who battle will be worthy of double honor (see 1 Sam. 30:21-25; 2 Sam. 23:9-10).

The seventh stage is "*perhaps,*" which sees an upswing of confidence in the hearts of the people. We must encourage people to let go of the past as positive signs begin to develop in the church. Inevitably, in transition, things are said and done in the stress of the moment that we may not be too proud of. There needs to be ample opportunity for forgiveness and restoration of relationships. It is best, if we can manage it, to keep short accounts with people rather than allow our pride to let things fester. The enemy will exploit tension into separation if we allow him to do so. At this stage, people are beginning to look up and think about moving up. Hope springs eternal from the heart of God. Some people naturally work it all out and figure that if they are paying the price anyway, they may as well have the benefits of the new dimension!

Interest begins to form in the new direction. The route back into the old thing has been effectively blocked off by the Lord, and only the way forward is open. I am sure Israel must have felt like that in the desert where the choice was Egypt or Canaan. No one wanted to stay in the wilderness! It seems to be a spiritual principle that God brings us to the point of no return.

There were many people who followed Jesus initially and who were thought of as His disciples. When people openly opposed His ministry, Jesus did not back down from His mission. His words caused consternation in some quarters, but He did not modify His terminology (see Jn. 6:41-71). Some of His disciples grumbled and left Him at this point. Jesus said to the 12 disciples: "Do you also want to go away?" He was giving them the option because He knew it would not get any easier for them. Peter's reply carried with it equal amounts of pathos and resolve: "Lord, to whom shall we go? You have the words of eternal life."

Sometimes that is just the way it is. There is nowhere else to go; we must stick with it. We have reached a point of no return. To go on seems hard; to go back even harder, and we cannot endure the place where we are! We limp forward in pain, more in hope than faith. As we move out, haltingly, it seems that God begins to meet up with us. Our morale begins to improve. We break through the clouds as the storm of transition begins to fade.

All around us people begin to be inspired as we move into the final stage of *"Here I come!"* Productivity begins to improve. The prophetic is flowing. Outside speakers, when they preach to us, resonate with us at the new level. We shake off the lethargy as faith begins to rise. People grasp the new vision and want to begin to sow into it. Encouragement begins to flow in many forms from many people. People are reaching out spiritually and helping one another to stand up. We need to spend a season blessing and encouraging one another, unwrapping the grave clothes and taking away the scales from one another's eyes by prophecy and prayer. There is a renewal of optimism in the hearts of the people as the Holy Spirit begins to move amongst us. Every church has to have a corporate vision of the long "dark night of the soul." It is in this time of pressure that the diamond of our character is formed under the stress of circumstances. The beauty of Jesus and the unyielding nature of the sons of God is formed in the fires of transition.

> *The prototype is not formed after transition, but during the process.*

Now the Holy Spirit begins to quickly strip away the rough edges to reveal the hard bright diamond beneath. This precious stone of the character of Jesus is now ready to be shaped into a beautiful jewel in the hands of God. The Holy Spirit is busy; expectancy is rising as we are launched on a voyage of discovery into this new realm of anointing. We are ready for change and are willing to experiment with our structures, our meetings, and our methods. We want only what God wants. He wants only what works for us. We leave the stereotype of our old ways and become a prototype church moving with substance as well as style as the grace of God covers our plans and strategies with His favor and blessing.

It may take many weeks and months to complete the process from "*Oh no!*" to "*Here I come!*" We all must be patient with one another. This cannot be rushed. The whole point of transition is that we come out of it different people to the ones who first entered. Let God have His way in the process. Change the program to accommodate what God is doing.

This is important! Do not try to fit transition into your current methodology and style of meetings. The prototype is not formed after transition but during the process! The pain of transition must be allowed to break our traditions in order to comfort and strengthen one another. This is where we take God out of the sanctuary and back into people's homes. Operating home-blessing teams, where we gather in the houses of people to pray and prophesy over people, marriages, and children is a significant move toward developing the prototype. With home blessings we can strengthen relationships with God and one another. Prophecy into each life and home puts a sword in our hand at a critical moment to aid people in the battle to secure their own destiny.

We can use these prophecies as weapons in fighting the enemy and as meditation aids in our devotional times (see 1 Tim. 1:18; 4:14-16). As we stand together and develop new ways of ministering to one another, the stereotype of how we have always had church is shattered forever. Even our public meetings will have different layers and levels of function, procedure, and activity. Constant change is here to stay as the Lord moves us from one dimension to another, in a continuous upward and onward progression. Let us not merely grit our teeth and endure it, but let us learn to relax in Jesus and enjoy it!

Chapter 7

Building a Prototype Church

*T*hings seldom happen quite the way we imagine they should. No matter how hard we plan and strategize, keep the chain of command small to avoid confusion, work through tightly defined parameters, and generally/specifically keep on top of things, it doesn't seem to matter. Some odd variable that we had not anticipated will creep into the mix somewhere and upset everything.

Imagine that you are at the hub of full-blown revival. There has been a powerful move of God that has torn down all your cozy ideas and practices about church. The wind of the Spirit has filled you and your church with a compelling need to evangelize and go up against demonic forces everywhere you find them. Even the weaker brethren are now emboldened to a far higher level of anointing than your strongest preachers had *before* the move of God began!

Thousands are being saved. Sick bodies are healed; demons are cast out; and the nation is being turned upside down. The body of believers not caught up in this new move are against it, criticizing it as dangerous phenomena and preaching dire warnings about control, manipulation, and mental ill health. The government is stirred up by the whole furor, and there are various investigations underway or planned against this supposed new cultic activity.

You have never seen such a level of power, grace, and holiness of God all at one time. The church is outgrowing itself month by month. Miracles are commonplace; the amazing and incredible presence of God seems to be everywhere. The team that you are part of, which is caught up in the epicenter of all this activity, is the most profound experience that you have ever encountered.

Of course, there are problems—problems that often are huge and time-consuming. However, as you pray for wisdom, the anointing to move forward is so great that godly insight seems to spring into your conscious mind with ease.

Every day brings a pressure cocktail of more people, more needs, greater opposition, further demonic attacks, fresh misunderstandings, calculated misinterpretations, added responsibilities, supplementary organizational problems to overcome, and extra requirements for advice, leadership, and ministry.

Everything is strained to the limit of personal and physical ability. Revival seems to be concerned with endurance and stamina as much as it is preoccupied with anointing and empowerment. You are in the midst of constant attack and blessing; of tiredness, pressure, and opposition; of trying to keep everything going smoothly so that more people can be touched and reached; of not losing people to poor organization and mismanagement.

> *We can always rely on God to mess up the calm, ordered ways of humanity!*

You do not want this move to blow through society, touching thousands of lives, but not see church built at the end of it. Indeed, it shows no signs of abating! The need to develop leaders and train people to look after others, the need for more prayer, and the demand for more workers is huge. You are caught up in the whole wonderful and demanding, exhausting mix of a move of God.

Suddenly, you hear that one of your core team members has started another move of God. This move is not in direct competition with yours, but it is nevertheless going to impact it in a significant way. The implications and repercussions are going to hit everyone, hard. You don't need this pressure right now. All your prayers have been focused on asking the Lord for wisdom and strength to keep this ship steady so that the work of harvesting souls can continue unhindered.

Other members of your core team are up in arms about this new move. Not only is this an additional pressure that will give your enemies greater ammunition against you, but you also are losing some key people who want to be a part of this new thing. Rumors abound. The brother at the head of this new move does have a dubious reputation for going off on odd and crazy tangents. As part of a team, he is fine; as a potential leader of something, he is a walking disaster. With a reputation for not thinking things through and a penchant for working outside of agreed boundaries, this brother needs love and careful handling.

Rumors increase—angels, visions, trances, visitations, audible voices of God. The new move has become a focal point for dealing with people of other religions whose leaders are now up in arms, shouting about holy wars, proselytizing, and religious persecution. The tumult around the work increases enormously.

Surely this is not right? How can this be God? Why, when there are apostles, prophets, and other fivefold ministries working in team, when thousands of people are praying daily for wisdom and grace, when the power of God is being demonstrated daily on every street corner? Why would God communicate to a non-Christian, a devout man of another religion? Why send an angel to a pagan, put a leading apostle into a trance, and then by vision and interpretation connect the two together? Why start a new move of God, a new revival, when the current one is turning the world upside down? Why choose this particular brother who is hardly noted for his calm, common sense rationale?

Incredibly, we now have three things happening on a major level within the world of the people of God. Firstly, the word of faith and hope is passed down successfully from one godly generation to another—the bedrock of all spiritual experience. Secondly, this "new" move of the Spirit is causing outrageous problems for the religious establishment of the day—not to mention the secular government. Thirdly, this upstart, outrageous, and frankly idiotic new thing is stirring up all the rest of the people that the first new movement of God (revival) was not concerned with. Confused? I can only imagine the uproar if it actually happened.

Of course, we know that it did happen. In Acts 10 is the biblical account of a second move of God beginning with God's sending an angel to a non-Christian. God then chose the most impetuous, reckless, and radical believer—Peter—to instigate a new move before the current one was even firing on all cylinders.

Trances, repeated visions, audible voices of God, angelic visitation, unclean contact with other religions and fake gods, probable demonic manifestations and the Holy Spirit falling on people before the message was concluded, an appeal given and response for salvation—all had occurred! This is not God! Is it?

Is it small wonder that the boys back in Jerusalem were demanding an explanation? I wonder how many seminary rules were broken by God and Peter? What possible theological thinking could be used to justify these insane events? What Scriptures would be quoted? Surely his explanation had to be founded on something more than just subjective experience: "I was in a trance; I saw a vision; I heard a voice; I went where the voice told me; I was in the house of an occult guy who had seen an angel; this angel told him about me (I don't know why me and not you guys!). While I was explaining the gospel, the Holy Spirit fell on them like He had with us" (see Acts 11:4-15).

Peter completes his explanation with these incredible words: "Who was I that I could withstand God?" (Acts 11:17)

Unbelievable, but scriptural! The early Church was in full flow of anointing and power—thousands entering the Kingdom of God; apostles and prophets interacting; evangelists being transported through time and space to keep divine appointments to bring salvation; teachers instructing new converts; pastors putting together systems of care and culture. The sick were being laid out in the streets, and society was agog with all the events of revival. No one dared to join the church with its radical expression of Kingdom life (see Acts 2:41-47; 4:32-37; 5:12-16); however, thousands were being added.

This is the stuff of dreams for the modern-day Church, representing the full range of all we are praying for and longing to see. "O, that we could have these same problems!" With all this phenomenal activity in the early Church, is it not strange that God wants to do a new work but cannot break into the existing structure of church?

We can perhaps better understand the dilemma in this modern time. The early Church was steeped in the culture and passion of revival. Why did they not receive internal direction in their apostolic prayer meetings? For some reason, the Lord could not break into the hearts and minds of the people He was using the most. A mind-set is a mind-set is a mind-set, even if it is surrounded by incredible events and extraordinary spiritual dynamics. We would assume that they would be wide open to every nuance of what the Lord was saying.

There is a lesson for us here. No matter how good we are at hearing the Lord, how excellent at obedience and faith, how in tune with the things of God, there is always something more in the movement of the Holy Spirit than we are currently experiencing.

It would seem that no matter how wide open we think we are to the things of God; layers of prejudice, hidden mind-sets, and current practices can be broken only by God's touch. It is not in our nature to perceive new things while still being jolted by recent events. We do become self-satisfied with blessing, so easily preoccupied by all that is happening—a lot of it no doubt good and incredible.

> *Is the structure of your church or network hindering a new Kingdom anointing from being birthed?*

Sometimes the biggest threat to a new move is not the old one that is not working, but the move that is still working and doing well.

Somehow I don't believe we will have a traditional revival, an all-encompassing wave that will hit a country and take everything with it. I don't think it will be an outpouring centered around key, international, and high-profile ministries.

I think it will be a people revival. I feel that God will use a nameless, faceless generation of people, unknown in the earth. It will be a Gideon's revival, led by the least among us who have been powerfully touched. Think about it! Will God use the high priest, church councils, and key ministries, or pick up a bunch of illiterate fishermen and sprinkle them with a mixture of different personalities with educated upbringings of varying types?

The reality is yes and no, either/or, both and neither; we don't know for sure. It will be different. He will come to people with open minds and hearts, people who do not set things in concrete practice. He will come to people who understand that with all that God has given us, with all He has graciously blessed us, we need to be mindful that there are new things God will want to do—which may not fit with what He has already given us.

This "people revival" may not be just one type. God only builds prototypes, the first in a series. We build stereotypes, many of the exact same type! We build stereotypes because we are not creative enough. The Lord does not build stereotypes because He is too creative. There needs to be hundreds and thousands of different types of church in order for the Body of Christ to accurately reflect the immensity of Heaven and the creativity of God.

In character, God is the Father of conformity. Everyone must be like Jesus. In creativity, He is the Father of diversity, expressing Himself as fully in the Church as He has in creation.

I think we will have dozens of revivals, each one specific in its application and operation; each aimed at differing elements in society, at varying people-groups. God is generationally inclined. "I am the God of Abraham, Isaac, and Jacob." There may be a children's revival, a young people's movement, and a move of the Spirit upon the elderly to release the Caleb anointing. It may be among families, the educated, the poor, prisoners, business people, the arts community, politicians, lawyers, even church people themselves! Keep an open mind and heart.

In the midst of revival, God has to send an angel to a devout man of a different religion because His own people are too pre-occupied with what they are doing—or their mind-set is too narrow—to hear what God wants to do next.

A Glimpse Into a Non-Christian's Heart

We must be conscious at this time that God is probably doing as much with non-Christians as He is with the Church. Like the scenario we have just read about, the Church is not aware of all that God is doing.

On a tour in North America, walking through a mall looking for a gift for Sophie, my daughter, I came into an experience of God that was unlooked for and profoundly disturbing.

I found myself with a heightened sense of God's presence, being stirred up to pray internally for people around me. I was intensely aware that my prayers were not satisfactory. I felt inef-fective in my words to God. I had desire but no insight. I needed to know more to pray better. I asked the Lord to show me what He was doing in the hearts and lives of the people whom I was observing.

I moved through the mall, praying in desperation: "Show me what You are doing!" After what seemed an age (indeed, I did lose track of time by several hours), my eyes were drawn to a young girl, probably aged ten years. She was with her mother, much younger brother, and a small baby, walking toward me. I felt the presence of God increase within my heart. I felt God's words rise up within me: "Would you like to know what she prayed last night?" I was excited. I could feel God's joy at opening this new door of intercession for me.

"This is what she prayed." I waited, hardly breathing, my excitement intense, and then I heard this: "Please, don't let my daddy rape me tonight." I thought my heart would break. I gasped aloud. I think I shouted something. Certainly people looked at me. Tears sprang from my eyes. I felt weak. I groped my way to a bench and sat with my hands covering my head. People asked if I was ill; I mumbled that I was okay.

Okay? Who was I kidding? The joy of sharing potential new insight had turned to horror and shock at what had been revealed. It wasn't just the insight to prayer. Somehow I had seen her cowering under the bed covers. I had felt the fear and anguish in her heart.

More horribly, I had felt the pain in God's heart toward her. I had touched His sorrow. I was wrecked. I could not handle it. I realized how one-dimensional my spirituality was. I wept for her, for myself, and for the Lord, who heard these things all the time.

I realized that He doesn't listen just to the prayers of Christians; He listens to the prayer of every human soul that is offered in quiet desperation. There is so much evil that we do not fight. The Church is so tolerant of sin and wickedness that we have lost our voice in the earth. We do not have a spirit that rages against injustice and will not keep silent.

> *True revelation destroys all barriers and releases us to flow with the fullness of God's heart.*

I prayed for that little girl off and on for days, until the burden lifted off me.

I have often been conscious of God moving amongst non-Christians. I hesitate to use the term non-believers because it is really inadequate. In desperate times, many people are desperate to believe in something outside of themselves that can provide help, comfort, and support. A non-Christian believer is a potential Christian in reality.

I have often prayed for people around me in airport lounges, restaurants, shopping places, and entertainment centers. It was mostly an act of warfare, asking God for words of knowledge so that I could pray effectively and tie up enemy resources in the process. I firmly believe that the Church does not give the demonic realm enough work to do. The demons should be reacting to the pressure that our lifestyle, worship, prayer, and activity put them under. Instead, they lead largely untroubled lives where they are free to terrorize humanity, causing the premature death, oppression, and ruination of millions of lives, as well as creating powerful opposition against believers who are really on the front line where Heaven meets hell every day. I want the enemy jumping around my life. I want to make him pay, make him work, give him no free ride. I want to lift Jesus higher and make all that is not of God pay attention.

In this context, my prayers were an act of war. Everything you do for God is an open act of aggression against the devil. In these new circumstances, I crossed a line into a different dimension of God activity.

I was caught up in one aspect of the work but realized in a more profound way that there were other things I needed to give myself to that were just as legitimate. God's breaking into my life this way had just constructed a larger and stronger context for the call of God on my own life.

A large part of my call has been to wake up the Church, to make her aware of her true ministry, to reconstruct the real Church of the Bible in modern times. If we want supernatural power, then we must return to our biblical roots, do away with rationalism, and develop a simple faith. Our theology should be that of slaves and ignorant fishermen: simple, purposeful, and intensely practical.

There is an elegance about God that is rooted in simplicity, honest relationships, and a dynamic expression of His heart. Being led by the Spirit is a dedicated dependency on the love of God. It comes out of a willingness to be governed yourself; out of the recognition that you have no rights, that you are bought with a price (see 1 Cor. 6:19-20). You do not belong to yourself; you are the property of another. Withholding even a part of yourself weakens your relationship with God and one another; your faith; your capacity to rise up in war; and your church's effectiveness in the whole community.

I have to say that, walking through that mall, I was not ready for what God wanted to do. I was not ready for what was on His heart. Just a glimpse of that dimension had a profound effect on me. It left me thinking harder than ever before about the role of the Church in humanity. I was, and am more so, profoundly uncomfortable with second-rate Christian activity. I need to rearrange the priorities of my own life. There is more than what we have experienced in our churches. Some of us have bridges to cross and hard decisions to make just to become involved in all that God is doing. Early settlers in America burnt the boats that brought them to the New World as a sign that they were not going back. Some of us have boats to burn—a stand to make in the realm of the Spirit.

There is a divide between what we are doing now (as good as it may be) and the true spiritual dimension that we should be occupying.

Without a doubt, God is still speaking to non-Christians today, outside of mainstream church activity. Using Acts 10 as a backdrop, let us attempt to recognize a number of factors if we are to experience a fresh move of God in our own works.

Recognize Your Time of Visitation

Each time the Lord does something new, it will probably counteract something He has already done. With God there is usually a layering process going on in the Spirit. He is moving the Church into successive new dimensions of understanding, experience, and activity. Each element is accompanied by a revelation of His principles and a testing of His purposes.

Whenever God does something for the first time or whenever He reveals His heart to a new generation, He also sets a precedent and creates a principle by which we know Him that way forever. Our understanding and exposure to God's unchanging nature must be updated and expanded with each new level of experience in the Spirit.

Each spiritual breakthrough to a new level is preceded by a breaking out of old patterns of thought and behavior. We love getting a breakthrough, but we do not enjoy the cost of breaking out. Each promotion to a new dimension of the Spirit will make our current experience of church uncomfortable. Things become less familiar to us than they are right now.

With the passing years, we become very familiar with how our church works. We are clued up on its pattern, its function, and structure. When God does a new thing, He interferes with our comfort zones. He will not have us taking good cheer from anything or anyone except the Comforter He has provided.

We become comfortable with how the church moves. When God begins to do a new thing, we are discomfited. We easily get out of the habit of understanding how the Lord moves. We too readily confuse what we are doing with what God is doing. They are not always the same, and indeed, on some occasions, are radically different! Many of us will confess that we are more familiar with how the church works, than we are with God.

We are acquainted with the routine of church to such a degree that a new move of God is viewed as a major threat to what we have learned by experience.

Recently in our home church, Tony Morton, the senior team leader, said these words regarding our worship, our services, and church in general: "Guys, listen, we worship God one way one week, and a different way another week. Let us not get into such a routine that we cannot spot when the Lord wants to do something new among us. It may be nice for us to sing all those nice songs

> *We need the practical theology of slaves and ignorant fishermen that is grounded in a simple, purposeful, and intensely practical ministry.*

that give us those good feelings, but we have to understand something. We are here to do what God wants. We are having church for Him; He is not doing church for us! There is a subtle difference here, which we are coming to appreciate."

Increasingly, we are coming to a place where we do not recognize the church we have joined. This may be a good thing! If the church you are in has not changed significantly in the past five to ten years, you must question its corporate relationship with God. Clearly, you could be missing something. God is moving us from one dimension of relationship with Him into another realm of Holy Spirit activity in church life. To bridge that gap, He is messing with our mind-sets and comfort zones. When our comfort zone is disturbed, so is our personal security. This leads us to ask questions about the foundations of our security. Is our security in what we are doing, in the familiar of church life, or locked into the heart of God?

The personal security issue is currently quite strong in many churches. God is taking churches through new times and seasons of change. With the onset of change comes the opportunity to reappraise and rekindle new depths of relationship with the Lord Jesus and one another.

If you are in that place of unfamiliarity and are feeling vulnerable, cast your heart onto God in a deeper way. The change that God has thrust you into must become internal first. He is drawing you, touching you, and provoking you to giving Him more of your life. You may be excited and apprehensive at the same time. Do not rush this experience. Savor it; be changed by it; find the Lord Jesus in it; deepen your friendships in church because of it. Take every chance to go deeper in every way.

What you gain during this time will be significant. The Lord has come to you; recognize the visitation for what it will release to you, not because of what it will cost. We all are being drawn into a deeper place of relationship through vulnerability and inadequacy. God offends the mind to renew the heart. Peter recognized that the Lord was moving and submitted to the flow of the Holy Spirit even though he was led into territory he had never before encountered (see Acts 10:28-29).

Change Your Mind-set

By far, the greatest hindrance to a new move of God is the way we think about the old one. All his life Peter had been brought up in a particular way. Although acknowledging the presence of God in his reply (see Acts 10:14), Peter feels safe in his tradition to obstruct the cause of God and disobey the Lord's command. "Not so, Lord!" That is, "No way, God! I have never done what You are asking me to do, and I am not starting now." Tradition is bigger than God when we put it first.

Without a change of mind, Peter cannot move into the fresh anointing and new ministry that God is releasing. I previously stated that each new visitation is accompanied by a revelation of God's principles and a testing of His purposes.

Each thing that God does, involves a test of our submission and commitment to Him. Can Peter be trusted with the new move of God? The answer lies in his ability to cast off a mind-set that has long governed his life. It is like God to strike at the very heart of our past experience in order to release us into a new move of the Spirit. We are not talking here of salvation or the very root of our involvement with God. We are talking, however, of a fundamental practice that was a significant part of Peter's experience and tradition.

A change of mind was demanded as a prerequisite to participating in a major new move of God. Peter was horrified: "Not so, Lord!" He did not understand that he was in a new day, a new era of the Spirit. He had heard Jesus say on numerous occasions, "You have heard it said...now I say to you," thus signifying major alterations to perception and practice. It had not computed though into any determined areas of change.

Peter had one way of thinking until God demanded a change of mind-set: "Do not consider things this way any longer" was the Lord's response to Peter's mind-set. When the Lord does a new thing, He releases a new mind to His people so that they can submit and be involved. A new dimension involves a new mind-set. The work of renewal in recent years did not compute with many churches. Instead of allowing the Lord to fulfill His purpose, they chose rationale, putting Scripture in line with their own mind-set to justify their non-involvement.

"Renewal does not fit in with what God is doing with us," they observed. Actually, it was their mind-set that probably did not suit the purpose of God. It was easier to point to phenomena as a way of justifying their behavior. The Holy Spirit may well have a different perspective, as we will discover as each one's work and life receive judgment, either in this life or the one to come.

Zacharias could not change his mind-set when presented with an angelic visitation and prophetic word about a new son (see Lk. 1:5-20). He was struck silent as a result of his mental and spiritual disobedience and unbelief. "How shall I know this?" is an extremely arrogant question when faced with a heavenly being who is representing Almighty God. Whenever intellect is raised above spiritual response, it always puts us on the wrong side of God.

> *The Lord will have no other security except Himself.*

It has been said that evangelicals have elevated cerebral Christianity above experience, whereas charismatics have kissed their brains good-bye in the pursuit of spiritual encounter.

Both mind-sets have to conform to the Lord in humble obedience. Mary's response, in an experience similar to that of Zacharias', seemed to be similar as well. "How can this be, since I do not know a man?" (see Lk. 1:34) However, in reality, it was very different.

Zacharias' underlying question really was, "How do I know you are telling the truth?" He questioned the integrity of the messenger who was rightly insulted and made this response: "I am Gabriel, *who stands in the Presence of God*" (Lk. 1:19). To question his integrity was to malign the Lord; therefore, a punishment was required to teach a lesson.

Mary's response was quite different. She was not questioning *if* it would occur, but *how* it would happen. Her attitude seemed to be, "Great. How will it happen, since I do not know a man?" The angel gave her an appropriate answer, to which Mary's response was, "Let it be to me according to your word" (see Lk. 1:34-38).

The issue is, we must be prepared to let go of old mind-sets and be influenced by God's thinking so that we enter into new paradigms of His calling and purpose.

Spiritual change begins with a renewal of mind. Romans 12:2 states: "And do not be conformed to this world, but be transformed by the renewing of your mind, that you may prove what is that good and acceptable and perfect will of God."

In order to prove the current will of God, we may need a release from our understanding of His previous will. In the past, His will may have been for meetings and mission to be conducted in a particular way. However, His will at this time may call for a fresh strategy and methodology. Unless our mind is changed, the new knowledge of His will remains unknown or unappreciated. We become ineffective and irrelevant. Transformation in reality always begins in the mind. (Read First Corinthians 2:9-16.)

To walk closely with God, we must win the battle for the mind. The close connection between mind, God, and heart must be recovered fully—not just the ability to understand the revealed truth of Scripture, but actually the capacity to know the mind of God in terms of our life. The Lord has thoughts about us daily. He knows what He wants to say to us; what our response should be; what and how He wants us to pray; what we should contemplate in study of the Word; what we must meditate on to expand our revelation of Him. He knows who He wants us to meet and the direction our life should take over a period of time. (What we call guidance, He calls relationship.)

His plans for next year probably began last year or before. He thinks long-term. A seemingly inconsequential meeting with someone today may have great repercussions in several years' time. Life is perceived in the Spirit first before it can be understood in the mind.

In the Acts 10 account, we read that Peter was greatly perplexed in mind as to what everything meant (verse 17). There was a great struggle going on in his head, which he was losing. The Lord had to tell him to go "doubting nothing" (verse 20). Peter still asked the men for the reason they had come because the battle in his thought life was still raging (verse 21). He went out of sheer obedience but still asked the same question several days later in Joppa (verse 29). Suddenly, as Cornelius was speaking, something clicked in Peter's spirit and he said, "*In truth I perceive* that God shows no partiality" (verse 34).

We need the mind of the Lord to understand what God has said and done in times past; to understand what God is saying and doing in times present; and to know what God is saying now about what He will do in time to come.

There is a quality of spiritual perception that we receive in our heart relationship with God that unlocks our natural mind and causes us to think on a different wavelength. The thoughts and the ways of God are altogether different from ours (see Is. 55:8-9). We have received the Spirit of God so that we may know about everything that God wants to give to us.

We are taught to think like God by the Spirit. He combines spiritual thoughts with spiritual words, revealing the mind of the Lord. The more we understand the mind of God, the quicker our maturity develops into experience and anticipation in Him. When we understand that the Lord is principle-centered and therefore unchanging, we relax greatly in our knowing of Him. We wait for Him patiently and willingly because we know He will come. We are no longer worried because we have learned in mind and heart that when God gives us a promise, His word is just as good as the action of it.

> *God has the right to change His mind about how we do things.*

Some of the wisdom and ways of God are difficult to comprehend at first. Generally, that is because we make our mind the critical point of reception and the focal point of belief. The mind is an instrument; it is the heart that receives acknowledgment. Your heart receives revelation; your mind receives information. Your mind applies what your heart admits. (Read Proverbs 3:5-6, especially in the Amplified Bible.)

There is a divine order created for your mind to find peace and rest before the Lord. The heart is for trusting and acknowledging; the mind is for understanding and guidance. The combination of both together, in the right order, will keep us moving on freely in the purposes and will of God. We have the mind of the Lord as we have His heart.

We love and trust God in all things. We express that trust in worship, praise, and lack of anxiety. The more we acknowledge Him and express our trust, the more the burden of worry is replaced by a depth of peace and rest. This is important, because it is through rest that revelation moves from heart to mind. Worry closes our mind to faith and peace. We cannot experience God when our mind is in turmoil.

Worship releases divine order. A heart full of trust and rest creates a mind of peace. Then faith is the vehicle that takes revelation out of our heart and into our conscious mind. Meditation is the combination of heart and mind working together to expand our conscious understanding of the Lord. It will release not only knowledge, but also a capacity to experience that knowledge now. Revelation and information produce transformation. The mind is renewed by its submission to the heart.

It is not just revelatory facts that the mind picks up from the heart. It is the Spirit of revelation itself. The Spirit that releases revelation to the heart is passed on to the mind—spiritual thoughts combining through spiritual words. It is the mind of Christ, who always acknowledged from His heart the words and works of His Father.

It is a cycle that occurs continuously at different speeds. Some cycles are annual, monthly, weekly, or even daily. A cycle begins and ends in God. Scripture links God's thoughts and ways with nature:

> *"For My thoughts are not your thoughts, nor are your ways My ways," says the Lord. "For as the heavens are higher than the earth, so are My ways higher than your ways, and My thoughts than your thoughts. For as the rain comes down, and the snow from heaven, and do not return there, but water the earth, and make it bring forth and bud, that it may give seed to the sower and bread to the eater, so shall My word be that goes forth from My mouth; it shall not return to Me void, but it shall accomplish what I please, and it shall prosper in the thing for which I sent it"* (Isaiah 55:8-11).

Water from heaven produces growth in the earth before returning to God. He is Alpha and Omega. Everything begins in Him and ends with Him. Even His love is a cycle. We love Him because He first loved us and His love affected our life profoundly.

Even so, revelation flows from God to our trusting heart, which is profoundly affected. The heart combines with the mind, bringing renewal of thought and transformation of life. Transformation of life occurs when mind and heart agree with the Spirit. These words are given back to God, released to return to Him in a variety of ways—through prayer, worship and praise, preaching and teaching, writing and singing, and the manner in which we live.

It is a continuous return that gives back to God pressed down, shaken together, and running over. Revelation is an investment of God into a human being, and He wants a return on it—hundredfold, sixtyfold, or thirtyfold. Your return depends on how much your mind and heart have successfully combined.

We must prove the will of God not only for ourselves personally, but also for the Church corporately. The will of God is changing; the nature of God is constant. Don't confuse the two. Whatever we know about God, whatever we understand or have experienced of Him, it has probably not prepared us for what He is about to do!

He is building a new prototype of church to cure our irrelevance, our ineffectiveness, and our powerless state.

He is changing our structure, renewing our practice of church, and overhauling our methodology in order to restore us back to our primitive roots. Cultural relevance is about the Church relating to the language and culture of Heaven, not about making ourselves understood by the world. Power breaks through! We spend time, energy, and resources to present God in a modern way to a sophisticated civilization, and then wonder why the effort and outlay produce such a meager return.

The manifest presence of God can do more in one moment than we can do in weeks of activity. The Great Commission is better and more easily fulfilled by a people who are God-conscious in mind and heart, totally sold out to His life, love, and purpose.

Has your thinking been endorsed by the Spirit of God? Is it okay for you to think the way that you do currently? What is the effect of your current thought-life on your holiness, integrity, faith,

> *If you always do what you've always done, then you'll always have what you've always got... which is insane!*

relationship with God, harmony with people, witness in the world, understanding of the Word, and practical relevance of the church in vision and operation? Just a little homework for you!

Is God wanting us to break out of our current thought pattern about church into a new expression? If we always do what we have always done, then we'll always have what we've always got...which is insane!

Have we submitted our current thought processes to God so that He is free to interfere with our mind-set to bring change? By this, we do not mean just a mental assent in the direction of God's right to change things. Remember, mental renewal begins in the heart—loving God before our own comfort and lifestyle, recognizing that we belong to Him and are His to use how He pleases.

With God, it is an affair of the heart first. It's a love relationship that puts our life into His hands on a daily basis. Our mind can play tricks on us if our heart is pretending to love God.

Is our current mind-set preventing us from entering into a fresh experience of God? I have been stupid in this area on many occasions. In fact, I have a history of letting my mind dictate to my heart what it can/cannot believe, think, and do. My question these days as I hold my life under a microscope at certain times is this: "Is this still okay for You...is my thought-life interfering with something You want to show me or speak to me about?"

If we change our mind, He will change our heart. If we change our thinking, He will change our emotions. Fresh experience in our relationship with God alters our perception of spiritual reality at that point and leads to a redirection in our thinking. As we go through the cycle, we come to a point of transformation where we are ready to go to the next level.

Before I became a Christian, I had a certain mind-set about God, about church, and about the Bible. Experiencing God really blew my mind. When I came into a personal experience of God

Himself, it altered all the states of my thinking on those levels. I realized that, to become a Christian, I had to change my mind enough to let God come into my life in a fresh way. He broke through the barrier of my thinking to touch my heart. As a non-Christian, I was living out of divine order; my heart came after my mind. Divine order begins with the heart preeminent before God. Our relationship with Him is an affair of the heart. Many people become Christians but do not realize that they must maintain the new order. They do not place any emphasis on worship and praise as a primary means of maintaining trust and faith. The mind rules all.

The way we come into salvation is the way that our spiritual journey is governed. Experience God in the heart, bring your mind into joyful submission, and receive a spiritual transformation. A change of mind-set begins in a loving heart.

Walk by Faith

Faith never stays the same. Every level of spiritual growth is determined by the increase of faith that we generate. There is a cycle of faith that is revealed in all circumstances. Initially, as a situation begins, we may find ourselves facing a measure of insecurity and vulnerability. Mostly this is caused by uncertainty concerning the situation we are in and how it will turn out. People want to understand everything (there's nothing wrong in that), and at times will focus on their desire to comprehend something rather than make expressions of trust.

If we are to grow in faith, we must deal with the inadequacies and maintain our security in the love, grace, and power of the Lord. Every promise of God comes with a potential for trouble as well as the means of supply and fulfillment. Trouble and difficulty can breed insecurity and fear if we allow ourselves to feel that exposed.

Walking by faith is learning how to stand in the day of trouble, believing God and His promise, and expecting the supply of God to be realized and fulfilled. The greater the promise is, the more enormous the difficulty. The size of trouble we face may determine the level of rest and trust we need. The greater the problem is, the stronger the potential for insecure behavior and feelings of weakness.

The stronger your stand before the Lord is, the bigger your breakthrough into provision. Many people learn to live with a cut-down dream or insufficient resources, often because they have not understood the cycle of faith. As you prove out in trials of your faith, you will learn the endurance necessary to lack nothing in times of struggle and battle (see Jas. 1:2-4; 1 Pet. 1:6-7).

When we have learned to stand, endured the trial, and seen the supply provided by God, our faith has proven out in the struggle. Eventually at each level, we pass from faith into knowledge by the constant experience of the goodness and truth of the Lord.

For example, I no longer believe that Jesus Christ is Lord. After many, many years of seeing God in wonderful action, I *know* that Jesus Christ is Lord. When I first began the walk of faith, I had to choose to believe that God was in control and that He was Lord. Now with the experience of His Lordship gained over many years in significant troubles and battles, I have an expectancy of His Lordship triumphing over all forms of oppositions. I can revel in the battle because I know the outcome: Jesus Christ is Lord. I still have to stand and endure the circumstances, but it is unthinkable to do anything else! It is not a faith issue anymore because my understanding of the Word and my experience of God are combined together. I have passed from faith to knowledge.

So when I come to believe for new things, my faith is founded on what I know. I know that God is faithful. He is steadfast. His Word is true. He is good. He does not lie. He is unchanging. On my best or worst days, I can have the same relationship with Him because He is so constant and consistent. He is the same—yesterday, today, and forever. This is a great source of strength and security. We love an unchanging God.

> *Every problem comes complete with its own provision.*

On many spiritual levels of life, that is the cycle. What was an issue of faith, produces endurance as we stand in trust waiting for the provision in the promise. As our faith proves out in the testing, we inherit the supply and we pass further in the dimension of faith toward knowing God. We become comfortable with His dealings and eventually come to a place on that level where we *know* God is true. Then the cycle begins again—only at a much deeper level and with higher stakes to believe God for!

The temptation, when we hit a new dimension of experience, is to want to build it directly on the old familiarities. We have become comfortable and feel good where we are in our believing. New dimensions return us to the beginning of the cycle—having to stand up under insecurity, feelings of inadequacy, and vulnerable thinking. Faith is an issue again, and the stakes have risen! "We walk by faith, not by sight," says Second Corinthians 5:7. God will find us new situations where we learn to trust Him again. It is a lifelong lesson and hopefully a passion.

Peter had to arise and go without misgivings. He, no doubt, had plenty of questions and reservations. When people ask us to do something we don't understand, our normal procedure is to ask why. We need information so that we can be convinced of our actions.

It was a new dimension for Peter that was about to open up. He was unaware of the total magnitude of what God was asking. He had enough trouble with the concept of stepping into a Gentile house. This was a huge problem. There is an important lesson to learn here in faith. The size of the obstacle in front of us will be dwarfed by the opportunity being released behind it. Whole nations were being lined up behind the house of Cornelius. All Peter could see was a houseful of Gentiles.

There is a second important lesson here that we all must learn in our walk of faith. God never explains Himself before the event! He did not sit Peter down and give him ten reasons why he needed to walk with Him in this next dimension of the Kingdom. He gave enough revelation to help Peter walk by faith and be trusting and obedient. If there had been any more instruction, Peter would not have had a faith test; he would have walked by sight and understanding. Here was an opportunity to develop Peter in relationship with the Lord through faith. God would not miss the chance to grow Peter in this way.

God doesn't give you the information that will make you feel good because He wants to increase your faith and deepen your relationship with Him. The only way that happens is by Him taking you out into that place of insecurity, uncertainty, and vulnerability. Here you become dependent upon God's nature or you fold under the pressure. You learn to hold onto Him and realize that He has a strong grip on you!

There is a new place of fellowship in the Lord to be enjoyed in trials of faith. The passage of insecurity is designed to strengthen your grip on God. We learn to move in God, not leaning on our own understanding, but guided by the Holy Spirit. Like Abraham, we can move out in God not knowing where events are leading but trusting God to get us where He wants us to go.

Trusting without fully understanding deepens our faith and creates in us a capacity for obedience, which is part of God's goal. He will deliver you to the very part of His nature that He wants to be to you. He will take away your security in things so that He can be your security. This is personal. He wants to be everything you need. Therefore, all situations are designed for you to become dependent on Him.

Through dependency, the friendship of God draws near. He sticks closer than a brother. This is the place where the mature in God are separated from the babies in Christ. Mature people know that the trial is the place of release. They have learned that if they stand fast in the day of trouble, something will open up that is bigger than they expected. Days of trouble therefore become exciting to the mature in faith, because where the stress is, the anointing is present!

We have to learn to go without misgivings. That is, we have to go not allowing our questions, concerns, and reservations to prevent us from moving out on what God has said. We will understand, but only as we move out. Revelation is an "on-the-road" experience, not a static observation. Revelation is a journey, an expedition of faith. The Lord will take us into a place where our vulnerability will be showing. He will ask us to do the impossible, which will increase our feelings of inadequacy and insecurity.

If God does not speak initially, He always speaks eventually. Everything becomes clear—in retrospect, through other people, by revelation, or through a study of the situation itself and a growing perception of how God works.

Vulnerability to a point of almost complete insecurity comes, only to be relieved by a belief in His presence: "I will never leave you nor forsake you" (Heb. 13:5b). In your inadequacy, hold on to the One who can do all things in and through you.

At this time of testing, some people cannot handle the training in maturity. They look for excuses why they cannot carry on. They point to the fact that the situation is impossible; what they are being asked to do is inconceivable; the resources seem unobtainable; everything is impractical. Meanwhile, the Lord Jesus smiles at you and says, "Nevertheless...I will be with you!" That is your only comfort. For many people, brought up in an information-mad society, it is not enough. Their misgivings are too great; they are bigger than their capacity to trust and obey. They look for a way out, always taking the advice of other people who have not learned to walk by faith.

Maturity is where we look for a reason why we can hold on to God, persevere, stand up and be counted, be included in what the Lord is doing, and take the opportunity to do something we have not done before. A real faith walk has adventure attached to it. Adventure is risk. Risk involves the potential for success and failure. Failure is averted only by staying close to the presence of God, gritting our teeth, and holding on to Him.

> *The size of the obstacle in front of us will be dwarfed by the opportunity being released behind it!*

As we break through in the situation we are in, there is a corresponding advance in faith and a greater development in our relationship with Jesus.

God has not called us to do the reasonable, the possible, or the fashionable. The calling of God upon each of us will probably create tension in the people around us (see Chapter 4). That is why Scripture talks so much about relationships and the need for loving friendships and personal accountability in the church. Grace and love in relationships play a key part in knowing and walking with God. In the tension of warfare, new situations, and times of testing, we have to learn to walk in faith with each other until our experience helps us to see how we can connect on this new level.

For relationships to progress, they must of necessity go through periods of realignment in order to establish a reconnection at a higher level. This will be part of the difficulty in a new move of God. We have to reestablish our connections at a much deeper or much higher level. The people around us whom we knew on the previous level are disjointed with us, unless they reconnect in the new realm where God has moved us.

It is inevitable then that some friendships do not make the transition—but not because of disagreements or rancor. It is just that the direction of our heart changes as God moves us into a different dimension of calling. All our friends in high school do not make the transition with us through college, university, or employment. It is a natural part of life.

Even if we remained in the same church, any real progress in God will draw us into the orbit of different people or a radical readjustment of current relationships. Tension means there is something happening. God makes provision for tension. He supplies the oil of the Holy Spirit. Only the Spirit of God, generously poured out, can prevent tension from becoming friction. If we all really want the best for one another, we will see how we can reconnect at the new level.

We are learning how to walk in faith with God and with each other until our experience helps us to see what each of us is talking about. God is going to ask us to do things that are impossible. He is going to ask us to step out into things that are invisible. The only one who can hold us and sustain us is God Himself. And that is the whole point of it. If God called us to things we could do, we would do them without His grace and His blessing. We would then

take the glory away from the Lord because we have achieved something in our power and not His. He understands human nature
only too well (see Judg. 7:2). But because God calls us to the impossible, and we cannot do it, and yet we feel this tug and this pull on
our life, we have to depend upon God so much more. The whole
point of why God does it this way is because every new level of
faith He calls us to creates in us a new desire for dependency upon
Him. That is why He throws us in the deep end. That is why He
takes us into that place of vulnerability. It is not our certainties He
wants! It is our inadequacies, our vulnerability. And He will deliver us to that place again and again, at successively deeper levels.

We will find ourselves doing things that we always said we
would not do, just like Peter here in Acts 10:28 (NAS): "And he
said to them, 'You yourselves know how unlawful it is for a man
who is a Jew to associate with a foreigner or to visit him; and yet
God has shown me that I should not call any man unholy or
unclean.' "

"It is unlawful, and yet God has shown me." To obey God,
Peter had to go against his upbringing and all that he knew,
because God was declaring something new to him.

Sometimes what we know in our experience can prevent us
from moving forward into something new. All the understanding
and experiences that Peter grew up with did not prepare him for
this situation. It was not just off the road of his personal map. It
was a different map! All those experiences were legitimate for him
in terms of his upbringing, his understanding of church, and his
knowledge of God.

They brought him into conflict with the new thing that God
was doing. All his life he had dire warnings from the rabbi, the synagogue, and his parents about not mixing with Gentiles. "Do not
visit them or eat with them. It is unlawful." Suddenly, he is doing
something that he vowed he would never do, simply because God
is doing something new. He is discovering that his allegiance to the
Lordship of Christ is greater than his commitment to a previous
experience or understanding of church. How many of us would be

willing to make that transition today? How many of us have made unconscious vows about church?

"You will never catch me raising my hands. I'll never dance to God in church. I wouldn't be seen dead speaking in tongues! Praying for the sick, casting out devils—not me, no way!" Peter is in the same situation. "It is unlawful, *and yet* God has shown me." This is where relational departures begin. God has shown you something, but not your friend. Your mind-set, like Peter's, has to change.

Hopefully, your friend can make a readjustment. This is the difficult concept to grasp here. Some people are catalysts for the realignment and readjustment of others. Peter stepped out in faith and obedience. He knew he was in trouble at this point. He simply preferred to be in trouble with men rather than with God.

In Acts 5:29, when Peter was brought before the High Priest, the Council, and Senate, and commanded not to teach about Christ, he responded, "We ought to obey God rather than men." A short while later he was in similar circumstances—only with one major difference. The men concerned were other apostles and friends in the ministry! Yet Peter's response had to be the same.

All ungodly vows will be broken as God releases us into greater levels of maturity. We are all going to find ourselves doing things that we promised ourselves we would never do in church. Break the vow now in private, before it is broken in public by the Lord.

> *In these days the Lord is making many realignments and new connections in the spirit between people, ministries, churches, and networks.*

So Peter, in Acts 10:28 (NAS), says, "You yourselves know how unlawful it is for a man who is a Jew to associate with a foreigner or to visit him; *and yet* God has shown me...."

There was something that had to be broken there in Peter's mind-set, in his lifestyle, in his upbringing. "This is not right, this is not how we do things, this is not how I was brought up, this is not what church is all about." Whatever there is on that side, there is going to be an "and yet." God is going to show us something different that will conflict with what we have understood in times past.

"It is unlawful, *and yet* God has shown me." Peter had to go against his upbringing and all that he knew because God was declaring something new to him. And for all of us, I believe that God is leading us into a new realm of walking with Him that will possibly take us down paths of conflict in various parts of our life. Is there a clash now between your current experience and your previous thinking? Resolving that clash is a faith issue, not an intellectual one. The walk of faith is one where reason and understanding must always be preceded by trust from the heart.

Many people went through that clash in times of renewal. The statement heard most often was, "God is offending the mind to reveal the heart." In other words, the Lord Jesus is not going to help us understand just so we can feel better. His priority is to help us walk into new levels of faith in complete dependence on Him. He requires that we trust in Him with all our heart and not lean on our own intelligence as a prerequisite for obedience. He helps us to understand as we submit and walk.

The walk of faith is one where reason and understanding must always be preceded by trust from the heart. In Matthew 14 when Peter walked on water, he only had one word from God to help him overcome his intelligence and his fear. That word was: "Come!" He said, "Lord, if it is really You out there, bid me to come!" And Jesus just smiled enigmatically and said, "Okay, come!" He did not say anything else to Peter. He did not give him any help whatsoever. On the basis of one word and his trust in God, Peter got out of the boat and walked on a substance he had no business walking on. It was a place of total vulnerability.

You may be in a period of tranquillity and calm right now, but I wonder what substance you are going to be walking on in the next few years that you have no business being on, or being in. I wonder how many of us are going to be walking in a place that we would think, *Dear God, never in my wildest dreams did I think I would be doing what I am doing right now.* I wonder how many of us are going to be quite so tranquil in the days ahead. If you have never been vulnerable before, you have got a treat in store. It is going to scare the life out of you. More to the point, maybe it will scare life into you!

Receive a Spiritual Perception From God

Revelatory perception opens the heavens. It releases new dimensions. It draws back a curtain before a whole new realm. Peter was actually in the Gentile house. He had stepped into the unknown. He was probably a mass of tension and stress, full of questions and concerns. He looked around in his obedience, and suddenly his sight changed. He opened his mouth and said these words: "In truth I perceive that God shows no partiality. But in every nation whoever fears Him and works righteousness is accepted by Him" (Acts 10:34b-35).

That was a major, significant paradigm shift for a man who had lived his life in one way, and then found God suddenly turning him around and redirecting him in a new way. One day Peter was a man with a message to only one people group—the Jews—and the next, God was using him to open a door to other people groups.

The point I want to make here is this: An encounter with God on a personal level leads us to a different encounter with God on a corporate level. I hope that is what we are going to find in the days ahead...that each of us is going to have a new personal encounter with the Lord. When that happens, it must lead us into a new corporate encounter with God. The individual expression of God that is growing up has to change the corporate culture and lifestyle of what we represent together. Otherwise, we are all going to be fed up and frustrated. Many are in that place of frustration right now.

I hope that enough of us in the church are frustrated right now, because that frustration hopefully will take us to a new place in God. The reason many of us are frustrated is that our own personal encounter with God is growing and the church structure is creaking right now. It needs to creak, and it is right that it is creaking, because we cannot contain God in what we have if He is doing something new in the lives of people. Our structure of church is obviously going to have to change at some point. If you are frustrated to your maximum right now, just bear with God. The culture and the shape of the church needs to be stretched because God is giving it a new shape.

Frustration occurs because we care deeply about something but cannot see a way through to a place of liberation. Our aspirations cannot be achieved without empowerment. We feel disenfranchised from the work of the church but still care enough to want to stay and pray and work where we can.

> *God usually explains Himself after the event, seldom before.*

Others around us do not comprehend our frustration. It is often just the quality of spiritual perception that divides us. However, we must make a distinction here. Frustration is not just a sign of spiritual desire and unfulfilled potential. It also can be a sign of human weakness and thwarted ambition.

The difference between the two is seen in how we handle frustration. What is developing in our character? Is it flesh and carnal behavior, or is it the fruit of the Spirit? We all are at different levels of our spiritual journey with the Lord. Frustration is a very important part of growing up in God. We cannot grow without frustration. It is how we handle it that is important. The Lord opens up a new horizon to us, and we begin to see new direction. Inevitably, we compare the horizon to where we are now. The ground in-between is called frustration if we are not allowed to traverse it on our journey of faith.

Some churches will not move at any price. They are settlers with occasional pioneers living amongst them, both types irritating one another! Frustration is a place to be occupied for God. It is a territory that must be claimed. It is a place of character development. Before we can insist on our inheritance in terms of vision and destiny, we must claim it through our faithfulness and integrity.

It is not enough to stand in that place and start moaning and whining about church. It is not enough to stand in that place and start complaining about what is happening or what is not being achieved. We have to stand in that place and begin to pray like we have never prayed before. We have to stand in that place and say, "Lord, what is it that You are calling me to be obedient about at this time in this place?" It is not for us to dictate and start whining about what other people are not doing. We have to do what we are called to do in fellowship with the people we can be in fellowship with.

We are looking for reasons to be included in what God is doing, not reasons to put ourselves on the outside. We are not looking to withdraw; we are looking to step in, to be the catalyst and keep the door open so that people who are not seeing it at the moment will suddenly gain new perception. We are here to pray. We are here to hold that door open, to prop it open with our own prayers and our own life, so that everyone can be touched with what God is touching us with.

Think about your personal encounter with God actually connecting with the corporate encounter of the church. There may be frustrations and changes in cell church—are you in one? Are you enjoying it? There are different approaches now to the way we pray and the way we worship. Are you resisting it, struggling with it, or yielding to God to find Him in a deeper way? There are new ways in which we are evangelizing, training, and teaching. Are you struggling with those?

Allow that frustration to take focus now and let the grace of God flow to you so that you may enjoy what He is doing. Change can be exciting rather than just uncomfortable.

An encounter with God on a personal level leads us to a different encounter with God on a corporate level. Let us enjoy our frustrations for what they really are: opportunities to pray and to hold the door open for other people. Do not step out; rather step into something with God, knowing that He is doing something.

This is the nature of change. We grow out of one thing and into another. Growth causes problems. Growth changes our identity. It births new relationships; therefore, we will have new connections. If you have got a glimpse of something new, what God probably is going to do is reconnect you with other people. Even the people you are friends with right now, you may need to reconnect with on a different level. People we used to have fellowship and fun with at one level, suddenly start to move in something different, and we think they have gone a little strange. We are going to have to reconnect with them at a new level.

It may not be that long since our last shaping, but God is giving us divine acceleration in these days, and so we are shape-changing really quickly. We are going to move through several different shapes and types as God remolds us into the prototype church that He really wants us to be.

So please do not get upset if things are changing fast. Blame God, because *He* is moving fast! And look at yourself to see if you are moving fast enough with what God is doing! An encounter with God on a personal level leads you to a different encounter with God on a corporate level.

New connections can be costly. It may mean that we have to move on from where we are to a new church where we feel there is a place for us. Sometimes we have simply outgrown our spiritual place but still enjoy the relationships in the natural. That can make life very hard for us. Our desire to move on in God is as great as our desire to remain friends with people who do not see our new spiritual perspective. It hurts. There will be misunderstandings. We will suffer in the misinterpretation. Motives are questioned, rumors abound, judgments are made, and villains identified.

Keeping our mouths shut and our hearts open is the best way forward. We will be killed for it, but death is part of life in spiritual progression. Be humbled. To fight back is to resist the grace of God. Put things right in private and give the devil no ground at all, especially in public.

If we are staying where we are because it is the place of God for us, it may still be tough. People who are used to dealing with us on one level may have trouble readjusting to us on a different level. We earn the right to be treated differently. God is developing the one characteristic that will enable us to inhabit this new realm and remain there. It is called patience. Part of patience is the capacity to be faithful when people do not see it the way we see it. Working that one through requires a strong dose of long-suffering with kindness. As these qualities grow in us, the inward change gathers pace and we become more like the person of Jesus. Insisting on external change without that internal conversion to the character of Jesus leaves people with a distinct lack of confidence in our perspective or our ministry. Sometimes in order to defend ourselves, we have to attack someone else. This is where our integrity wears thin. Attack and counterattack create opposition and greater capacity for division.

Old wineskins split because they have become so rigid and inflexible that they cannot cope with the action and re-action of new wine settling down. Churches split because people have become so settled in what they have that there is no further desire to explore new ground in God and new territory in the supernatural realm.

> *Your frustration is tailor-made by God to improve your maturity.*

In these times of change, we all must examine ourselves for signs of new desires in God. We must look more closely at our fellow travelers to understand what God is doing with their lives. How do we reconnect with the new things we are seeing in one another?

What is your current encounter with God all about? Are you seeing and understanding everything in proper perspective? What changes are being worked into your life by the Lord? In transition, the ability to reflect on your own life with critical honesty is extremely vital. Whatever answers you gain will provide you with big keys that may open up whole new realms.

Know what the Lord is doing both in you and through you. Keep these apart, especially in times of stress. Otherwise, you will demand corporately what God is challenging you with personally. This is a well-documented problem (especially with prophetic people) that all of us fall into periodically.

Being aware of what God is doing within our lives will give us information about what He is preparing us for. For example, if the Lord is dealing with a sin issue, He is preparing us for purity. God does not expose particular sin unless He has the immediate antidote to replace it with. This has to be good news for people with besetting sin.

If it is a faith issue, He has already planned a walk of faith for us, so we can look at our current situations more positively. If it is our comfort zones that are being stretched, He probably wants to be our security, so that is what we must look forward to in the crisis that we face. If we face the situation by looking at what God wants to give us in and through it, then we will grow accordingly.

We must remember to be kinder to ourselves and one another. We have not passed this way before. It is normal for us to feel uncomfortable. Let grace and mercy carry us forward.

Corporately we have not been on this journey before. We have no road map to make us feel secure and knowledgeable about the way ahead. Have mercy on the leadership in the transition process. Try to get an external guide who has either building wisdom, a pioneering spirit, or an understanding of process and transition.

We are going into a new country, a new realm of the Spirit. Since we have not been there yet, it is no good looking at the elders and expecting them to have all the answers. They may have the answers that help us walk the next couple of steps, but they probably won't have the answers for the next year or two. Things are changing, and we all are having to walk so much more closely with God and so much more closely with one another. I have a sense in my heart that our friendships and our relationships need to be improved upon. Whatever we own in friendship and relationship in our church must be improved and honored. Bless what we have right now and let understanding and grace come into our hearts now one for another, because we are going on a journey we have never been on. It is going to cause some tension and conflict, so let us fall more in love with God and let us love each other a whole lot more in the process.

Embrace the Vision

A move of God can be held up or fail to materialize altogether if the vision that God has given is not adopted by a significant worker group within the church. Personal encounter leads to corporate change. What we believe together as a body creates the climate for what will happen. Unfortunately, the opposite of that is also true: Corporate unbelief creates a negative environment where nothing can happen (see Mk. 6:1-6).

Faith creates the culture for what God wants to do. What are we in faith for at this time? It will affect the way we pray and work. What do we mean by *culture*? I guess it depends on where we are. It has many meanings. People say that culture is civilization, breeding, customs, lifestyle, education, and enlightenment. It is all those things. A friend of mine works in a laboratory. For him, *culture* is a place of experimentation, where new life-forms are grown!

Faith creates culture that is positive and conducive to change. Faith allows us to experiment in the grace and call of God. In God's Kingdom laboratory, He is experimenting with different prototypes of Church. As ever with our Creator, there will be many kinds, not one stereotype. We are growing a new life-form as a church, bringing together a new identity, a new corporate culture that reflects the will of God.

Peter embraced the vision that the Lord gave him. He had questions and reservations, but he went where God told him to go. He did not hang back, and neither must we. By embracing the vision that God had given him, by being obedient to what the Lord wanted, Peter stepped into a revival message. It clearly was not a good one, because he had to be interrupted by the Holy Spirit! That actually proves that we do not have to have a great message or have everything together. Faith, obedience, and a willingness to step out for God will attract the Holy Spirit with power into our midst. *That* is creating an environment! Peter stepped into something that God was inspiring.

I wonder what new perception of Church we are going to come to live with in these times? These are really exciting times when God is changing things that need changing in you and in me. I think we do need some kind of sober reflection on what that means for us as people, what it means for us in our family—in our relationship with our spouse and children.

> *In transition, the ability to reflect with critical honesty will provide keys to open up whole new realms.*

What does that mean for us in terms of our lifestyle, as a family in the house of God? What does it mean for our relationships here in the church? What does it mean for our perception of church? What does it mean for our ways of "doing" meetings? There is a new perception of church that eventually will have to come to us, and it will discomfit us before we feel glad about it. But then that is the nature of change.

We also must appreciate the fact that we are going to be misunderstood. When you pioneer, you are always misunderstood. If we read Acts 11:1-17, we see that everyone took issue with Peter about what he had done. That is, all those who were not there while he was doing it, who heard about it secondhand, criticized it. And that will always be true. People from a past paradigm that we may have moved away from will want to take issue with us about what it is we are doing now! And so in Acts 11:3 it says, "You went in to uncircumcised men and ate with them!"

Everyone took issue with Peter. What I find fascinating here is that it was only the people who did not go with him who took exception to what he was doing. They did not understand what had happened because they were not there and involved. That is a fact of spiritual life. If we are not there and involved, it is hard to understand what God is doing at times. There is no substitute for being there. Revelation is positional. We have to be in the right place when God is moving to catch the Spirit of what is happening.

Examine the moves of God recently, in Toronto and Pensacola, and see the criticism that they have experienced. Look through Church history and view the criticism that people, who obeyed God and did something new, experienced. God is going to want us not only to start a new move, but also stay with that move and see it through. That is going to be our prime responsibility: seeing it through. It's not just starting something; it's having the guts and the courage to stick with it, through the fight that is around it, and see it through.

Our secondary responsibility is satisfying other people's mindsets, questions, and opinions about what it is we are doing. When it happens, don't get mad! I am still learning not to get mad when people question what I am doing. I think it is important that the rest of the churches call us to account. It is important in my own ministry that I am called to account for what I am doing. But when that happens, all you can do is give your testimony and point to your fruit. Show them your works by your faith, because faith is defended only by works. Fruit inspection is good, isn't it? It should be encouraged. Of course, fruit inspectors with love and manners would be a wonderful bonus!

We are going to be a people, I hope, who convert our opposition into a new move of God for ourselves. When all else fails, do what Peter did: Blame God!

If therefore God gave them the same gift as He gave us when we believed on the Lord Jesus Christ, who was I that I could withstand God? (Acts 11:17)

I suppose a modern-day Peter would put it like this: "Guys, I couldn't stop God from moving. I was giving my message, preaching quite well, and suddenly, the Holy Spirit interrupted me and fell on people. End of message! All I could do was get them baptized. It really wasn't my fault."

I have a feeling that we are going to hear that excuse a lot in the days to come!

> ### *What is your new wineskin going to look like?*

Chapter 8

The Process of Transition

Part 1

The world around us is full of change. These changes are not just technological. Keeping pace with man's inventiveness is amazingly difficult. No sooner does a breakthrough piece of engineering hit the market than it is made smaller, more compact, and more powerful. Whatever you buy is out of date before you learn how to use it properly.

International boundaries are changing; different nations are forming or re-forming. Economies everywhere are going through profound change with the realization that no economy will ever be safe again. Some changes affect not only the way we live but also our perception of who we are as human beings.

Despite the immensity of change taking place in our world, very few of us have learned to deal with change in a healthy way. Without being aware of reasons why, we seem to put up instinctive and devious barriers to anything remotely looking like change. There is something in most people that profoundly dislikes transition, and it will cause them to do amazing things in order to not have to go through any change at all.

Transition is an adventure. But it is an adventure into the unknown with all the attendant risks that the uncharted can formulate around us. Change provokes our hearts because it challenges the status quo. It makes us feel uneasy and vulnerable because it takes us into territory where we have never before been. We are happy to talk about Abraham going out without knowing where he was going, simply trusting God to get him there (see Heb. 11:8). However, when it is our turn to make the journey of faith, it is a different matter. God has His own road maps for times such as these. The old ones are useless to us, and the new ones are filled out as we go!

Every change involves a letting go of one thing to reach out for what is next. It is death by installments—the slow death of our mind-sets, our attitudes, perceptions, and paradigms with apparently nothing obvious to take their place. That is, we only see the replacement concept as we journey. We don't just see it, though; we experience it. Sometimes our experience is first, and we go through something that we understand only in retrospect. It is important therefore, if we are to journey with the Lord into new lands, that we build in time to reflect and review where we are and where we have come from. Our road map to faith must be kept up to date and relevant for anyone else coming after us.

Pioneers draw the maps; they seldom enjoy them! Every day's journey into the new is accompanied by a slow and, at times, painful letting go of the old. There is a death process to be worked through in transition. Future fruit comes from present death (see Jn. 12:24).

> *In transition God gives us a new road map of faith.*

The Holy Spirit will, if we allow Him, teach us how to be present to the moment with God. There is a God-consciousness that is so compelling that we need never worry again. There is a peace so profound that it is unshakable. There is a rest in God so potent that the enemy fears it. (Rest is a weapon against evil.)

In order to be alive to God in this way, we must surrender to Him and to everything

He brings. He allows in His wisdom what He could easily prevent by His power. The dying daily that is Paul's description involves a death-to-self process. Change is the pivotal point of that process. If you enjoy God's life, you cannot fear change. Where He is present, resistance has died.

Death, the understanding of change, liberates us to experience the adventure of new things. We welcome the risk because His life fizzes in our bloodstream. He sparkles with new gifts, new realms, fresh anointing, and different challenges to faith and love.

His great power will pitch us into battle with no thought but that His great love will shield us from the enemy. He is careful and carefree at the same time. Change is an opportunity to grow more like Him and to continue the sampling of all He has to offer. He Himself never changes; that is part of His beauty. He is so utterly faithful and unchanging that we always know exactly where we are in His heart.

He wants to impart that same unchanging nature to us so that we can partake of this aspect of His divine nature. Though unchanging in Himself, He causes ceaseless change round about Him. To know Him is to be changed by Him. He loves the journey that we are on. He has carefully thought through all the stages that we will experience. Death and life combine in Him. Unchanging changeableness is part of His mystique. Find meaning in Him, and you will understand your journey so much better. Everything begins and ends in Him, the Alpha and Omega of change.

The inevitability of change is made enjoyable by His presence. As we submit to each process, our appreciation of the journey grows and our faith increases. Change comes from within. Everything that God does in us comes from the inside to the outside. That is why our inward development is more important than the outward circumstances. If we give the Lord Jesus the ground He requires on the inside of our life, then each present set of external challenges shall diminish, if not disappear.

We will be excited about change because we are excited about the Lord. Our road map is being drawn as we experience life in

Christ. If we keep hitting the same landmarks in our life, it is because we have probably resisted change from within.

Change helps us grow, and growth is part of life. Without challenge there is nothing to overcome, so faith cannot grow. This lack of expectation creates a smallness in mind and heart.

Process Is Relational

Transition is a process; it is a series of steps and stages that take us from one realm to another. There is a rhythm to life and a cadence to walking with God. Each of us must be in tune with our inner man before the Lord. When Jesus spoke in parable form, He spoke of shepherds, fishermen, and farmers, putting people in touch with the rhythm of their existence and teaching them the movement and the tempo of the Spirit life.

In non-technological times, people lived at a different pace or beat. They were in tune with nature and its ways and processes. Their ability to survive depended on that knowledge. What is true in the natural is true in the Spirit (see 1 Cor. 15:46). Our walk with God is not separate to our employment track or our natural affiliations.

These days people live by clock and calendar. We schedule people into diaries depending on actual time, not the rhythm of our life. In other days, people did things after sowing, plowing, or harvesting. The natural seasons were the only calendar they wanted or needed. These days we are governed by deadlines, time constraints, and schedules. Few people eat when they are hungry, sleep when they are tired, or get up when they are rested. If we woke up two hours early, most of us would stay in bed because it wasn't time to get up.

All this is very well, but what is the point? The point is we have lost access to our rhythm—the ability to flow through life from within, to have the form and essence of our life be prescribed by our inner voice.

Our world is too functional, too structured and contrived. There is little rest and peace in the process of how we are forced to live. God ordained that our lives should fit a natural and spiritual process. Society and civilization largely have robbed us of both. Physically we are made up of a procession of movements. Psychologically and spiritually the same creative process applies.

For example, rest is an important process for all three areas. Physical rest in sleep, peace of mind, and the act of trusting and not being anxious are part of our rhythm of life before God. Food intake is good for the body, just as reading or conversation is for the mind and prayer for our spirit.

The world is full of functional paradigms whilst we were created to live in relational ones. The loneliness and lack of friendship and companionship we feel is damaging to our health. "It is not good that man should be alone" (Gen. 2:18b).

Relational process is about the journey we make with God and one another. The functions of life now rule us. Everyone wants to know what we do rather than who we are. People define their life by geography, job title, and performance. In this busy functional paradigm, we seldom have real time for people. We have surface relationships with many people. We wear social masks of politeness that hide our fears, worries, and inner thoughts. We do not reveal our true inner self because we are afraid of rejection. We want to be loved but the process of real love involves the true revelation of self, so our fear of rebuff does not allow us to go deep with people around us.

Transition is about the journey of relationships as much as anything else—learning to trust, to be open and honest, to understand and be understood, to accept and approve and in turn find acceptance and approval. Transition is about connecting with one another as we draw the road map of life in the spirit together. It is about connecting through our fears and concerns, dreams and aspirations, joys and delights, dislikes and annoyances. Whenever we hide

> *Modern-day believers have little or no rhythm with God or His creation.*

part of ourselves for fear of discovery, we disconnect or fail to connect with people at that point.

Process Involves Crisis

Transition usually throws us together in circumstances that are far less than ideal. Transition involves crisis. Crisis leads us to process, through which our road map will deliver us to a new place of promise if we faithfully complete this particular leg of the journey. It is hazardous and arduous but exhilarating and inspirational, all at the same time. The difficulty lies in the fact that we don't see transition coming, mainly because we do not live from within.

When we live from the inner man of the Spirit, we detect nuances—like a sailor detecting subtle shifts in the wind, or a farmer the smell of early rain. These signs of change cause us to reflect and move closer to the person of God through prayer and worship. We begin to ask for grace and wisdom because we feel something is changing. Our early warning system is working. Most churches have an early warning system. They are called prophets. Or they could be people with a prophetic/intercessory gifting.

The difficulty is that the prophet speaks about change and transition when we are all in a place of safety and blessing. Seldom do churches take such a word and process it internally. The prophecy is given so that we can make subtle changes to our perspective, the way we position ourselves before God, and our petition to Him for us to be faithful in the coming crisis. Many people leave storm warnings too late and put themselves in places of needless risk.

If we lived in a relational paradigm of sensitivity to God and one another, we would go through life evenly and with more calm.

A friend in the ministry, Steve Chua, once told me that the Chinese word for crisis is made up of two concepts involving danger and opportunity.

The danger comes through disruption. Crisis will often involve a storm. We are caught up in a tempest of different circumstances colliding together. It is a time of commotion, assault, agitation, passion, strife, and outburst.

Every spiritual storm has two halves. The first breaks upon us and finds us ignorant and confused. Maybe we didn't heed the early warning system when it sounded the alarm; possibly our internal man was not in position and listening. Suddenly we are in the midst of crisis and our relationships come under intense pressure.

Process Is Primarily Internal

If people have no internal frame of reference, they lash out, under pressure, externally. Because they are involved in a functional paradigm, they connect on that level. Other people are at fault because this or that did not happen; we relate through function. We get angry and frustrated and look for a way out on a physical, emotional level. We stop to ask why this is happening on a physical level, but our answers at this stage do not give us the wisdom to see beyond the natural. The outer man sees the danger and reacts to it—lashing out indiscriminately, apportioning blame, living on survival instincts of self-preservation. Our prayers are for deliverance and escape.

The inner man understands the danger but also recognizes the opportunity that God is presenting. Our inner perspective helps us position ourselves in line with God's objective and pray in accordance with His will. Those living from the inner realm see beyond the natural into the realm of the Spirit, so they wait patiently and with praise and honor for the Lord Jesus to reveal Himself.

Transition is about revelation and the process needed to make it real and experiential. We miss the profound truths and the deeper works of God when our paradigm is functional and not relational. If we are unprepared when the storm hits us, we take it on board in our soul, not our spirit. Our soul is the outer man reacting through our body, the outermost part of our being.

We have a conflict of two natures within us: the spirit versus the flesh (see Gal. 5:17). Our soul and our carnal nature (flesh) interact together. Our soul is made up of our mind, emotions, and will. These elements can be drawn inward into the realm of the Spirit through the attention and faithfulness of the inner man toward God.

Alternatively, they also can be drawn into an external perspective through relationships, circumstances, and influences. This external perspective with no inward support will be the vehicle through which worry, fear, anger, bitterness, and rejection can take hold of our hearts. We will be agitated, vexing, and difficult to live with.

Revelation is the revealing of who God is and what He is doing. It impacts our lives and changes our viewpoint. It divides spirit from soul, enabling us to live before God and experience what He is releasing to us (see Heb. 4:12).

Though our outward man is crumbling under the assault of life and circumstances, our inward man retains a balance before God, which brings a constant renewal (see 2 Cor. 4:16-18). The inner man does not look at what is seen but goes beyond that to a level of perception that is more powerful and life-changing.

> *Transition is a journey in relationships.*

In all tribulations and transitions, it is the revelation of God's intention that allows an amazing strengthening to be released into the inner man by the glorious power of the Spirit. There is a change within that enables faith to rise and understanding to appear, causing us to be filled and to abide in a realm of power that can achieve more for us than we ever thought possible in the circumstances.

Transition is about the discovery and connection of the inner man of the heart toward God (see Eph. 3:13-21). It is about discovering the rest of God (see Heb. 4) and being at peace in Him. It is restoring our relational paradigm with Almighty God. It is about breakthrough into an inner place of the spirit and learning how to remain there. Your inner man is the restful presence of Jesus in the external turmoil of your surroundings (see Mk. 4:36-39).

This is the opportunity that God is giving to us in the crisis of transition. He is holding out the very process of inward change and development. In crisis we put our lives firmly into His care and we obey Him implicitly! Crisis, transition, and process open a door on a personal and corporate level for the people of God to come to know Him, experience Him, and be changed by Him. Crisis is the door of inward opportunity opening through the danger of external circumstances.

The Spirit searches all things in our lives and enables us to know the mind of the Lord (revelation) as well as to experience what God wants to give us in the situation (see 1 Cor. 2:10-16).

Many times the storm breaks over us and we are unprepared for it. If we are used to living from our spirit, we can retreat there to our secret place and wait patiently for God. If we have not fully learned that discipline of grace, we may succumb to worry and fear. Then we will be tossed to and fro by circumstances and unsurrendered thought-processes. The inner man of the spirit is the anchor for the soul.

Here, in our distress, the kindness of God will reveal itself to us. He really wants us to succeed in crisis. He wants us to go through the door of opportunity and not be sidetracked by the difficulty in the situation. He will give us a second opportunity to succeed.

Every storm has two halves divided by peace (the eye of the storm). Churches going through difficulty need apostolic or prophetic presence to give them Heaven's perspective. These gift ministries can enter into a situation to bring peace and provide revelation. They stand with one foot in our past and the other in our future. They can tell us where we have been and where we are going, and they can bring both together into our present to help us make sense of where we are now! They give us the revelatory rationale for what is happening.

Having understanding does not save us from the second half of the storm. However, now, through the input of revelation, we have a compass reading to take us in the direction that God wants us to travel. Therefore, we can endure the change because we know what God wants to achieve. Now we can let go and let God have His way.

On a personal level, we may be going through tough circumstances that we are failing to process internally. We need to look and listen for the sweet voice of reason to come to us. It may come in a sermon, through a book we are reading, by a Scripture we are studying, from a prayer we receive in ministry, in a letter or card, through a prophetic word, or just in a telephone call from a concerned friend. The point is, it will come! Many times, we miss it because our soul wants to hear only about deliverance, so we sift every word and discard those not compatible with our soulish desires. The inward man knows that process is the key to all God's dealings with His people. Life is a journey. A friend of mine, Mary Dennison, once told me, "Don't get so hung up on your destination that you forget to enjoy the journey!"

Soulish activity often leads us into realms of protectionism. It puts a hard exterior, a protective cover, over our sensitive areas of mind and heart. Like a bulletproof vest, it protects the wearer from any adverse circumstances. The spirit man finds his protection in the love of God. He knows that God is our secret place, refuge, fortress, high tower, hiding place, and holy habitation.

When the soul protects itself, it doesn't realize that the hard outer casing also prevents relationships from forming with God and people. The wearing of this casing is irksome. Not only will it give you a form of protection, but it also encases all your irritations. They are locked in with you!

The inner man gets rid of such things by having open communion with God and people. The outer man is imprisoned by these things until release occurs. Worries, fears, frustrations, and irritations begin to adversely affect our personalities because they have no place of release. We become angry, resentful, bitter, and vengeful in all that inner turmoil. Our health suffers, and we are unhappy, negative, and contemptuous in our personalities.

If we have no way of dealing with these issues, they simply stay with us. They never leave. They act on the inside of us. Each unresolved issue becomes another layer that has to be peeled off if we are going to enjoy life. The accumulation of unresolved issues grows into a barrier, a shell that covers our heart and emotions. Frustration is the result of all these unresolved conflicts. We have a short fuse; we get exasperated easily. We feel thwarted by other people. We do not want to allow them to have a viewpoint. We listen only to give our opinion. Whilst they are talking, we are formulating our riposte.

Transition cracks the shell of our personality and breaks open our hardness. Frustration is a key to development. Part of our frustration is caused by a history of disappointments and unresolved issues, creating dissatisfaction and unfulfillment. We half expect to get thwarted again and so we get our shot in first. We have learned how to see the flaws, the cracks, the negatives in situations and people because our protective shell looks to guard itself against intruders.

> *The inner man of the spirit is the anchor for the soul.*

Process Releases Potential

Through the prophetic side of my ministry, I have had hundreds of contacts with people who were very negative toward me because they were under the illusion that I could see right through them. Actually, I prefer to see the good in people. No one can hide their rubbish for too long; truth will always come out. A prophet looks for the treasure in the earthen vessel and brings it to the surface. We are on a treasure hunt, seeing people with the eyes of the Lord Jesus—the kindest person I have ever known.

God always speaks to our potential. Gideon was alone, frightened, angry, and disillusioned. He had lots of questions and reservations and a tremendously low self-esteem. When God came on his scene, he was hiding away, making bread in a winepress (like you do when you're depressed). There were so many things the Lord could have said. He could have ministered deliverance or rebuked him for his lifestyle and attitude. Instead, the Lord spoke warmly to him: "Hello, Gideon. The Lord is with you, O valiant warrior!" (see Judg. 6:12)

God spoke to what was noble in Gideon, and it rose up within him. Whatever we speak to in people, rises up! If we speak to their flesh and find fault, the flesh will rise up and there will be an angry frustration. If, however, we speak to their spirit, to their potential, then the treasure of Christ that is within them will surface. We will find that as the treasure rises, people automatically deal with any issues in their life that prevent it from being revealed. In this way, prophecy is an inspiration to enable people to change and an encouragement to see themselves as God sees them. It releases the wonderful presence of the Comforter to enable them to deal with any rubbish in their lives. We simply have to love God and all His ways. The kindness, the grace, and the thoughtfulness of the Lord are outstanding!

However, when people do not know how the Lord thinks or works, they tend to think the worst. So people have blanked me out in various ways in order to not be exposed. They do not understand that God is more interested in exposing their potential than He is in the stuff it is buried in!

Our frustration has to be cracked open. Signs of pain are usually signs of resistance as well. It shows us where we need to be healed. In the natural, a cut or a bump denotes the area needing medical care. So in the spirit, our pain is a pointer to our healing. Frustration also shows us where the point of breakthrough is going to come in our shell. Frustration is the key to our ongoing resistance. It tells us where the hammer of the Lord will apply itself to the hard shell around us. Your frustrations and pain are clues to your transition. The process will involve God breaking into those areas to bring healing, release, and empowerment. He loves you too much to let you stay in that place!

Watch for the signs; the Comforter will open your eyes and teach you if you ask Him. He is quite brilliant at this aspect of relating to God's people. Enjoy Him!

In the mercy of God and out of our abiding relationship with Him, we are better equipped to perceive transitional moments and seasons. This gives us the power to choose to cooperate ahead of time, which is very significant in our relationship with the Lord. We can become prophetic in our own development, thwarting the plans of the enemy as we grow in our spirit. This can be a pleasant and welcome experience—maintaining our tranquillity of mind and heart despite the pressure of life.

Other areas of transition are unseen and also unpredictable. We only learn how they are going to turn out as we walk closely with the Lord. Indeed, that is the point of some changes and upheavals. As well as helping to shape the direction of our heart and life, they also deliver us to a new level of dependency on the Lord Jesus. At first, they make us vulnerable, insecure, and inadequate, which is excellent. Actually, these are three of the entry points into the grace of God where we stand in hope of His glory. That is the reason why Paul was so pleased with weakness (see 2 Cor. 12:7-10); he knew it was an entry point into God's grace. He became both most glad and well content. He had a revelatory rationale for what was bothering him. He knew the process that God was using (through the difficulties he was encountering) to bring him to a new place in the spirit. Paul's revelation of God's grace was not big enough for the level of warfare he was experiencing; hence, the thorn in the flesh. It was allowed by the Lord to bring Paul into a deeper relationship with Himself. The best way to combat darkness is to receive greater light. Having an increase of revelatory rationale for the events of life is a prerequisite for greater spiritual growth.

Three Stages of Transition

We see in Scripture that transition has three defined stages. Each one incorporates particular elements that we need to walk through in order to grow in the way that God has planned for us. In the heart of God, transition is the way that He has designed for us to approach Him and become like Him, using the circumstances He has allowed. Nothing is left to chance; everything has been ordained.

God is very principle-centered. Whenever He reveals Himself, He shows us His nature. He gives us the ability to understand His mind and His ways. When God says or does a particular thing for the first time, He sets a precedent. He establishes a precedent, and by it we know Him forever. We add that information to the storehouse of what we know about His faithfulness and unchangeable nature. Briefly, the three stages are *closure*, *conversion*, and *commissioning*.

In closure, God brings the past to an end. He closes a door on the enemy, hurts, wounds, and poor decisions we made previously.

This involves forgiving and forgetting on His part and on our part, which sets us free to pursue Him with a clear conscience.

Our frustration and pain are clues to our transition.

Second is a conversion experience in which we undergo significant transformation and change of heart. This normally takes place in a temporary vacuum that God places around us to help us concentrate on Him. Because this experience is very different to our normal walk with God, it can appear to be chaotic. On the surface nothing much is happening. However, underneath and inside we are very busy with God, being redeveloped internally.

Finally, there is a commissioning—a new mandate, an appointment in the Spirit. It is a release and a sending-out to fulfill a particular birthing. A metamorphosis has taken place—a new birthing and beginning in the purpose of God. We are renewed, restored, and revitalized in the calling of God upon our lives.

Through this process—which must be understood and complied with in its fullness—we are given the real opportunity for breakthrough into a new place in God. The work of God is never compartmentalized, so we must be prepared for overlap and interaction between the stages. By that, I mean God is always doing several things at once. He will work back and forth between stages, using elements of one to help us break through into another.

For example, we can see this process in the life of Moses. Closure came when he killed the Egyptian who was beating a Hebrew. He was exiled from the palace and his country, and sent to wander the earth. One way of life was about to come to an end. However, before God could pick up this man, he had to be changed into a different type of individual. The wilderness was where God set to work on Moses, converting him from an arrogant Egyptian prince to a humble shepherd used to hardship. Moses needed desert training as well as transformation. When this process was advanced well enough (it is never complete at this stage), the Lord appeared in the burning bush to commission Moses for the calling that had been set aside for him.

Moses was to become a prophet of God. One of the fascinating aspects of the prophetic call is the sense of going through things ahead of time. Prophets experience in their own life what they will prophesy to others. Joseph was a man sent beforehand to prepare a way for Israel. Moses went through a carbon copy of Israel's experience on a personal level.

We will use Israel's journey as a guide to both a personal and corporate journey. Firstly, we will examine closure from a personal perspective to see how we individually may cope with transition. Secondly, we will view transition from a broader, more corporate context to give us some impressions from that angle.

Stage 1: Personal Closure

One of the most difficult things to preach about in church is death in the form of being crucified with Christ. It is a paradox that Christianity begins with closure. Death to self; repentance from dead works; reckon yourself dead to sin but alive in Christ (see Rom. 6:11)—these are all forms of closure.

When Jesus hung on the cross, His last words were, "It is finished!" (Jn. 19:30) It was closure, an end to sin. Through His death, man would have a new beginning in God. It was a closure of the Old Covenant and a beginning of the New Covenant. In creation, God made everything before He made man. His last act of creation was to make man in His own image. Then God rested on the seventh day—closure. Adam's first day was a day of rest. All the work had been done; he entered into God's rest. (See Hebrews 4:3-4.) Adam was formed as an act of closure to the process of creation.

So, in the New Covenant, we enter into the finished work of Christ on the cross. When He died, we died.

Romans 6:3-11 is all about closure. I recommend that you read that passage. It is rich with ending and beginning. He who has died is free! Our old self was crucified with Him.

Much of the failure in the Church today occurs because people do not live in the truth of their baptism. "Buried with Him through baptism unto death and walking in newness of life" is talking about the process of transformation. We see the process in

Romans 6–8. Chapter 6 concerns closure in death. Chapter 7 is the change of heart process: "For the good that I will to do, I do not do; but the evil I will not to do, that I practice" (7:19). It brings us to the realization of verse 2 in chapter 8 that "the law of the Spirit of life in Christ Jesus has made me free...."

Christianity begins with closure. It starts with a celebration of an ending that we were not part of when it happened, but can enter into by the goodness of God. We don't celebrate death; we normally lament it in our western culture. In the east it is a triumph, in the west a tragedy. New birth delights us; death causes grief. Throughout our life, we have so many opportunities for closure and new beginnings. A good closure releases a good new start. We can't have a fresh start without an end first. For a Christian, death is closure in the time-space world and a beginning in the eternal world of the Spirit.

Life teaches us that we cannot experience a fresh start until we deal with the closure preceding it. Failure to deal with closure means that we carry on the unfinished business of our past into the present and future of our life. In other words, we are condemned to making mistakes because we did not get closure from them in the first place. We carry them with us because we have not off-loaded them. They will dictate the pattern of the new start we desperately want.

> *Transition is the way that God has designed for us to approach Him.*

Take a moment and think. Reflect on your life. How much baggage are you carrying from the past? How many times have you made the same mistake? What governs your thinking—optimism or pessimism? If it is the latter, possibly you need closure on something that still haunts you. There is a whole self-help industry at work in the world because millions of people need help with closure.

Many people minimize the importance and impact that real closure can bring. People talk about forgetting the past and getting on with their life. Closure is a mental, physical, and emotional process. It requires closure in all three areas to really end something. In the

Romans 6–8 process, we see that the physical act of baptism is important to closure (6:3-4). We are encouraged to consider ourselves dead (6:11). This is followed by the emotional agony of release in Romans 7:24-25:

O wretched man that I am! Who will deliver me from this body of death? I thank God–through Jesus Christ our Lord! So then, with the mind I myself serve the law of God, but with the flesh the law of sin.

Romans 8:1-2 goes on to state that there is no condemnation to "those who are in Christ Jesus, who do not walk according to the flesh, but according to the Spirit. For the law of the Spirit of life in Christ Jesus has made me free from the law of sin and death." Never underestimate the importance of closure. If you have ignored it in the past, then you may need to consider the possibility that you are in denial. You have closure in your mind, but you have locked away your emotions, and now you still feel crippled by the past. If you are unable to trust, love, or commit yourself, you need closure. If you have wept buckets of tears but can't forget or forgive, you cannot enjoy a new beginning.

We manage our sorrows in different ways. Denial occurs when we minimize an ending. Self-protection is another form of managing grief. It occurs by not getting involved, not letting people get too close. We need the emotional support of others.

In 1995, my wife and I went through a particularly painful time of transition. We were leaving one network to join another. It was a time of realignment in our lives. I had been part of one apostolic team and now was joining another. We were moving churches but not relocating. We were staying in the same city. There was nothing wrong relationally; I simply needed a stronger apostolic base as my home church. I wanted to be rooted in a church that could challenge my life and develop my ministry. I wanted to be part of a local church where I could put into practice the apostolic and prophetic revelation that I was processing. I needed accountability at the level I was functioning at in the spirit realm. This was not possible in the church where I was based. This is not a reflection on them; they simply were not an apostolic center.

I spoke to various people in the network. There were several places we could have relocated to so that I could have stayed within the network that I had been part of for 13 years. When it came down to it, though, we had no permission from God to leave Southampton, which was where we lived. So it meant a painful process of change for all of us. We all wept, it seemed, for months. Our pain was great. It would have been easier to relocate. It was hard to make new friends when our old and dear friends lived just around the corner. My wife, Heather, found it particularly difficult. I could travel with my ministry and therefore process some of my pain on the road. She lived and worked in the city. I felt so bad, putting her through all this because of my ministry, my calling. She followed me out of sheer love. She had not heard the voice of God for herself. She put herself in the hands of God and came with me. Our life was painful for several months. I watched her putting on a brave face. I cried for her. I raged at myself for bringing her into such grief. It was a great loss.

Eventually, I fasted and prayed for her over several weeks for her to hear God through the sorrow. I remember the day she got closure. It was a Sunday morning, and I felt lost in the worship, lost in God. His presence was heavy around me. Suddenly, I heard her voice coming through the microphone on the platform, exhorting and encouraging the church. Heather returned to her seat, and we held hands, not speaking. I looked around at the hundreds of people. Several of the elders had tears in their eyes, as did we. We all knew what it meant, and we were grateful to God. The sorrow still had to be processed, but we had closure; we could now have a new beginning.

I remember my own closure in this time of distress. It was at a staff prayer meeting on a Tuesday morning. Several of the guys prayed for me, and Lynn Swart, our worship leader, sang a prophetic song over me: "Welcome, son; welcome, welcome, welcome, my son." There were several verses, but it always returned to "welcome, my son." I cried. She kindly put it on tape for me. I still play it occasionally, years later.

As a family, the move has been brilliant. We have settled in and are all functioning in new ways and at new levels spiritually.

We are making friends, seeing people, and developing new relationships. We miss our old friends, yet we are enjoying our new ones. I miss the previous apostolic team; still, I'm enjoying the current one. I have lunch and dinner occasionally with guys from the old team. I keep in touch with some people. We all are busy working in different Kingdom vineyards...life goes on. Transition is painful and enjoyable.

We exchange the ending of one phase of our life for the beginning of a new one. It is in the gap between closure and commission that real conversion occurs. The gap between them represents our capacity to put off the old and think about the new, prior to putting it on. The gap is the place where we come to terms with everything and say "good-bye" and "hello"!

We also need to understand something here that is important. There are different types of closures. Some are absolutely final in all respects, like the death of a loved one or changing jobs. It is a defined end where you no longer see your deceased friend or work in the same building or city. It's over!

> *We cannot experience a fresh start until we deal with the closure preceding it.*

Some closures are partial and ongoing, such as a child growing into an adult. Some parents want to hold on to the young cuddly child who was so innocent and said the funniest things. Now we have this hulking, six-foot being with a different humor and a mind of its own! If we want to enjoy the present relationship to the full, we need to let our children grow up. Otherwise, we permanently embarrass them, or worse, make them angry because we don't recognize their adulthood.

Young love turning to marriage changes into parenting with all the responsibilities, planning, schedules, and thousand and one things to do for young children. It irrevocably changes how we live and love. Many people survive that transitional process because, in their love, they are willing for closure and new beginnings. In the gap, most marriages go through difficulty where real adjustments have to be made to process their marriage onto another level.

Some marriages do not make it because people want to return to young-love experiences. They cannot move on to a mature relationship because they never got closure from the time of being carefree and without responsibilities.

Some closures are big and final. Other closures are relatively small endings and beginnings in a mutual transition that is ongoing within relationships of meaning and significance. What we must bear in mind are these truths:

- Closure is a part of a life process, if we accept it.

- We do not lose our ability to enjoy life and people in closure.

- Closure allows us to focus on the new beginning that is coming.

- Our capacity to possess life and appreciate everything actually grows through our understanding and participation in transition.

Sorrow and loss do not have to be permanent conditions. To make the most of life, we must learn to progress through the variety of experiences we encounter and learn to arrive at new beginnings.

There are two reactions to closure that we can experience, and both are extremes of behavior. Firstly, we can underestimate the power or impact of closure. We do not take it seriously enough. This reaction may reveal itself in denial or self-protection, as we have already discussed. We simply try to shrug things off as "just part of life's rich tapestry." We get rid of people or things quickly and move on to new pastures. Some people have a whole history of broken relationships and loves because they underestimated the impact of closure. Therefore, they never learned how to make a new beginning really work. Their excess baggage tripped them up time after time.

Secondly, we can exaggerate the power and impact of closure. People commit suicide after a love affair breaks up because their sense of loss seems so permanent. They feel that their life is over. Some successful career people fall apart at retirement. Powerful, go-getting executives suddenly can lose the ability to make decisions.

They drift through life, taking up one thing or another but can never recapture their glory years. People lose their fortunes and put a gun in their mouth. When people exaggerate the impact of closure, they have lost sight of their next new beginning. In the anguish of their misfortune, they fail to convert their ending into the potential of a new beginning.

There are three stages that I have identified in my own personal journey. No doubt you could probably find more stages or define them differently. I hope this feeble attempt to define the process encourages you to do better!

Closure Involves a Reaction

In relationships, a closure can begin far back with a growing unease that leads to disillusionment. In many cases, disillusionment can be a critical part of growth if we allow it. However, we may react positively or negatively to disillusionment.

Disillusionment is the breaking of our illusions. We all have illusions about ourselves and one another. The grass is always greener somewhere else. We get starry-eyed about people until we get to know them properly, and then we become unhappy with the reality. However, disillusionment can be healthy if we process it properly.

Actually, the breaking of our illusions is very positive because it can lead us to a greater reality of one another that strengthens the relationship. I thank God that there are some people who know my weaknesses and frailties both as a human being and as a minister. As a leadership, we try to practice disclosure—the humbling of ourselves in shared weakness. In main church meetings, it is one of our requirements in preaching that we tell a story against ourselves, using personal failures as examples, to make a significant point.

I am aware, though, that at times disillusionment can come through very hurtful ways. Our growing disenchantment with people or a living situation causes a reaction inside us. We can no longer tolerate or play down certain events and circumstances. Staying in the situation may require such an odious change of heart (one that is injurious to our faith or personality) that every-thing within us reacts to the idea.

Some situations weigh heavily on our conscience. We cannot make agreement with people no matter how much we love them. There is a very great problem in some church circles with leader-ship being out of control. Some leaders rule over their people in a very unhealthy and ungodly way.

The proper structure of authority in the church is firstly God; secondly, the infallibility of Scripture; thirdly, the conscience of the individual; and finally, delegated authority recognized through apostles, prophets, and local eldership teams.

Learn to arrive at new beginnings.

True leaders, ones with a fathering heart, will always teach people how to live in and before God. They will not violate people's con-science but will nurture it and appeal to it in times of tension. The apostle Paul spoke about how "by manifestation of the truth commend-ing ourselves to every man's conscience in the sight of God" (2 Cor. 4:2).

Also, in the context of wanting to please God and appearing before His judgment seat, he makes this statement:

Knowing, therefore, the terror of the Lord, we persuade men; but we are well known to God, and I also trust are well known in your consciences. For we do not commend ourselves again to you, but give you opportunity to boast on our behalf, that you may have an answer for those who boast in appearance and not in heart. For if we are beside ourselves, it is for God; or if we are of sound mind, it is for you (2 Corinthians 5:11-13).

In some churches and organizations, delegated authority is placed ahead of conscience. Leaders control how people think and behave. People are not taught how to grow up in God, but how to submit to leadership. In some cases, to have a different viewpoint than your leaders is seen as being rebellious or a troublemaker. The process of alienation begins so that your "Jezebel spirit" does not contaminate the rest of the body. In my understanding of the Jezebel syndrome, the problem was with designated leadership using prophecy and power to control and manipulate the people (see 1 Kings 16–21; 2 Kings 9).

Leaders are meant to be so in love with God and to display such great humility and servanthood that, by their fathering spirit and example, they provide a model in self-government. They teach people about self-control (one of the fruits of the Spirit) and how to live in their conscience before the Lord. Paul spoke to Timothy about the hypocrisy of liars, seared in their own conscience as with a branding iron (see 1 Tim. 4:2). We must not destroy one of the main qualities in people whereby they can receive progressive truth. The conscience of our people must be as highly prized by the leadership as the development of their inner man of the spirit.

Disappointment can lead to frustration, which is another facet of reaction. We can blame others, get mad, or get even. Moving in the opposite spirit to what you are experiencing is a difficult but attainable discipline. Jesus spoke about it in Luke 6:27-28: "But I say to you who hear: Love your enemies, do good to those who hate you, bless those who curse you, and pray for those who spitefully use you."

If you move in the same spirit that your opponents move in, then you establish your own carnality rather than the nature of God.

In reaction, we often suffer a sense of loss and grief. We grieve and sorrow for how things have turned out—at least we should. If we leave angry, we will take longer to process how we feel.

If you feel compelled to leave or are unable to stay in certain circumstances, you must do this next step *before* you go. If you do not, you will wander in an internal wilderness until the effect on your heart is resolved.

Closure Requires Reflection

Before we withdraw physically from a situation, people, or circumstances, we need to question ourselves and our motives. We must review all the circumstances, taking on board the opinions of friends and seeking the viewpoint of mature people. We also must correctly diagnose the real reasons why we are disaffected. Finally, we must recognize our own part in the failure as well as the failings themselves and deal with them positively and effectively.

These four elements of examining internal motivation, seeking external reviews, coming to an accurate diagnosis, and recognizing our failure, are a critical part of our reflections. If they are done as humbly and as honestly as possible, we can face the circumstances with an open heart and deal with our excess baggage accordingly. Reflection is the unpacking of all the mental and emotional baggage that we gather in the process of gaining closure.

If we work through these with honest transparency before the Lord, then our closure will be a positive learning experience and our capacity to be joined elsewhere will happen much more smoothly. Failure to reflect and learn will mean that the bitterness and the hurt will remain with us to adversely affect our ability to relate in the next place that receives us.

Question your *internal motivations*. Examine yourself first. Look at your own attitudes. Take the plank out of your own eye. Write down a list of what you have done wrong as well as what has been done wrong to you. Weigh each list accurately. Be harder on yourself than you are on others. Most of us want mercy for ourselves and judgment for other people. Be tough on yourself. Be kind to others as much as you can without getting sentimental and trite.

Apologize for what you need to repent of in terms of your own words and actions. To be sure, your apology may probably be used against you. Your "confession" will damn you in the eyes of others, but probably not your real friends. Remember, this is about gaining an effective closure so that in your next new beginning, you do not start out with a millstone around your neck!

Gain the viewpoint of others. Do not live on your own perspective. Have an *external review* if you can, using people who have maturity in these matters, but also using people in the situation itself. There should be a mixture of people for and against you, but who have a love for the truth.

Remember, in reflection, you are processing your own attitude as much as diagnosing what went wrong. Review all the possibilities. If you can, fast and pray before the Lord so that you can receive personally damaging truth that will lead you to repentance and change.

> *People are not taught how to grow up in God, but how to submit to leadership.*

Remember also, there is a huge difference between truth and perspective. Truth is a Person. His name is Jesus. Truth is what God says in Scripture. Everything else is perspective. In emotional difficulties, no one tells the whole truth and nothing but the truth. Our version of events is shaped by how we feel and their effect on our life. Our thought processes can be influenced by a number of things, such as our general disappointment and our particular reading of events. We do not have access to how other people felt or how their mind was working at the time that something happened. What they thought they said, what they actually said, what they really meant by it, how we heard them say it, and what effect it had on us are probably all going to be wildly different. That's perspective!

We will never get to a place of total truth, because the event will mean different things to different people. If everyone were to examine themselves thoroughly instead of each other, if we had a real desire to win one another's hearts, we would stand a good chance of not separating over general issues (see Mt. 18:15-17).

Relational difficulties in most cases cannot be resolved, only harmonized. Harmony is the simultaneous combination of several tones blended together in relationship. Tones that are opposites, or that are running parallel but not together, can be blended with other tones that are mutually relational to both to create a common sound—a harmony.

In relational difficulties, we find just such a disparate grouping. There are people on opposite sides of the fence to us; people on parallel lines with us but still with a slightly different track; and people who agree that both sides have something to say and that they can see the truth in both. Tension is one of the ingredients of relating in depth. There is no movement without tension.

Church is a people paradox. Relationships in church (or any people group for that matter) are about holding different personalities, ministries, visions, and perspectives in tension with one another. Tension does not mean there is something wrong; it means there is something happening! We do not want to have the Frank Sinatra style of relating together: Do it my way or take the highway.

If you look at the Gospel accounts of the life and ministry of Jesus, you have four versions. Each account is complete, yet incomplete. That's the paradox. We don't use them against one another to contradict one another. We agree where we can, and we celebrate the different nuances of each author. The point is that all the Gospels agree on the main elements of the Kingdom message. That's what we look for, that's our harmony; everything else is a bonus.

We will probably have to agree to disagree over some issues and come to a place of broad agreement over the central issues without compromising ourselves.

Find people you can trust either within the work or associated with it enough to comprehend the tensions. Their role is to be impartial and provide an effective sounding board. Do not be upset if they spot the flaws between your perspective and your behavior. They are not here to agree with you. They are here to listen and help you process your own mistakes as well as to provide comfort and support in the difficulties you are facing.

An important part of reflection is making an *accurate diagnosis* of your disillusionment/dissatisfaction. At this point, you may be of two minds as to whether to go or whether to stay and work it through. An accurate reading of the situation minus a strong emotional context hopefully will provide you with enough raw data to make informed decisions regarding your process through the situation.

Your identity as an individual plus any ministry you have within the group may be the most threatened here. Your sense of belonging may be severely disrupted. Do not get personal. Try and retain some objectivity. Having an external review before beginning real diagnosis helps to bleed off unhelpful emotions that may unnecessarily color your perception.

We want cold, hard facts at this point, as devoid of subjective input as possible. Don't window-dress it; tell it like it is. The questions you are asking yourself here are these: "Can I live with it? What is the cost of staying? Will things really change here? What is the track record of this church actually working things through to a point of effective change? Is there a history of broken promises or good ideas not being implemented? Do I have confidence in the people? Do I fit? If so, where do I fit in? Do I still want to belong here? Is the cost of leaving more than I can bear? What will it take for me to stay? Is that attainable?"

Do you get the idea? You are using diagnosis to build a picture of what is happening. The point is, you are trying to find yourself in the jigsaw puzzle of answers. Can you connect, or will you declassify yourself in terms of your belonging? If you cannot belong, then you must leave on the best terms possible and in the right spirit.

Hopefully, these deliberations will lead you to the final part of reflection, which is *recognizing your failure*. This is an accurate description of how the situation failed overall and the part you played in that failure.

In reflection, we need to come to a true point of understanding the reasons for failure. This is chiefly how we gather wisdom to ourselves via retrospective revelation. This is the wisdom we learn through our experience of success and failure. What worked and what did not? Most of us learn how not to do things first, which is why we need mercy and kindness toward one another in these situations. Many people criticized Moses, but he was the only one doing it! It is easy to sit on the sidelines and snipe at other people. There is a simple rule in relationships. According to Jesus, it is "do to others what you would like them to do for you." Simple, profound, and powerful. So why do many people not practice it more often?

> *In many cases, relational difficulties cannot be resolved, only harmonized.*

When you have gathered the list of reasons for failure, ask yourself, "What could I do differently next time?" By the way, if you're not yet ready to ask that question, you probably need some deeper help for your emotions.

There is always a next time. Someone far better, more intelligent, and more anointed than myself once gave a definition of victorious Christian living. Are you ready for it? "If you're not up, you are planning to get up!" Well, okay, I thought it was good, and I'm the one who wrote this book!

Learn from your experience, and your chances of not repeating it will increase dramatically.

The second aspect you must reflect on in your recognition of your failure is what your particular contribution was to the failure. Was it your attitude? Your lack of commitment? Did you engage in negative fellowship or criticism? Were you an influence for strife, backbiting, and jealousy? Analyze your verbal communication and your non-verbal signals. Withdrawal or general lack of commitment normally manifests itself in such actions as coming to the meeting late, sitting at the back, not joining in the worship, reducing your tithes and offering, and not responding to ministry times, to name but a few! Be honest; don't spare yourself. It is better out than in.

In reflection, one of the chief elements you must analyze and review is the issue of your personal identity. Your identity is based on who you are in yourself with God. Ideally, it is not based on your function, position, title, status, wealth, physical looks, intelligence, or abilities. These will undoubtedly add to the luster of your personality, but they do not define it. A.W. Tozer said that character is what you are in the dark. When everything is stripped away, who are you? Closely allied to that is what you can do in terms of ability, gifting and personal vision, and call.

If we depend on external things to maintain our identity, we will fight tooth and nail to protect that part of our identity. Relying on external things to define identity often creates a mask or an image of what we want other people to see.

Who am I, Graham Cooke? I'm an introvert, and I love my personality. It is a gift of God to me. I'm quite shy and reflective by nature. I adore silence. I have my moments of madness in humor and can be quite funny. I know hundreds of people who are better than me at what I do, but I do not feel inferior to them. I love being with them, and I actively seek out my betters to learn from them.

I love depending totally on the Lord. My personality tends to sit easily with God's requirements for vulnerability, inadequacy, and weakness as prerequisites for knowing His strengths. I do not like platforms, and I do not find it easy to be a speaker on public view, though I am often told that I am good at it. I blame God for that.

I work best under pressure. I do not mind tough situations. I relish the battle. For me, spiritual warfare is about the majesty and supremacy of Jesus, not the power of the devil. I like cold beer. And soccer. I don't want recognition; I prefer anonymity. I want to beat the devil, to make him pay. I like a glass of wine with a meal and lots of friends to share it with. I love the way the Irish speak. I want Scotland to win the World Cup at soccer (they have such passion). I want England to beat someone, anyone, at cricket. For those who are not familiar with this archetype English sport, it's too long to explain. Actor Robin Williams calls it baseball on Valium, but that may give you no help in understanding it!

I want the Church to be full of the manifest presence of God. I want revival everywhere, especially in Wales. I love the easygoing humor in America. I want my own land and to design my own house.

I can't believe I'm still married. I don't deserve my wife, Heather; she is too good for me. I would like to be as intelligent as my son Ben, or as madcap, brilliant, and totally committed to things as my other son Seth. My daughter thrills me.

I want to empty hospitals. I want to see a Mount Carmel showdown on international TV between the psychic channel people and real prophets of God! I want evangelicals and charismatics to fall in love with God and one another. I love the way Catholic people pray, worship, and love God. If I could be any type of vehicle, I would choose to be the old-style, long wheel-based Land Rover with no frills but stripped down and ready to explore uncharted areas.

I love resting in the Lord. Every day I want to be as tranquil as He is. Rest is a weapon. I want to steal the devil's key people from him. I love the movies. I like blues music. Native American culture is brilliant. I wish I could work with more African-American churches. I love the sound of Africans singing without music. I like hot spicy foods. I wish I could cast out calories into really thin people to even the spread. I love the mystics and their writings. I love being with creative people. I like being the server at parties in our home.

If I could have the last 25 years all over again, I would make more mistakes. They occur mainly because we are doing new things and going in new directions. I want to do more of both!

"Okay, okay, that's enough," I hear you say! Do you get the picture? Identity is a mix of who we are, our dreams and aspirations, how we feel, and what we are like.

> *In times like these, it helps us to remember that there have always been times like these!*

If you could write your own job description for your personal role in church, job, etc., what would you list? If you could write your own obituary, what would you want others to write about you? How do others see you? If you feel brave enough, you could try to reflect on yourself a little.

Closure Necessitates Redirection

First the ending, then the beginning—that is how process works. It may be that we need closure over some issues so that we can stay and continue with people in the situation. Our continuity, however, must take a different form. We need to reassess the basis of the relationship so that we can find a new way forward. Life is full of such negotiations. Often, we do not appreciate the value of someone or something until it is almost taken away from us. The sense of potential loss galvanizes our hearts into a reassessment of what we value most.

Redirection in its basic form involves a release. Our mind-sets and emotions are liberated along with our desires to formulate a new path for ourselves. Release occurs on two levels—first the natural, then the spiritual. We come into a new season where change has had a positive physical and emotional effect. We feel better; we are much happier; we think, act, and speak differently. This empowers us into a release in spiritual terms. We gain wisdom, insight, and revelation. We grow in grace and vision. We become empowered. We blossom in this newfound freedom. Others note the change and see the benefit.

Sometimes this is preceded by a period of solitude and prayer as we come to terms with our decision and seek to make it work.

Alternatively, redirection may mean a total withdrawal, a disengaging from the situation and the people in it. Closure is leading us away to extricate ourselves completely. Our continuous reaction to events, coupled with our reflection, combine to convince us that departure is best for all concerned.

Our leaving must be good and honorable to God. This is a priority! We do not want to reap bad things in the future; therefore, we must sow good things now. Redirection not only involves a release from our current circumstances, but also a discharge into a new start. This may be defined up front. We may feel that we know where we are going. Indeed, God, who is always previous, may have mapped this out for us and already begun to open doors and make a way. We may have definition as to the future and the beginnings of a road map of reality to take us there.

On the other hand, we may have only the revelation that it is time to go but no clear sense of direction. We are waiting on God and probably being misunderstood at the same time. Christians have a great capacity to misinterpret what they do not understand. For some reason, we feel debased by uncertainty and in some way, demeaned by our lack of coherent direction.

Redirection works best in peace and faith. God will make a way. It is in His nature to guide and open up new horizons to His people.

Abraham was the model for a man who went out not knowing where he was going, but trusting in God to complete his journey. Moses went to Egypt not knowing many things but still trusting the Lord. Sometimes, endings are not neatly packaged, or quick and easy. They can be long and drawn out, which will test our patience and our relationships with the Lord and with the people around us.

Try not to box things up just because you are impatient for closure or because you want to prove to detractors that something is happening.

Redirection involves the release of new vision, a new lease on life, a rediscovery of calling, and a new base of anointing and significance to build from. The flow of our life changes, and the water level in our spirit rises. We speak with more passion. We are free. We have closure, and we now feel that nothing can hold us back.

We need to stop at this point and go on to the next chapter to try and understand the next pieces in the jigsaw of transition.

Chapter 9

The Process of Transition

Part 2

*W*e've already discussed process and, in particular, the need for closure. That stage is only one facet of the multiple-stage process of transition. The next piece in this jigsaw is *conversion*.

Stage 2: Conversion—The Cycle of Change

Everything has a season and a rhythm (see Eccles. 3:1-8). All of created life has built-in instincts that enable it to function in the various cycles of living.

These instincts are supplemented with knowledge and certain experiences that form learned behavior. Knowledge of climatic conditions will aid animals in hunting, feeding, and seeking shelter. Interplay with other creatures will enable them to discover prey or hide from an aggressor. The functions of their lives are determined by various cycles, such as preparing for winter, resting, mating, and raising their young.

As humans, we also have a certain inner knowledge that we can draw upon to sustain us through the cycles of our lives. In our relationship with the Lord, we learn that there are cycles of anointing, relationship, ministry, lifestyle, revelation, and church building. (More of that in another book!)

In transition and process, we think of departure, destination, accomplishment, and arrival as our major goals. The Lord, however, thinks of the journey and relationships as His significant targets. Our thinking must come into line with His. A journey that could have taken 11 days eventually lasted for more than 40 years because Israel's thinking was not aligned with God's goals.

Our focus must not be on our ultimate destination in our walk with the Lord but in what will take place as we journey with Him. Transition is always about particular change. If we are to survive transition and not be killed by it, we must discover what it is that the Lord wishes to change in us. Transition and process then are about giving the Lord what He wants and receiving from Him what He wishes to release. At the heart of transition is a willingness to discover and submit to the dealings of God at this particular time. For Israel, their transition concerned firstly a rediscovery of personal intimacy with a close and personal God. Secondly, it was about making the transition from a nomadic tribe of slaves and refugees into one nation with identity, commitment, and purpose. Thirdly, it involved learning how to fight again in a disciplined manner.

> *Transition is always about particular change.*

All these elements were put together in one mass of transition to prepare them to take new ground and enter into their inheritance. Transition must be broken down into its different elements so that we can understand events, submit to the Lord, be changed personally and corporately, and inherit the various promises that the Lord has made.

The main point to grasp in any transitional time is not concerned with our eventual destination but with the experience of traveling with the Lord on the journey. That is why prophecy is progressive in nature. It builds through various cycles and upon certain experiences, linking past with present and future. We are all travelers journeying with the Lord at His pace and in His timing. He is preparing us both internally to walk with Him personally and externally to overcome the enemy and various obstacles and opposition.

The point is, we should enjoy the journey and not complain about the process. It is there for a reason! Mature Christians find that reason and embrace it by submitting to the hand of God. We should arrive at our destination radically changed by the journey itself. We should be different people on arrival than we were on departure. This is where Israel significantly failed. They grumbled and complained at the beginning, throughout the journey, and at the end as they reached Kadesh Barnea. Their outlook had not changed. They would not enter into Canaan because of their unbelief about God, themselves, and their understanding of the process of change. Grumbling and complaining radically affect the development of faith, our ability to inherit all that God wants to give us, and our capacity to enter into the warfare that His presence provokes around our lives.

The wilderness is a strange place. It is a place of no distraction where we learn to relate, submit, and serve the living God. In transition, we are strangers learning how to live together at a deeper level. Even good friends will learn new things about each other—pleasant and unpleasant—as they journey along this new road. Moses described himself as a "stranger in a strange land" (Ex. 2:22 KJV). He had to get to know himself in a new way. He had to come to terms with his weakness and inadequacies. We learn how to discover God, ourselves, and one another in transition. A major part of transition is facing disillusionment. This is the breaking of our illusions about the Lord, ourselves, and one another. The process of change will deliver us to a place of total reality. Although painful at first, it is then sobering as we consider our own actions and lifestyle, but it finally is exhilarating as we become liberated to be ourselves in the loving-kindness of God.

The end of transition is a new beginning where we enter into a new identity and a new phase of being. Prior to that happy event, we must be converted to the goals and purposes of God. More than that, we must be transformed into His very nature. There must be a reformation process so profound that we lose our own personal identity in the struggle and have it so reformed with God's personality that we are radically changed.

Then, when the commission comes upon us from the Lord, we will respond in His nature and not our old style of thinking. The reaction of "Who am I that I should go to Pharaoh?" must give way to the more intimate response of "I will be with you" as we learn to live in the heart of God.

Preoccupation with ourselves and our inadequacies must give way to a revelation of God as the great "I Am." "I Am" will go with us. "I Am" will be present on the journey. "I Am" will do the work as we stand before people and situations that are bigger and more formidable. The conversion process is designed to lead us away from self-reliance into a more intimate place of surrender to all that God is and can accomplish.

When we are fully converted to God's ways, then we can be commissioned with His authority and power to take the land and enter a new beginning. Conversion means that we no longer get in the way of all that God wants to do and accomplish. We cease to be conscious or unconscious resisters and instead become willing vessels in the hands of a sovereign Lord.

Conversion is concerned with how God changes us from that insecure reaction to a more intimate and faith-filled response. We learn to walk on holy ground. We learn in transition how to walk in the name and nature of God. Challenge promotes conversion to His ways. He will be with us on the whole length of the journey. Sometimes in manifestation, He is clearly revealing Himself. Other times through hiddenness, He is teaching us the walk of faith. We learn that God is always present whether we feel Him or not. Many Christians walk by His presence in their feelings and then switch to faith when they cannot detect Him emotionally. Of course, some believers cannot make the switch because their emotional dependency is too great. Conversion is about walking by faith constantly and only using our emotions as a bonus when they agree with faith. More importantly, it is about discarding emotions when they are not in alignment with the Spirit of God.

Our authority before God, the enemy, and the people will rise up in this time of conversion. Like Moses, we can stand before a powerful and implacable enemy and say, "Thus says the Lord: Let My people go!" (see Ex. 5:1)

When the enemy refuses to capitulate at that point—as he must if God is to eventually destroy him—we must ensure that we can stand the heat that will follow. If athletic medals are gained on the training ground and not on the track, then our authority is gained through our conversion period and not at our commissioning celebration!

Jesus said, "The prince of this world has come, but he has nothing on Me" (see Jn. 14:30). That is because He had gone through His own conversion experience from the carpenter's son to the Messiah in the 40 days of fasting in the wilderness (see Lk. 4:1-14).

When He returned and began His ministry in earnest, people had problems with His identity. "Is this not Joseph's son?" they asked themselves. They could not equate His new message, authority, and power with the Jesus they grew up with.

Transition has particular stages that need to be understood and submitted to in the will of God.

For Him to read Isaiah 61 and then proclaim that it was being fulfilled in Him, divided people in their opinion of Him. Some were amazed at His gracious words; others were filled with rage and drove Him out of the city (see Lk. 4:22,28-29). Something happened in the wilderness that transitioned Him from one type of sonship to another. Conversion is the process where we put the past to rest and take up our new identity. Our past will catch up with us if we do not deal with it at this time. God will allow the devil to come after us (see Ex. 14:10-11) so that we can have a present that is free of our past. Just like Israel trapped between the Egyptian army and the Red Sea, we will always be caught between a rampant enemy and an obstacle to our faith. This is where we give up and go back in an unbelieving lamentation of worry, fear, and doubt; or where we stand still in faith and see the salvation of God (see Ex. 14:13-16).

The dilemma of faith is nothing new. It will return in various guises to enable us to grow spiritually throughout our lives. Conversion is where we put down roots of faith and strengthen the ground of our relationship with God. As we minister, the life of God flows from our root to our branches, producing life and fruit. Left unchecked, we will always transfer our life and experience of God into what we are doing. Pruning is God's way of restoring us to being rooted in our being, not just branching out in our doing. Pruning ends the cycle of growth in productivity and fruitfulness, and begins the process of enlargement by establishing an expanded root system that can support the greater fruitfulness to come.

A lifestyle of constant communion and response to God will produce a consistent and even distribution of change continually throughout our lives. No major surgery is needed once we totally submit to the perpetual and immutable law of life in the Spirit. Constant change is here to stay! We will live by the dynamic spiritual law found in Romans 12:1-2. Constant presentation of our lives before God on a consistent basis will have a continual transforming effect on them, enabling us to live on a higher plane of the Spirit where the will and approval of God are experienced at a deeper level.

Habitual discipline is an attitude of the Spirit. It is a vital part of our walk with the Lord, which aids in making straight paths in our relationship with Him. It is literally to watch every step (see Heb. 12:4-17). Lack of attention to discipline will cause it to be stockpiled in our lives. Discipline never goes away! We can ignore it and disobey through our nonresponse to the Holy Spirit. Noncompliance builds up until eventually we have a deposit large enough to guarantee chastisement from the Lord.

We can stumble over the rock and be broken, or it can fall upon us and crush us (see Mt. 21:44). This implies a choice that we must make before the Lord. Clearly, brokenness is going to be a part of our spiritual experience. We can choose how this happens. Submission to God's dealings releases discipline on a continual basis, which although painful, is releasing and wholesome. A constant series of small alterations is infinitely better than facing one huge change. Continual evolution is better than major revolution. The Spirit must win out over the flesh.

Discipline that is stored up is released as chastisement. God will bring a scourging to us if we make it necessary. The point of discipline is to yield the peaceable fruit of righteousness. Discipline is an exercise in conversion, walking before God in a way that is acceptable to Him.

The conversion phase is where we learn to stand still and see the salvation of God, which He will work in us. There is the promise and provision of total deliverance combining into a message of complete freedom. There is the joy and the hope of a real and lasting authority to overcome all obstructions and bring us to a place of anointed release. We see all these declarations represented in the keynote passage in Exodus 14:13-16:

> *And Moses said to the people, "Do not be afraid. Stand still, and see the salvation of the Lord, which He will accomplish for you today. For the Egyptians whom you see today, you shall see again no more forever. The Lord will fight for you, and you shall hold your peace." And the Lord said to Moses, "Why do you cry to Me? Tell the children of Israel to go forward. But lift up your rod, and stretch out your hand over the sea and divide it. And the children of Israel shall go on dry ground through the midst of the sea."*

This is Moses' prophetic revelation, released to Israel in desperate circumstances. The conversion is the middle ground between closure and a new commissioning as we move toward our inheritance. It is the place of maximum vulnerability and weakness. It is the place of apparent desperation where we learn how to hold on to the Lord and be changed by Him. No conversion to God's nature and purpose means no commissioning to enter in and possess our inheritance. Canaan can be taken only by fighters. Warriors are produced in adversity and are converted to God's ways and character in the process of trial and testing.

Closure is letting go of the past. Conversion is stepping into the process of necessary change and submitting to the Lord. Conversion consists of two elements. Firstly, it is knowing the Lord as the great I AM of our heart and to be still and know His presence. Secondly, it is to learn how to walk in faith, not fear; to stand firm in God and not ourselves; and to be of good courage as we walk forward.

The rod of Moses, which signifies the power of release and freedom, must be lifted over our hearts. We must learn the power of the Spirit working through us as we journey with the Lord.

Egypt was initially a good place for the people of God. It represented salvation. Salvation, however, is not a destination, but a starting place. Jesus is our destination; being filled with all the fullness of Christ is our destiny. He is our inheritance, our Promised Land. There is so much more of our God that we must discover and experience as we are made in His image.

> *Constant change is here to stay!*

Israel outgrew their environment and had to move on. Whatever spiritual development we have made is never enough to allow us to put up tents and camp in one place of experience (see Mt. 17:1-8). Every one of us will outgrow our environment on several occasions before we finally meet the Lord. Our choice is to complain, be fearful, and cling to what we have; or to move forward knowing that the Lord is leading us and guiding us into a new dimension.

What works for us on one part of our journey may work against us later if we are depending upon knowledge and experience rather than relationship and obedience. That is why the Lord gives us transition. It is the transforming power of the transition process that breaks us out into a new experience of God.

The evidence of conversion inherent within transition does not lie in our arrival at some fixed prophetic point, but in our experience of the process and the journey itself. Old mind-sets are not easily forgotten or cast aside. If we do not put them away, they will return to haunt us later. The worst place to live is between memories of the past and an uncertain future. Anxiety and regret can cause us to want to return to the Egypt of what we know, rather than press on to the unknown of Canaan.

The Israelites' story is about real closure on the past, a conversion to the ways and attributes of God, and a commissioning anointing to take up their inheritance and fight. These are the prime goals of transition.

We will have to struggle with our emotions of leaving and cleaving. We have become familiar with Egypt. It suited us once and was the answer to our prayers. Now we must leave it behind. Like Abraham, we find ourselves on a journey not knowing where we are going. We will of necessity feel vulnerable and inadequate. We are learning to rest in God's sufficiency. Trust replaces the frantic need to know. We realize that if God does not speak initially, He always does eventually. We are content to trust in His nature and wait in His presence. We are participating in the conversion process.

This is a critical lesson to learn. Our identity and destiny are being reforged in the desert of our conversion process. When our personal identity is affected strongly, we feel vulnerable and powerless. At this point, we are susceptible to various forms of attack, both human and demonic. We cannot fully answer the questions regarding who we are or where we are going. Our critics have a wonderful time questioning our fitness, our goals, and our ability to achieve anything. We are written off by people who do not understand transition and who will most likely fail their own testing and transition when it arrives. What goes around, comes around.

All we can do is trust the Lord and allow ourselves to be misunderstood. We can talk about the process, but what people want to hear about is the destination, not the journey. The more anxious and inadequate we feel, the more we are open to suggestions. We seek explanation to form a reality map. We are having powerful spiritual experiences at this time, and we believe that these should be backed up by real revelation concerning vision, destiny, and identity. When that is not forthcoming, we can look around anxiously, looking for clues. Taking comfort in the most subjective and nonsensical quasi-spiritual output of other people, we can enter the twilight zone of bizarre Christianity. Trying to justify ourselves to others puts us at risk of missing God altogether. Our souls will fix on little clues here and there. We attempt to put these random occurrences together into a coherent spiritual road map. We cannot tell the difference between an event that has no significance (there are plenty of those in life); a red herring from the enemy designed to distract and disorientate us; and a God-incidence that provides momentum and continuity. We tend to lump everything together and formulate a meaning.

We are being challenged to draw on resources that only recently are being formed within the church. It is a powerful time of being open to new levels of freedom, empowerment, and opportunity. Healing—both spiritual and emotional—is taking place. Transformation is happening. We need objective direction to package everything neatly together. We want to arrive at a destination—*any* destination. After so much hardship, we want the sense of accomplishment that comes with achieving a goal. We forget that our goal is always God; for where He is, we are! The Lord may keep us in a state of weakness and vulnerability for a while longer. The *real* breakthrough comes when we find contentment in Him alone. We do not need justifications to explain our lack of direction. We no longer require a destination, a fixed point of arrival, a compass heading. We point the ship into the wind of the Holy Spirit and sail before Him...trusting, worshiping, and allowing Him to call out the course corrections as we go.

Of course, eventually our horizon will be made clear. Our identity and vision will unfold. Doors will open and miracles of deployment, logistical support, and distribution will take place. We settle into a new routine that delivers faith at a higher dimension of being. We have learned to relax, to be at peace and trust. Control has devolved from our hands to His. We are simply glad to be included in Him. Our leaders become facilitators and fathers. We see ourselves with new eyes of perspective. We learn to look beyond the natural into the supernatural realm. We can give an answer for the hope that is in us. It will not come in the form of an agreed vision or defined destination—not yet. That comes later. Our hope is in a Person.

We are a little like the disciples on the road to Emmaus. Something momentous is happening, but we cannot put our finger on what exactly it is. Our hearts are burning within us. Things are being explained, but the revelation has not yet penetrated. We are unconsciously waiting for that point of grace to arrive when our eyes will be opened and we will know as God knows. We are journeying with God, but He is hidden among us. God always works through either hiddenness or manifestation. Times of revealing are in His hands. He is faithful. As we trust and journey, our eyes will become open. We will be able to answer the questions and challenges of others.

We have not embarrassed ourselves by trying to give answers that the Lord has not given. We have merely suffered the rejection and ill humor of people who require evidence before they acquire faith.

Every spiritual environment created within the church will be outgrown as we move forward in the Holy Spirit.

Learn to wait on the Lord. Patiently set aside your own thoughts and emotional needs. It is here, when the worst has passed, that a person is at his most vulnerable. You can lose the race within sight of the tape. Do not undo all the hard work of submitting soul to spirit by giving in to the overwhelming desire for identity and direction—just be! Live in Him. Trust in Him. Put your energy into trust and worship. Don't ruin your progress by insisting on details of destiny. They will unfold when He is ready. Do not speak too soon. Stay in tune.

Perspective grows as we look at the Lord. Our hearts must burn within us before true understanding can take place. What is hidden is revealed as we journey and break bread in relationship with the Lord. Such intimate fellowship is always followed by revelation.

There is always a season of emptiness before fulfillment. Do not fill that void with your own attempts at truth and direction. They will become distractions. The best growth occurs when we let go. Lack of release inhibits re-creation. When things are without form and void, trust in the brooding presence of the Holy Spirit and wait (see Gen. 1:2). Creation is preceded by emptiness. See the emptiness as a womb. What is deposited initially is in seed form. Do not look at the seed and try to formulate a description of the life it contains; nurture the process of development, and life will come full term.

Formation releases revelation as we learn to embrace God fully in everything that happens. Enter fully into all that the Lord is doing and become occupied with Him, not just the recent events.

The valley is no place for making decisions. Wait until emotions stabilize before considering long-term vision and goals. In the conversion stage, many things will become different. People will change. The person who makes decisions at the beginning of the process might not be the same person who has to live with it, after transition!

There are no shortcuts to real spiritual growth. If we concentrate on running with patience, then the Lord will give us a divine acceleration at the right time. The more patient we are, the faster God moves. The more impatient we are, the more He slows things down! We cannot rush process or force transition to happen quicker than God wills. To everything there is a season.

Learn to express trust in prayer. Keeping short accounts and enjoying regular feedback on where we are in transition is a positive response to the process. Trusting the Lord and not leaning on our own understanding will enable us to recognize the opportunity when it arises. Perspective is seen best through the eyes of Jesus.

Keeping a journal of events in the church as we go through transition is wise. A written record will be invaluable to us later on. We can chronicle our dreams, prophetic input, our learning curve, and various insights, prayers, and experiences.

Taking time to redevelop existing friendships as well as finding new relationships will anchor our hearts into the nature of God. There will be lots of signposts and markers that will explain our journey in terms of where we have been, where we are now, and where we are moving toward for the future.

It is important to note the seasons of the soul—the time when something dies and something is reborn. Constantly becoming a new creation is a vital part of our continued spiritual growth and development.

Receive Desert Training

When we surrender to the process of change, we discover the unchangeable nature of God; thus, our confidence and security in Him grows. This stage of conversion is also about undergoing desert training. Israel was prepared for battle during the 40 years of their conversion period. Deserts do not normally last this long. Remember that the Israelites' story is a national perspective, not a local church one. In local church, we are dealing with far fewer people, so the transition has a different focus.

Nations can and do go through long seasons of development and difficulty. In the church, we experience a more localized form of transition that may or may not be linked to the national Church scene.

Moses was the only one among the Israelites with any desert training. Prophets and pioneers always go through things ahead of time on behalf of themselves and the wider company of people. It was in his own exile that Moses developed his personal inner resources to learn how to live in a hostile environment. Our personal inner resources before God are then used by Him to develop the corporate inner resources of the company of people traveling with us.

The enemy is dealt with in closure. "The Egyptians whom you see today, you shall see again no more forever." In the conversion period, we must deal with the inner life of the church. People grumble and complain in the wilderness because they have no desert training, a poor relationship with God, and little trust in leadership. Moses represents the indwelling Christ in touch with the Holy Spirit. We must learn to live with and serve "the great I Am."

We all have an "I Am" within us. We must learn to rest in the finished work of Christ and relax in His goodness. The desert is

> *A vision of God must take precedence over a vision for my life.*

about dealing with crisis. We must learn to stop complaining and develop a new covenant in the promises and intervention of God.

The conversion stage involves a crisis situation, an opportunity to react or respond, a direct intervention by the Lord, and the establishment of a covenant for Israel or a black mark through a failed test. Israel's first test occurred almost immediately after their famous victory at the Red Sea in Exodus 14–15. After closure, they were led into conversion in the form of the wilderness of Shur. The eventual water, when they found it, was bitter. They grumbled and complained. Moses responded to the Lord. God directly intervened and made the water sweet. Exodus 15:25 says, "There He made a statute and an ordinance for them, and there He tested them."

We are tested by the principles of God. The pattern for testing was set thus:

1. Crisis situation.
2. Opportunity to react and complain or respond and believe.
3. A direct intervention of God that produced breakthrough.
4. The establishing of a covenant or the earning of a demerit through failure to pass the test.

In desert training, God will give the church a whole series of tests to prepare, train, and then equip them to take the land. Our capacity to convert to the ways of God has a direct implication on whether He can trust us with our real destiny and inheritance.

Israel misunderstood the process of transition. They failed at the conversion stage and did not inherit all that God wanted to give them. They failed the tests that God set to train them. In doing so, they tested God's desire to fulfill His purpose over their lives.

Initial belief in the prophetic word (see Ex. 4:29-31) turned to unbelief and grumbling after Pharaoh had increased their workload (see Ex. 5:20-21).

Complainers and grumblers 1 — Covenant keepers 0

The joy of deliverance from Egypt turned sour as they complained by the sea when Pharaoh marched after them (see Ex. 14:10-14).

Complainers and grumblers 2 — Covenant keepers 0

The joy of victory over Egypt and their triumphant marching and singing gave way to resentment and grumbling at the waters of Marah (see Ex. 15:22-27).

Complainers and grumblers 3 — Covenant keepers 0

Each time, they never learned anything positive from the wonderful direct interventions of God. Crisis found them reverting to type, behaving in the flesh and not living by the Spirit. Conversion from slavery to desert warriors was clearly not working.

The grumble about lack of food (see Ex. 16:1-4) came on the back of God's provision for water. They learned nothing of God's heart and responsibility toward them.

Complainers and grumblers 4 — Covenant keepers 0

The Lord was even gracious enough to repeat an earlier test involving the provision of water. Tests that we fail are repeated until we pass or disqualify ourselves.

Moses had to strike the rock to cause Israel to see and know that God was intervening to bring provision (see Ex. 17:1-7).

Complainers and grumblers 5 — Covenant keepers 0

When Moses had not returned from the mountain, the people reverted to type as they had been taught in bondage (see Ex. 32:1-10). Despite the plagues in Egypt, the evidence of God's power and deliverance; the crushing of the enemy by the Red Sea; and the constant provision and intervention of God; Israel was not prepared to keep the covenant. Even God's words at Marah to hear and obey His voice went unheeded (see Ex. 15:25-26).

They failed to give earnest consideration to God's voice and to doing what was right. This is the reason for the desert place and the necessary time of conversion.

6 - 0 to the complainers and grumblers!

Despite the building of the tabernacle and the cloud of God's glory and presence being manifested to all the nation, Israel continued to grumble and exhibit unbelief. The Lord sent a fire into the camp to consume some of them, yet they still continued to complain about the food (see Num. 11:1-8).

Complainers and grumblers 7 — Thankful and grateful people 0

Even the leaders in the work were infected by the continuous grumbling and complaining of the people. Walking in the Spirit is always about creating environments that are faith-filled and positive toward the Lord. The devil is the prince of the power of the air. He lives in the atmosphere. Our attitude must displace environmentally unfriendly atmospheres that detract from the Spirit. Miriam and Aaron both succumbed to a critical spirit among the people. They also were plainly jealous of the standing that Moses enjoyed before the Lord (see Num. 12). They murmured against Moses before the people and only understood how foolish that was when it was too late.

Murmurers 8 — Faithful people 0

> *We are tested by the principles of God.*

The spies who gave a bad report filled with unbelief provoked another bout of murmuring. As we continue through conversion toward commission, there will be those who have no vision for where we are going. They will accurately diagnose the difficulties ahead but will fail abysmally to incorporate any faith-filled perspective. Their unbelief will drown out the few prophetic positive voices, which leads to another crisis situation (see Num. 13:25—14:3).

9 - 0 to the unbelievers in the midst!

Their final act of unbelief and final testing of God's patience occurred when they wanted to appoint a new leader so they could return to Egypt (see Num. 14:4-12). Once again their reaction was to stone the faithful rather than to repent of their unbelief. The Lord's response to Moses' gallant attempt at intercession was to deny this unbelieving people access to a place of inheritance (see Num. 14:22-24).

When we fail our tests, we unconsciously test the Lord. At some point, our continued failure and bad attitude will disqualify us from the next stage of the moving of God. We must learn to develop the inner man, the "I Am" of the inner Christ. The wilderness helps to scour our lives of the effects and influence of the past and helps us to find fresh faith to walk with the Lord. The correct pattern to establish in transition is thus:

- a crisis situation
- leading to a positive response to the Lord
- followed by His direct intervention
- which results in the establishing of a covenant relationship that honors His name.

In New Testament language, it is establishing the pattern of Ephesians 4:22-24:

That you put off, concerning your former conduct, the old man which grows corrupt according to the deceitful lusts, and be renewed in the spirit of your mind, and that you put on the new man which was created according to God, in true righteousness and holiness.

Constant miracles did not prevent Israel's disinheritance. They were guided by a cloud during daytime and a pillar of fire at night. God's provision faithfully followed them. They won battles they should have lost. But they never outgrew their unbelief or the slavery attitude of complaining and murmuring. They were not prepared to stand up and grow up. They were not ready to give up their old ways and practices. When left to their own devices, they congregated around a symbol of their bondage: the golden calf.

In the desert and conversion period, our capacity to sin has to suffer a meltdown! We must make decisions to move away from the old into the new. The inner work of the Spirit must take priority in our thinking, acting, and communication.

Desert training is about preparation. The number 40 in the Bible generally refers to a period of preparation. In conversion, we receive time to prepare. Crisis situations are sent to prepare us as a church. Old attitudes have to die, and new ones have to form. It takes as long to happen as our obedience takes to grow.

In the conversion period, one of our prime assets is the faithfulness of core people in the church. Israel believed in the Lord *and* Moses, His servant (see Ex. 14:30-31). Sadly, their initial confidence was not strengthened by the crisis (which was the intention), but weakened.

Many people imagine that we move straight from the old into the new. This is not the case. We must be converted to the new place by testing; otherwise, we may encounter what appears to be a new place before we are actually ready for it.

The period of conversion between closure and commissioning is a vital time of preparation and growth where we shake off everything that would hold us back. We learn obedience, trust, and how to make positive responses to God in the place of adversity. Without this period, we do not gain the spiritual dimension necessary to receive anointing and power for the warfare of inheritance that is to be accomplished. In conversion, we learn to walk with the Lord in humility, depending upon Him for His provision and power.

When we can receive blessing in adversity and be faithful to God in times of crisis, then we are ready for the violent confrontation of entering our inheritance. The conversion period builds up immunity to adversity in our system. We learn how to stand and walk with the Lord. It is our training and proving ground where we develop the response necessary to please the Lord.

Adversity always follows breakthrough. Real breakthroughs have two elements. There is a breaking out and a breaking in. It was one thing to break out of Egypt, but an entirely different scenario to break in to Canaan. The period of conversion is situated between these two points in order to ratify the first and prepare us for the second, which is breakthrough. The initial release and blessing of transition will give way to necessary adversity as we are trained for battle. Abram had trained men, born in his house—318 of them—to pursue the men who had captured his nephew Lot (see Gen. 14:14).

> *The conversion period enables us to outgrow old habits, traditions, and customs.*

In conversion, the Lord trains our hands for war and teaches our fingers to fight (see Ps. 144:1). Only when we have stood our ground and learned the appropriate lessons will we be ready for the commissioning that follows the successful completion of training.

Stage 3: The Commissioning

It is vital that we complete the work of the previous stages before we think about entering the land.

The commission begins with the internal work of preparation as we change through closure and conversion. We must come to a new place of readiness to fight. The church must confess the warlike spirit that will be required to enter into the next stage of transition.

We will never be 100 percent ready for battle, but our hearts must be awakened to the need to fight. Our churches must produce warriors. If they don't, our inheritance will be unrealized. Leaders must be aware of the potential of their people. To take a nation, we need the modern-day equivalent of David's mighty men of valor (see 2 Sam. 23; 1 Chron. 11).

Josheb-Basshebeth killed 800 at one time. Eleazar stood his ground against the Philistines and defied them when all of Israel ran away. He fought himself to a standstill, his sword stuck to his hand, presumably with blood. Israel returned to plunder the spoil from his victory. Shammah defended his own piece of ground and won a great victory. We need people who will not run when the going gets tough.

Abishai killed 300 men with a spear. Benaiah killed two huge men from Moab and a lion in a pit on a snowy day! He also killed a spectacular Egyptian giant with his own spear. These men were fearless warriors who could be counted on when the battle was hot and fierce. Are we producing people capable of doing exploits for God?

These men were ready to fight. They understood what it took to take a nation. We need people who possess great internal awareness of God and who understand the battle that is to come. Like Gideon's army of 300, representing less than one percent of the original number, we need people who are alert and watchful. Choose such people and develop them. Empowerment should follow the recognition of such internal awareness and readiness to fight.

Our desert training will equip and empower people. Our hands-on development will cause us to fast track the people who stand up well under pressure. Leaders are not here to take pressure off the people; neither are they present to cause pressure to come. They simply recognize that obedience results in pressure, and they use the stress to develop the anointing in people. Where the stress is, the anointing is present. We look to see on whom the anointing is resting. We mentor such people, so that they can go from strength to strength.

In corporate transition, we are observing how people handle themselves personally. We also watch their capacity for teamwork alongside like-minded others. Our personal transition will have benefits and healthy repercussions for people around our lives as we learn to live under the hand of the Lord. Needless to say, our failures here contribute to the downward spiral and potential demise of the corporate work. There are four types of attitude within the church, symbolized by well-known mathematical marks. There are people who add (+) something to us by their obedience and love for God. There are people who multiply (x) faith and anointing by the passion in their lives. There are people who take away (-) from the faith environment because they are negative or always taking and never giving. Then there are the people who are divisive (÷) because of unredeemed aspects of their own character and personality.

Battle may come upon us unexpectedly, but we will have people readily adaptable to any current situation—people who can make a good response in tough times. We must develop people who can rise to a challenge and overcome whatever obstacle presents itself.

In commissioning, the Holy Spirit releases new vision to us that reveals our destiny and sense of direction. We need people who have strong desires for God. We must have people who have a will to inherit, no matter what the cost. Israel had that type of people in the tribe of Gad. They had seen the land that they wanted. Their desire to inhabit and possess the land was strong. They came and asked for their inheritance to be given to them (see Num. 32). They also had a sense of responsibility to bring the rest of Israel into their own inheritance. When challenged about their motives by Moses, they were able to convince him that they were not merely being selfish. They volunteered to pass over Jordan and be first into the fight.

They had a love and responsibility for the rest of the people, which manifested in their attitude: "We will not return to our homes until every one of the children of Israel has received his inheritance" (Num. 32:18).

There are people in our churches now who have this same unselfish spirit. Our people need mentoring so that they can determine their own inheritance before the Lord. Then they need the added example of our leadership to enable them to serve others as we enter new territory as a church.

Only as we fight corporately can individuals come into their own inheritance and possess what the Lord has set aside for them personally. If we develop people individually, without the corporate context, we will not take ground. We will probably lose anointed individuals who become involved with their own ministry rather than being a catalyst for the joint work of the whole body.

People should be encouraged to determine their personal burden and vision. They also need strategy and resourcing to

> *Crisis situations are sent to prepare us for the next dimension of the Spirit.*

enable them to determine where their lives and ministries fit with and alongside others in a church. As we pull together, we develop one another. Part of this determining our vision will come through involvement in the work. To find such guidance, the Holy Spirit will usually put us to work. In the process of serving and working together, we become more clear about ministry and goals.

There is a point where the personal must surrender to the corporate. There is a place too where people must be encouraged to see where they fit in and relate to the whole church. It is a mutual partnership based on love and respect. It is an ever-changing, constantly adjusting working relationship based on an unchanging friendship of love and trust. It is a paradox that works. We learn to let go and surrender ourselves to the Lord and one another out of mutual love and respect. We look out for the interests of others and not merely for ourselves. In love, we esteem others as more important as we follow the example of Jesus (see Phil. 2:1-8).

There is a place in ministry where there is no clash between personal and corporate anointing. It is on the altar of humility and meekness that we surrender our lives to a calling higher than the personal. Many churches will not develop a corporate anointing because there is little or no example of surrender and unselfishness being handed down throughout the work. We get what we model.

We are in partnership with God and with one another. Transition represents death to personal ambition but release to a surrendered personal anointing that seeks to combine itself with significant others. When soul submits to spirit, we are happy and healthy.

When we seek to preserve our personal anointing and exchange churches, we can still end up with similar relationships. Selfishness is only undone by surrender. It may not necessarily change in better company! We can divorce, remarry, and make the same mistakes. Having two left feet on the dance floor will not be affected by a change in partners! Something fundamental in how we perceive ourselves in relation to others must be radically altered if we are to become an asset and not a continuous liability.

The quality of our surrender determines the anointing in the ministry. The Father only commits to what He sees of Jesus being manifested in His people. The issue is one of trust, not necessarily of ability. Does God trust us? At the very least, our prayer must be that God would trust us enough to release His power and anointing in overcoming proportions. If the stages of closure and conversion have gone well, this question will be already partially answered in a positive manner.

If we have not responded fully to all that the Lord is seeking to do internally, then we do not have a new beginning, but merely a change of location. The power and authority of the commission comes from the Lord Jesus. The ability to enter in and the capacity to move in fullness within this authority comes only from a heart radically changed and surrendered. In England, we determine a person's maturity by the amount of opposition it takes to discourage them. People must grow up spiritually into a place of surrender and rest before God. Being occupied with Jesus is a prerequisite for becoming a champion of God on the battlefield of life and church.

If we are not planning full repentance and surrender to the Lord, if we are not opening our hearts and lives up to the love and scrutiny of significant others, then we cannot have a new starting point. The power of a new beginning will elude us. Our attempts to start over will be revealed as artificial and ultimately bogus. We cannot fake a new beginning. Lack of real surrender will reveal the pretense. Our power to fully embrace the commission that God wants for us is diminished or enhanced by the quality of our internal response. External change without internal redevelopment is not a new beginning. It is rearranging the furniture in the same house. As my Texan friends say, "Same meat, different gravy!"

We must learn to live in the present moment with the Lord Jesus. Abide in His presence and allow the Holy Spirit to complete the inner work. The desert is always about finding the Lord and ultimately finding ourselves in Him. In the desert, we learn the clean, pure, fresh joy of the Lord in all things. He is so incredibly happy in Himself, and He seeks to impart to us this sense of delight in everything. He trains not only our hands for war, but also our eyes to see beyond the natural into the spirit realm. He teaches us how to behold Him. Jacob said, "Surely the Lord is in this place, and I did not know it" (Gen. 28:16b).

Life in the spirit is about learning to see the signs of God's presence everywhere we look. He is present to the moment with us. If we are unhappy in the desert, we will not be happy invading Canaan. The desert is about the joy of just being! It is not about doing. It is falling back into the everlasting arms and resting in Him. It is preoccupation with the person of Jesus—receiving His joy, learning how to overflow in His grace, being filled with the love of God.

> *The power of corporate anointing is established on the altar of personal ministry.*

In the presence of God we learn gratitude and thanksgiving. He does not give us what we deserve. His mercy and loving-kindness bestow upon us blessing that breaks our hearts with appreciation. He is the kindest person I have ever known. I have lost count of the number of times I have been ignorant and stupid. I have blighted my life with sinfulness and hard-hearted responses. My arrogance has been a stink in His nose. My deceitfulness has been shameful.

Yet, He has broken my heart with His kindness. I have stood flinching in His presence and He has loved me. I have felt His arms around me tenderly when I should have felt the rod on my back. When I could not bear His presence or the company of His people and cast myself away, He would turn up in my life and take hold of me. With great patience and loving-kindness He would bless me, draw me into His presence, and teach me to stay. He taught me to have pleasure in abiding and resting...to be touched only by Him...to not be moved by circumstances, but to rest and respond to what I eventually saw Him doing. He taught me simply to wait until He spoke or created, and then to flow with Him.

He taught me that there were no good days and no bad days, only days of grace. Some days the grace of God allowed me to enjoy what was happening. On other days I learned, in His grace, how to endure circumstances and people with a peaceful heart. On the days of mixture, I learned how to rejoice fully in good news and how to respond to Him gratefully through bad tidings. He is all in all—Alpha and Omega—the first, the last, and everything in between.

In the desert, we live present to the moment with God. We learn patience. We do not rush to get to where we want to go. We revel in the journey because the presence of God is the prize. Our high calling is to know Him as we travel through whatever circumstances we face.

The Lord Jesus has ways of surprising us. He creates out of apparent nothingness. Big events that seem to carry great portent, yield nothing, while innocuous circumstances turn out to be of momentous consequence. Then, just as we have figured out His way and pattern, He does the opposite to lovingly, and with great merriment, teach us that there is no substitute to a true walk of childlike faith and simplicity.

God loves a paradox and will always show us the other side of the coin so that we stay continually aware that life and indeed the universe were created to be extremes held together in tension. This is the reason why preparation, readiness, trust, and obedience are so significant in our relationship with the Lord.

Commitment to Change

Constant change is here to stay as we love and follow the Lord. Never focus on change as an end in itself. Learn to look into the face of God and be guided by the light of His presence. Make it a goal to live each day under His smile. Being with God is a continuous challenge to our soul but a great delight to our spirit. The soul resents change. The spirit revels in the closeness of God and will do anything to abide.

As the commission takes hold of us, commitment is required from our hearts. This is best made from our innermost being, not the outer man of the soul. Commitment requires trust, discipline, obedience, and sacrifice.

In the natural, we know that to be good at anything requires a responsibility to train properly and a commitment to operate at the highest level of our ability. Anything less will reduce our achievement and sense of fulfillment. There is a personal loss when we do not fulfill our potential. There is a corporate loss when we do not contribute to the church our real abilities. Everyone suffers when we accept mediocrity.

Commitment is part of our commissioning. Commitment to servanthood and stewardship within the church is to accept that we will not look out for our own needs only, but also for those of others with whom we are in fellowship. Like Gad, we not only possess our own inheritance, but we move out corporately to enable others to possess territory also.

One of the intriguing elements of accepting the commission of God is to face the possibility of failure. We risk ourselves in order to bless and release other people. We often will not know how a particular enterprise will turn out as we contemplate a beginning. That is why faith is an adventure that carries risk and danger. There will always be some twists in the plot as we pursue the call of God.

People of lesser faith will stand and watch. People of fear will criticize. There will be times of mockery as we hit that place where the path twists away from the goal and we appear set fair for failure. People reject us and our vision at this point, as we hit the swamp of negative circumstances. Where the stress is, the anointing is present. It is only in the middle of the problem that the real provision becomes available. If we bail out of the venture before we actually hit the problem, we will never realize the providence of God. Every problem comes complete with its own provision. Commitment keeps us on track, believing in God's ability as the swamp of negativity slows down our progress.

Incredibly, we discover that, as we continue, it is the shedding of unbelieving people that creates the buoyancy that enables us to progress more quickly through difficult terrain. Removing the dead wood of fear and self-preservation creates a lightness of spirit that takes us through and beyond into the place of promise and fulfillment.

If we are living in that external place of the soul, the circumstances will fill our vision and can lead us to a place of bankrupt faith. However, if we face the challenges of our commission from the internal hiding place of the spirit-man, God Himself will be the object of our attention.

The soul (like Martha) interacts with our world and is painfully aware of the challenge and the risk. Our spirit (like Mary) has chosen the good part of resting at His feet and is fully occupied with Jesus. We choose where we live. Are you anxious and burdened, or waiting and restful?

> *Real spirituality arises out of being present to the moment with God.*

We all have a spiritual Canaan to conquer and an inheritance to possess. The art of overcoming begins internally. We must learn the way of the warrior—how to overcome fear, weakness, unbelief, and lack of commitment.

Israel accepted their commissioning and pressed into the land of promise. They were desert-trained by Moses but took possession of Canaan under Joshua. Both men are symbolic of a type of Christ, the One who brings us out in order to take us in.

Crisis and process go together and form the pathway of transition. Every new level reveals a new devil. Of necessity, the devil we are about to meet in this new dimension must be bigger than the church we represent. It does not matter what we defeat on the previous level and use as a footstool to climb into this new place. When we enter the new level of anointing, we once again become like David in the presence of a new Goliath. The bigger and stronger the opposition is, the greater our capacity to grow and put on Jesus. The more powerful the forces against us are, the stronger the anointing will be released within us. A powerful enemy only serves to release the more compelling majesty of the Lord Jesus. Hostile resistance is overcome only by God's sovereign rule within our own hearts.

The Caleb anointing is needed to quiet people's fears, with its declaration: "Let us go up at once and take possession, for we are well able to overcome it" (Num. 13:30b).

We also need a Joshua spirit to declare this:

> ..."*The land we passed through to spy out is an exceedingly good land. If the Lord delights in us, then He will bring us into this land and give it to us, 'a land which flows with milk and honey.' Only do not rebel against the Lord, nor fear the people of the land, for they are our bread; their protection has departed from them, and the Lord is with us. Do not fear them*" (Numbers 14:7-9).

Problems emerge at every new level of power that the Lord releases to us. Our resources are fully challenged, people leave, and finances diminish. Fear surfaces as we look at circumstances. The desert trains us to look at God. Desert-trained people have gone through inward conversion to the mind and ways of God. Problems become catalysts that quicken us in the spirit. Canaan is God's territory; it was already won in His heart when He released the promise of it as Israel's inheritance. "Their protection has departed from them, and the Lord is with us" is the cry of a man under commission and longing to press in.

Awareness of God is the key to unlocking the crisis. We see the Holy Spirit as the architect of events as God's plan and purpose unfold. He will show Himself mighty on our behalf. Desert people have learned to look beyond the natural to see the hand of God at work. The people who gathered in God's supply of food also will partake of His provision of power to overcome. Those who have been clothed by God's indestructible apparel also will be cloaked in His formidable appetite for battle. The provision received and enjoyed in the desert becomes a symbol of all that God releases for the conquest of Canaan.

Transition is the journey from conflict, pain, tension, fear, risk of failure, and rejection to a place of inner peace and tranquillity. Our destination in transition is the very heartbeat of God—to be released in His calm assurances, faith, and the will to press in and lay hold of the inner territory of the Spirit. A Canaan is within us: It is Jesus, the high calling and ultimate prize of God.

In the desert we learn to become watchful and ready. Crisis precedes process, which is the journey of inner change to a place of transformation. We are being made in the image of Jesus as we travel with Him. We must understand also that we cannot make new decisions regarding our future if we do not get on the road of transition. The crisis allowed by God to provoke us to move out is given for a specific reason. It is the critical turning point of our life.

If we do not move, it is because we are rooted in our old mind-sets and paradigms. It is only as we journey with the Lord that the landscape of our thinking and awareness begins to change. We learn to adjust to a different spiritual terrain as we travel. We suspend our previous way of thinking as we learn this new road. We learn how to respond in a new way. Like Abraham, we do not know where we are going, but we recognize that we are on a journey of discovery. Before we commenced the journey, everything frightened us. We had more concerns, reservations, and doubts than positive faith. Now that we are traveling with God, we are excited about this journey of discovery. We are leaving the old ways and entering a new path.

Change often appears chaotic. As we look for the hand of God, we see the bigger picture as well as some of the finer detail of His handiwork. A crisis has the potential to be a turning point or a catastrophe, depending upon our awareness of God and our inner perspective in transformation.

If we do not physically and spiritually set foot on the road, nothing will change. We may understand something of the process, but if we do not surrender to God, we will go nowhere. We will simply settle for map reading instead of taking the journey, which is like going to the finest restaurant and only reading the menu without tasting the food!

God Is the Goal of Transition

In transition, the dominant need in the hearts of the people is for revelation. They want direction, vision, and a sense of purpose. If they know where they are going, they may be able to understand the reasons why certain things are happening. On the surface, this

> *To overcome,*
> *we must*
> *learn*
> *the way*
> *of the*
> *warrior.*

seems fair and appropriate. Yet there are times when the Lord does not work that way. He is in sole charge of how and when our circumstances receive explanation. There are times when God will insist on trust being established before intellect is rewarded (see Prov. 3:5-6). However, in transition situations, He has another goal. Initially, He will not give us revelation, but comfort.

He wants us to embrace our relationship with Him and go deeper to a whole new level of submission and trust. Eventually, revelation will come to us in the form of vision, direction, and purpose. Prior to that happening, God will give us Himself. Moses asked for a revelation, an explanation of who was sending him to rescue Israel. All he received was a cryptic "Tell them, I Am has sent you" (see Ex. 3:14).

God gives Himself to us, so that we might receive Him fully. We learn to rest in Him and express our love and trust in acts of worship, peace, and prayer. In doing this, the Lord sends out a signal that relationship with us is His highest goal, that understanding and practice must permeate the church. In transition, we must major on our relationship with God and our friendships with one another. God is promoting a greater love among His people.

Revelation will always follow people who make the first two commandments a priority. On these two commands hang all the revelation centered around the words of the law and prophets (see Mt. 22:40). People are comforted by revelation, the knowledge of how and why things occur. God wants us to be comforted by His presence. Only then will He give us the greater wisdom to perceive the nature and purpose of life events.

We will never fear change if our spirit-man is living in the changeless core of the nature of God. Transition will enable us to decide the place from where we will live and move and have our being. If we choose an external perspective, we will be subject to all the influences on that level of awareness.

But if we choose the inward path of the spirit, we become subject to all our internal reflections of the Person of Jesus. He dominates our perspective by His Person, by His peaceful and tranquil spirit, by His calm thoughtfulness and assured confident manner. God will shake everything that can be shaken so that our assurance and confidence is in Him alone. The external storms of life become the internal rest that rocks us to sleep in the arms of God.

Lying back in the everlasting arms is an act of peaceful surrender to God and all His ways. We feel everything through Him so that our response is grounded in real tranquillity. One of my personal goals is to be a peaceful man with a tranquillity of spirit that creates rest and peace for people around me. That calmness of spirit comes only from an awareness of, and the surrender to, a loving God.

Letting go and letting God have His way is a prerequisite for internal change. Allowing His perspective to change our mind-sets means that we will learn His thoughts and His ways. Transformation is about internal surrender to the will of God. This may lead us to be misunderstood, rejected, or even abused by other people. That is not our concern. Becoming God-conscious is the best way to help the people around us.

Initially, they may not understand us. We may well be rejected at first. However, as we are faithful to the journey the Lord sets before us, He will give us the right traveling companions. This is a painful part of the process—the leaving and cleaving. Some relationships are broken for a season as we cleave to God. New friendships form as we move on.

It is not callous to leave others behind as we continue to journey along a path they do not understand. Primarily, we are each responsible for our own journey, to faithfully and obediently follow Jesus in complete surrender. Tears are a part of transition. God has to be the goal. If we put our earthly friendships ahead of our heavenly surrender to the Lord, we will automatically damage our current relationships. We create a hole, a space for the enemy to exploit. Our disobedience will open an eventual rift that potentially will damage the very friendship we prize higher than our relationship with God.

However, it is as we surrender to God in our distress and tears over the people whom we are losing, that His love and grace comfort all people concerned. It may be that others will have a change of heart and travel with us. It may be that our parting will be sorrowful but not bitter. It may be that our paths will reconnect further down the line. All these things are in the hands of a loving Father. As we give ourselves to Him in complete abandonment, we also surrender into His care everything and everyone we love.

We are surrendering our attachments on every level to our desire and attachment for God. Many people try to make deals with God in this place. They believe that if this is really God, then everyone else will see it and want to come along. This is simply not true. If we make such demands on God, we are attempting to orchestrate His will, not surrender to it. This is a point of unconscious resistance that leads to an obstruction of faith.

Transition takes us through a paradox. Cleaving to God may necessitate leaving other people. People become confused at times like this because they do not fully understand the transitional paradox they are in. They are so used to the present paradigm that they have difficulty focusing on a different train of thought. People often say, "We have practiced this, and now you want us to do the opposite. Where does this new thing fit in with what we know?"

Probably the answer is that it does not fit. It is not meant to fit. Life is not a jigsaw puzzle where all the pieces fit together to form a picture. Jesus said, "You have heard that it was said...but I say to you" (Mt. 5:21-22). His new words brought a deeper level of insight into the life of the people.

Church is a paradox. We are told that the Church is a building and a city. Yet at the same time, it is a family and an army. How can the Church be

> *In transition God precedes revelation with comfort.*

a building, which is rigid and inflexible, yet at the same time be a body, which is fluid and constantly moving? The answer is, of course, that the Church is both. They are extremes that we seek to live within and hold in tension through our relationships.

The building represents the "being" aspect of our relationship, whilst the body represents the "doing" aspect of our ministry. Our relationships should be filled with non-negotiable love for one another. No matter what difficulties and differences occur, we are to be rigid and inflexible in our love for one another. We will not be moved away from the goal of loving, caring, and honoring one another.

The body represents our ministry, which is full of challenge, vision, faith, risk, action, warfare activity, and stress. Tension comes when we relate together on the basis of our doing things together, not on the foundation of our being together in Christ. The building takes precedence over the body. Just as our physical body goes out of the house to work each morning, so the spiritual body comes out of the house of the Lord to minister.

Real balance is living within the spiritual paradox that God creates around us by His presence! It is holding on to both extremes in the peace of God. The way to find life is to lose it, which is a paradox. The way to receive is to give. Show me your faith by your works. If we embrace both, we will have both.

Transition takes us through a paradox, a tension of extremes that must be understood and practiced. Resistance will occur if we put God second. Sometimes it is only in surrender that we catch sight of the paradox and our understanding begins to form. Resistance inhibits revelation. Surrender broadens and deepens our revelatory rationale. Renewal of the mind overcomes resistance. In the tension of transition, do not enter into personal judgments about others. Practice the surrendering of your thoughts. Take them captive to the Spirit of God. Release only the good thoughts; imprison the rest (see 2 Cor. 10:3-6).

As we allow God to search us and know us, we begin to see the strongholds of refusal to let go and surrender. Only by holding firmly to trust can we demolish every obstacle and break through into a new paradigm. If God is our goal, then our comfort is found in Him alone. Many people focus on how they feel about change and resist it for that reason. They are made uncomfortable. Initially, change is not about comfort but about surrender and obedience. Comfort occurs eventually as we make the required adjustment. If being comfortable is our goal, we cannot change. It is best for us if we make our surrender a constant experience and not merely an occasional one. If we make God our goal, then constant change and surrender is a life issue before Him, and His comfort flows continuously in our lives. Comfort and change can flow together if we live in constant surrender.

Trust the goodness of God. If He is our goal, we will more easily become partakers of His divine nature (see 2 Pet. 1:4). Surrender releases faith, peace, and confidence in the ability of God. Resistance increases tension, fear, and judgments. It is the opposite of surrender. This is where our mind needs retraining.

Lack of surrender to God diminishes our capacity to renew our thought-life. Our responses therefore become conditional to our current experience and mind-set. If God is the goal of our life, then our thinking becomes prophetic. A visionary aspect enters our thought-life, making us look ahead in anticipation. We develop the ability to look backwards and forwards, bringing events of the past and vision for the future into the present day, helping us to make sense of where we are now!

The process of transition is made up of closure, conversion, and commission. Closure to the past brings release and new freedom. A conversion through our desert training remolds our thinking and practice into the mind and ways of God. This is followed and completed by a new commission as the Lord releases the authority, power, and anointing to take the promised land of our inheritance.

> *The true Church is a paradox,*
> *a contradiction to the world,*
> *an oddity, a puzzle...the enigma of God.*

Chapter 10

Character and Transition

Part 1

*I*t is so exciting to walk with God, especially through these days of obvious change. Prayers we have prayed are finding answers. Dreams and aspirations are coming alive in our midst. I have never known a time, in all my walk with the Lord, when His presence has been so profound and tangible. His love, kindness, mercy, and generosity are everywhere, it seems.

To be able to express love for God in worship is a great honor. The love and affection of Jesus for His Bride is enormous. To be able to reciprocate that love to honor His personality and the way He works is a great blessing, one that we do not deserve. To be included by a God who is so inclusive is a great honor.

To know what the Lord is building and to be able to place ourselves in His path, so that we are not obstacles to the world of change but participants in His great endeavor—this is our prayer. It is to perceive the hand of God at work and not spoil it by being carnal.

We need His wisdom, grace, and truth to touch our church situation in this time of change. We must have revelation that provides impetus to the Spirit and a rationale for our thinking.

Transition has a character attached to it. Transition is not just about changes in structure, style, and strategy; it is about diversity into new prototypes as well as conformity into the image and nature of Jesus. There is a provocation of the Spirit on all levels within and around our lives. In transition, the war between the Holy Spirit and the flesh is intensified. We learn how to hunger and thirst after God in a disciplined and not purely spontaneous manner.

Transition is about being made uncomfortable by events, as well as being comforted by the Holy Spirit. Transition is about pain, difficulty, and suffering as well as about a new joy and peace in believing. It is about forsaking sin and abandoning oneself to the cause of God. It is about our sacrifice and His glory.

Whatever we have to give up is negligible compared to the majesty and greatness of His presence. Whatever we give of ourselves is returned back to us pressed down, shaken together, and running over. He gives Himself. The prize is still knowing Jesus in all His fullness.

Transition is also about warfare and perseverance; it's standing our ground and discovering Jesus as the Warrior King. It is about perceiving His majesty and supremacy in such a profound way that our life radically changes. We become real warriors, not just weekend soldiers.

> *Real transition will always conform us to the image of Jesus...anything less powerful is merely structural change!*

The whole world of the Church is going through a transition whether we like it or not; whether we understand it or not; whether we are prepared for it or not. Jesus is coming whether we are ready or not! Heaven is pressing down upon us, bending us out of shape. We have not built a church capable of welcoming the manifest presence of God. We have built a church for our ministry, not His.

In transition, everything heats up. The flesh gets hotter under the collar because it is being burned up. Passion for Jesus increases.

Excitement rises up in worship, and our prayer becomes more fervent. The temperature is rising. The Holy Spirit is infusing us with a new energy so that we can rise up out of the tiredness we feel. Transition *is* tiring. We need God's power to stand up under it. Transition is about laying down everything we are and taking up everything that He is. Transition is necessary upheaval.

It is the passing of one dimension and the release of another. In the difficulty of changing over, we console ourselves with the fact that we asked for all this! Remember all those prayers of "Lord, change us; do something new; pour out Your Spirit in a fresh way. Father, we don't want to be stuck in this place; we want to move on in the Spirit"? Remember those? If you prayed anything remotely like that...it's your fault!

After the prayer comes the frustration. This is the irritation, the aggravation that is sent by God to provoke us to more prayer. Frustration is the provocation of God to enforce change quickly. It will not leave us alone; it grips us. It makes us examine the old and explore the new. Frustration is the plank of wood that bridges the chasm between two dimensions. We know it is risky. We can go only one step at a time. However, we have found that it is more faith-destroying to stay where we are than to risk the adventure of change. Put your foot on the plank and let's go together.

New Model Churches

There are going to be hundreds of different types of churches, all finding their place together in the Body of Christ. The next dimension is taken up with a very strong Kingdom ethos. No single church will rise up with the whole revelation, anointing, or understanding of what God is doing.

No single church will be the prototype. In cities, towns, and rural areas we will find numerous types of church, each holding a piece of the jigsaw. It is only when we bring the pieces together in a Kingdom setting that we begin to demonstrate that Kingdom desire that sits closer to the heart of God.

Building church without a desire for the Kingdom puts a restraining order on it from Heaven in terms of how far the work can go. If we do not build with Kingdom in mind, then we build something that reflects our own ego. What we are constructing has its foundation in empire—a personal domain of the anointed man of God whose own anointing is greater than the church he has built because his people are passive observers of all that God is doing with him. How tedious it is to be part of a church where the anointed one is sold out to his own ministry.

In His mercy, the Lord has allowed us time to grow up and work these things through. Transition is about the destruction of empire and the refocus on Kingdom. It is better for us to fall on this rock and be broken and humbled before God than for it to fall upon us and crush all that we have built in the name of Jesus...but with an eye out for ourselves.

We must humble ourselves and put everything into His hands so that He can decide whether we are trustworthy. If God did not own the getting of our ministry, He will not own the having of it— not without making Himself unrighteous. If we cheated others, broke our word, trod on people, used and discarded people, or promoted ourselves to get where we are, we need to repent right quick! Make restoration where God leads you, because the shaking has already begun.

Other churches matter. Say it every day: "Other churches matter. The Kingdom is more important." Establish the Kingdom and build the church, in that order. As you build the church, build Kingdom into your people. Other churches matter. Pray for them; have a heart for their growth. Have a desire to participate in the development of the whole Body of Christ across the whole area.

It will not guarantee revival. However, the water level of the Kingdom will rise enough in our hearts to prevent us from building our own empire, however small. If we plan to be inclusive and work with others where we can, at least the Lord will not have to shake or dismantle our work later on. We can build a net between churches and cities. Each church will represent a knot in that net, a place where certain lines meet and join together. When the net is strong enough to bear the weight of what God wants to do in Kingdom, we will see some action. God works according to man's preparation and placement. The early Church was in one place and of one accord when Pentecost came. Can our sense of preparation and placement be any less?

The Lord is sharpening the Church at this time. He is putting a cutting edge on what we are doing. He is raising up a prophetic Church, one that is led by every word out of His mouth. It is a Church led by the Spirit, not one necessarily with systems, zones, or management strategies. The ministry of the Church will reflect God's relaxed but disciplined approach. On the surface it looks chaotic, because God is not a manager; He is a facilitator. Underneath the action, though, there is a calm order that arises out of God's character and nature.

Many leaders are not restful people. They are activity-oriented, or organizationally productive. The basis of order comes from within. It is the anointing to be at rest, calm, and peaceful before God and man. It is the capacity to step back into God in times of tension and trouble, to know His rest and peace.

The work of the church is full of the tension of many differences in ministry, many dissimilar people, and many contrasting applications of gifting. The capacity for chaos is endless. A little organization around this is fine. We need enough strategy to keep things moving in broadly the right direction. Too much organization will stifle creativity, spontaneity, and initiative.

> *Divine order is Kingdom first, our church second, my ministry third... "Seek first the Kingdom"; everything else is added.*

Organization may create order in the world of business, education, and research, but it does not create order in the church. The church is a supernatural body, one where the chain of command is less obvious. It is the goal of leadership to teach everyone how to hear God's voice and to be led by the Spirit. It is the goal of leadership to train, equip, empower, and release the saints into the work of the ministry. It is the goal of leadership to follow after God so closely themselves that they become a model, a pattern, and an example worth following. It is the goal of leadership to facilitate, through friendship and trust, a proper framework for accountability that is powerful and relational without being based on some armed forces structure.

It is the goal of leadership to produce whole, healthy Christians who can take initiative, be led by the Spirit, and cause the enemy endless trouble. If our structure and chain of command is too rigid, we make it easy for the enemy to stop us from being effective. If the majority of our people are capable of releasing salvation, healing, and deliverance as well as leading a small group, then we have a church based on interdependence that is difficult to pin down for the count. If the enemy opposes one part, another part rises up. When persecuted in one area, we rise up elsewhere; when attacked in one spot, we pop up somewhere else; when opposed in that part, we return to the first place and recommence.

In the church, too much order removes the supernatural edge that truly confounds the devil. Too much order makes us predictable and very, very ordinary. If our people spend more time learning about order, structure, who to report to, how to make referrals, chains of command, and accountable organizational behavior, they will not develop the initiative, creativity, order, and spontaneity of the Holy Spirit. We will have a man-centered ministry, not a Spirit-led one.

I like organization. I believe in structure. However, I would love for more leaders to be restful, peaceful, facilitating, trusting, and calm individuals in God, so that they can operate these things properly.

If we want the approval of God, we will have to face the annoyance of the world. The new prototype of church will anger the world. They will preach at us in anger because we have dared to go back to our roots. They like us to be familiar, predictable, and toothless. Obviously, familiarity is good when it relates to the character of the church—its kindness, goodness, love of people, mercy, and reliability. People should be able to count on the nature of the church being one with the character of our Lord.

However, in many places the church has become an institution of convenience. We give but we have no voice. We can comfort but we cannot challenge. We are seen but are not heard. Tolerance has been stretched to embrace sin—to cover it without dealing with it. We do not have the disapproval or enmity of the world; we have their derision and contempt.

There is a new prototype of church emerging that will clash with the world and institutional Christianity. A prototype is the first in a series. The Church will rediscover her radical edge, but not by playing with the world's toys and using them differently. Real radical behavior in church is grounded in the supernatural. It proceeds from the mouth of God; it emanates from simple obedience to His ways; it emerges out of Holy Spirit boldness to follow the plans of God with fervent faith. It is to be willing to look foolish in order to confound the world.

We all will be pioneers in this next move of God. His plans for our churches will mean profound changes to the structure, vision, personality, and effectiveness of our meetings, missions, training, and discipleship forums. We will see a radical change in leadership style and methodology.

When building a prototype church, all our mistakes are public. One thing we should note here: Real pioneers do not criticize other pioneers because they know how hard it can be to build something new. Settlers usually make the most vicious of critics. They haven't done it themselves and have no intention of taking what they perceive to be insane risks. Their credo is that it is better to snipe from the sidelines and then borrow the new thing once it has been proved out. Some even argue that it is their "refining" comments that have played a valuable part in maturing the original concept.

I guess we will find out what the Lord thinks of this type of behavior on the day of judgment. Unhappily for some, they will probably reap from what they have sown a little earlier than they would like.

When we go through times of testing with our new prototype, we will have an audience of both well-wishers and critics. Many critics have no honor and less mercy. It is true that the design stages will be fraught with problems. Our raw material is people.

Some can stand the strain and stress; others are caught out by the sacrifice and hard work. No one likes to fail. However, it is not all about success or failure, but primarily about learning and growing. It is about pressing on through the disappointments. It is about believing in the vision God has given and learning how not to do something before it suddenly clicks into place.

The Lord does not measure success by results, but rather by the faithfulness we display toward Him and His vision. Pioneering is about faithfulness to the call God has given us. Many of us are faithful only to ourselves. Self-preservation will always separate the true pioneers from those who progress only at other people's expense.

Some prototype churches will have a broad base of ministry; others will have a narrow field of operation. Some will look after several people-groups; others may base their ministry around one type. I know churches that cater for such groups as youth, people on the drug scene, and people of a certain nationality or economic type. It is exciting to see the many flavors that exist in the wider Body of Christ.

> *We need leaders who are restful, peaceful, facilitating, trusting, and calm individuals in God.*

True spiritual conformity is only ever about being made over in the image of the Lord Jesus Christ. Jesus came to put a face on God. "He who has seen Me has seen the Father" (Jn. 14:9). We are here to put a face on Christ. By our character, we demonstrate His nature.

The operation of the Church in ministry must reveal all the creative diversity in the heart of God. The broad dimension of anointing in the Holy Spirit cannot be contained within a single church, network, or organization. We must love and appreciate different ministries and befriend one another to help, shape, and support the full work of the Kingdom through the Church.

Sharing Perspective With the Holy Spirit

God is breaking us out of stereotypes. Prototype churches are often prophetic. They have groundbreaking concepts and people who understand the process of turning potential into something actual. They can handle frustration because they know it is a critical part of growth. There is no growth apart from a general dissatisfaction with the current state. This provokes us to move forward, to seek the face of God for a new initiative. This is how vision is redefined and where our calling is made clearer in our hearts and minds.

We often are provoked on two levels: firstly by satisfaction and secondly by comparison. God fills our mouth with good things and we are blessed. Some things are working well and we rejoice. By contrast, our blessed state in one area highlights a pressing need in another. By comparison, we are less happy and dissatisfied with this particular part of our life and ministry that needs attention. By contrast and comparison, our blessings highlight our needs. We enjoy the good, and we strive toward progression in the other areas. We simply want to transfer the blessing of God across every area of life and ministry.

To progress in the Lord through the tribulation of our current experience, we must learn to share perspective with the Holy Spirit. It is right for us to tell Him how we feel so that He can comfort us. However, comfort is not agreement.

There are times when God's words do not comfort—they sting! That is because we want God on our side. He has no side but His own! To be truly comforted, we must see our situation from God's angle. Comfort will come not by understanding God's perspective, but by adjusting to it. Real comfort comes through submission.

There is always more happening than we can see at surface level. Sharing perspective with the Holy Spirit will open up our situation on several levels, notably the conscious and the unconscious. That which is hidden has greater power of revelation than that which is obvious. It is the digging for truth that opens our heart to it; not merely picking it up off the ground. The things which are seen are temporal; that which is hidden is eternal (see 2 Cor. 4:18). What is happening on a visible, conscious level is quite different from what is being revealed through the hidden, unconscious dimension. The Holy Spirit who searches both wants to share His perspective with us, so that we may grow up (see 1 Cor. 2:10-13).

When we become a prototype, and when the Holy Spirit begins to move in the church in power, we also will come into a different level of warfare. We must understand this. If we are praying for power, we are unconsciously praying for battle. It makes sense now, doesn't it? If we are praying for anointing and power, we are unconsciously praying for battle and warfare, because that is what we will get. Along with the power will come responsibility; along with the power will come attack; along with the power will come a level of warfare. If we are praying, "God, take us into a higher realm," we have to understand the dynamics of what we are requesting.

One of my mentors in the very early days of my life was a guy who was mentored by Smith Wigglesworth. This man would say to me, "Graham, never ever ask God for patience, because the Bible says tribulation works patience." So you can say, "Father, make me more patient," and God listens to that prayer and says in reply, "I've got just what you need." Suddenly, our lives are full of trouble and we are thinking, *What did I do to deserve this? What is happening, Lord? Don't You love me anymore?* The Lord answers, "I am just answering your prayer." We are saying, "But I prayed for patience." He replies, "Yes, I know, but I am giving you the means to achieve it. Trouble works patience."

This dialogue begins in our heart because we begin to realize that prayer has consequences on both a conscious and unconscious level. When we pray for power, we are unconsciously asking God for warfare. It is in battle that God trains our hands for war, thus increasing our capacity for power.

If we pray, "Lord God, take us into a whole new realm of anointing" (which is a great prayer to pray, by the way), we have to be aware also of the unconscious factor that we are praying at the same time. Every time you go to a new level, you meet a new devil. The devil on the next level has to be stronger than the one on this level. We need to fight against a strong devil to make us a strong church! This is how it works; we have to beat the devil on the level that we are on first of all.

Are you aware of those awful computer games that children have? I used to play these games with my children. Even my daughter could thrash me. In one particular computer game we had to pick up a number of things before we could get through the door into the next level. There were about six chances of getting killed whilst we were picking up about 14 or 15 different objects, beating off those opponents, and escaping onto the next level. I could never make it out of the first level.

In fact, my daughter, who was about eight at the time, could get through to level 12 and would look at me in absolute scorn. I said to her, "Oh, sweetheart, Daddy is getting a bit old. I can't move my fingers fast enough." She said, "Daddy, the brain controls the fingers." Ouch, boy, is that perception or what? I could never get out of the first level. The problem was that if I did get into the second level, there I would have to pick up 30 objects and fight off 12 opponents who were bigger than those on the first level.

Every time you get to a new level you meet a new devil, and the new devil is always stronger. Why is he stronger? Because God is giving you strength. The strength of the opponent determines at least the strength that God is going to give you to survive on that level. You know the strength and the power that God wants you to have by the quality of the enemy coming against you.

> *If you want to be comforted, adjust your position.*

The point is this. We have to beat the devil on the level that we are on. As we beat him and make him submit, he becomes our footstool that we can climb on, to get into the next level. The first level is always about the flesh. The first rule of spiritual warfare is that we cannot take ground from the devil if he has got ground in us. So the first devil to beat is not the enemy—it is yourself. Who was it who said, "We have met the enemy and he is us"? The first enemy we have to beat is our own flesh.

The first level of warfare is always spirit versus flesh. The first level of contact and activity in warfare is always about dying to self and learning how to live in the Holy Spirit.

Jesus said, "The prince of this world has come, but he has nothing on Me" (see Jn. 14:30). The enemy's whole point of his temptation of Jesus was to get Him to act independently of God. The first battle is always against yourself, for we are partakers of the warfare that Jesus is always provoking.

The failure to understand the mind of the Lord in transition will have us running away at critical moments. If we have no revelatory rationale for current events, we will always interpret things in the realm of the soul rather than of the Spirit.

One particular year, I was working with a church that was going through a notably tough time of transition. There were repeated phone calls to my home in the UK, with several e-mails asking the same question: "Is there a word from God for us at this time?" It was not simply a word of prophecy that they were seeking, but insight that would help them progress.

I prayed about their circumstances for several weeks without any illumination. I was due to be with them approximately five weeks after their first telephone call. Eventually, I arrived in their city. The elders met me at the airport, the same question on their lips. I shook my head. Anticipating a hot shower and an early night after a horrendous transatlantic flight, I was amazed to be driven to the church where a meeting was in progress. The same question was on the lips of everyone I spoke to before and during the meeting. After a short time of worship, I was given the platform. I had nothing to say.

Whilst praying the prayer of faith publicly, I simultaneously prayed the prayer of the desperate, silently. As we waited on the Lord together, I felt Him ask me to recall previous prophetic words over the church. We had gone through them over a year ago. (I believe that prophecy gives us a faith-agenda and a prayer-focus.)

All these words had been concerned with gaining ground, fighting spiritual warfare, training up champions, and being a militant church. I remembered also some of the wonderful prayers that I had enjoyed in this church—prayers of passion and sacrifice; prayers that revolved around a desperate need to see God glorified through their lives. I recalled how impressed I had been with the quality and fervor of their praying in previous times. Their prayers were also about asking for a warfare anointing for themselves and the region.

Then I felt the Lord breathe these words into my spirit: "These current difficulties are not the work of the enemy, though he is active. It is not the result of persecution, though there is human opposition at work. This is not real warfare; nor are they on any battlefield of note. This is their training ground, not a battle ground. The word of the Lord is, 'Welcome to boot camp.' There is no word of deliverance. I am training them for the real battles to come. It is time to grow up and learn how to endure hardness as good soldiers of Jesus Christ (see 2 Tim. 2:3). This is not real warfare; it is training. I am toughening them up."

This did not go down well at all. As good soldiers, they had to fall in and stand up, not fall out and disappear. Until that moment, they had no revelatory rationale for what was happening, so they were at the mercy of an overactive imagination. They were ready to blame the enemy or point the finger at the leadership, the vision, and the church in general. When in trouble, the soul always wants a way out. The soul never likes to suffer and will always seek release if it can. If we have no revelation, the soul will interpret events to suit its own requirements. The spirit man, though, will always rest and wait until it hears God.

Understand the prayers you are praying. Reflect on the implications. Keep a log of prayers that you persist in. They will give you a valuable clue to the process you have embarked upon.

Order and Chaos

In the opening paragraph of his novel, *A Tale of Two Cities*, Charles Dickens begins with this narrative: "It was the best of times, it was the worst of times." This statement very accurately describes much of what we are experiencing in renewal and transition. There are so many wonderful things happening in the midst of real upheaval. At the point where vision is unfolding and we are reaching upward to see our destiny, the ground opens up beneath our feet and we find ourselves plunging headlong in the opposite direction. There is a divine contradiction at work here that we need to understand, for it will give us the real keys to incorporating transition and process.

Being part of a network of churches and having played a significant role in the transitional process of many churches, I believe that the Lord has given me some key insights into the nature, character, and methodology of transition. There is a pattern that the Lord is making known in these days.

God is in the business of enabling us to think and act like Him (see Is. 55:8-9). We are learning how to make adjustments in this area. We are changing from being a spiritually dry, consuming church that relies on the ministry of others to find their destiny, to becoming a living, breathing army of people who are productive and anointed.

> *On every new level, we meet a new devil.*

Order is always preceded by chaos. Whenever God restores order, something is being birthed out of the chaos He allowed in the first place. Everything is part of the whole with God. We look at chaos and say, "This is not of God." The Bible, though, points to chaos and disagrees with us. In chaos, God is disenfranchising the old order and birthing the new! Chaos is the overlap period between the old unsuccessful and now defunct period and the new model, pattern, and prototype that He is releasing in embryonic form. It is the establishing of this new type that brings order.

In Acts 2, we see the closing of the old system, which is Pharisaical, and the creation of a new prototype Church. There are 120 people in an upper room when the Holy Spirit falls, creating chaos. No one is sure what is happening! Within the chosen group, there is order because they know they are the prototype promised by Jesus. All people around them see only the events, which they interpret as chaos.

Of course, it is true of human nature that if we are not a part of something and we do not understand it, we always want to criticize it. We always criticize what we do not understand. There were people speaking in languages that they never learned. There were people staggering about in the streets at an inappropriate time of day.

Why does the Bible say that Peter stood up to speak? Probably because he was lying down at the time! Everything looked so chaotic; most people's interpretation of events was that people were drunk in alcoholic excess (see Acts 2:13). People were staggering around under the influence of God. A new order of church was emerging in chaotic circumstances. There were all the teething problems of bringing in something new, strange, and noisy. Everything was more than a little frantic.

This process is a viable part of transition and is best kept "in team" together. Do not be upset at the apparent chaos; rather, focus on the order that God is developing. At this level, church is messy. Most times, church is like a building site. I have never seen a building site look clean and tidy, and I worked on several in my earlier years.

In one part, houses are being completed and lawns laid. In another, foundations are being laid in a hole in the ground. In between, we have mess and chaos with homes at varying stages of development. The church will resemble this process at times. Even if we have the blueprint for growth and change, we will make a mess before we create order and growth. We need to rejoice at all aspects of the building program. Take pleasure in the completion of the finished article, and rejoice that something new is beginning. If we can learn to see the good in most things, our perspective will be more faith-filled than negative.

Our problem is that we have lived with a certain kind of order in recent years. It is the order of human beings engaged in a work of God, but not understanding how He likes to work. We build with our perspective on how it should happen, not actually how He likes to do it. Our version is sanitized and predictable. His reality is not always to our liking. He is a facilitator more concerned with people growing than with organizational correctness.

God works His own brand of order in the midst of total chaos. The creation story gives us unprecedented insight into how He loves to work. In Genesis, we are told that the earth was in chaos. It was formless and void; the words used are *tohu bohu*. There you have it! A totally biblical expression for everything being a mess is, *Tohu bohu!* This is my friend Lance Walnau's expression for complete and utter confusion, disorder, and a perplexing muddle.

Often, it is our failure to live where God is living that prevents us from seeing the order that He is imprinting on the chaos He is allowing. God is so restful. He is the essence of rest, totally at peace. Jesus is called the Prince of Peace because He manifested rest at every opportunity. He created peace around Himself. During the storm on the lake, He stood amidst fearful and anxious disciples and spoke out of who He was. He was totally unworried, and it showed.

Like the worried disciples with Jesus asleep in the boat, we often gain the impression that God may not care. In the midst of chaos, God is frequently silent. Why is He so quiet and silent? I think it is because He is teaching us how to rest in Him. He whispers so that we need to become quiet ourselves just to hear His voice. He speaks in a still small voice because He is teaching us stillness and truth. In Psalm 46, the psalmist begins with an earthquake and ends with, "Be still, and know that I am God." In chaos, God is bringing stillness and order!

The Lord operates from stillness. Whatever boat you are storming through at the moment, He is on that same boat wanting us to grow up enough to call on His peace ourselves. God creates order only out of chaos. He does not create order out of order! He takes the order that we have established around our ministry, and He injects it with new vision and purpose. This new depth of call will lead us to a place of vulnerability and inadequacy. This is a form of chaos because it removes the certainties that we were familiar with, thus creating a greater dependency upon God Himself.

Each new level of anointing and power demands a fresh understanding of process. Learning about the process of transition will teach us how to wait for the proceeding word of God—the "let there be" word that creates order out of our current perplexity.

The process that God prefers broadly follows the creative genius He displays in the Genesis transition.

The light of His word breaks into the confusion of our combined thinking and experience. Our rationale is expanded as we come to grips with fresh faith and insight. We begin to see different results as the word becomes real in our experience. There is heavenly interaction as we line up behind the purposes of God. The anointing grows into a lifestyle of walking before God at this new perception and participation.

> *When chaos surrounds us, the Holy Spirit broods over us... and God is creating a new masterpiece.*

Revelation leads to expansion. Expansion creates a solid faith foundation for a new level of productivity with the Lord. Interaction with the Holy Spirit leads us to a whole new anointing and lifestyle as we learn to rest in the Lord in this advanced dimension of the Spirit. In all of this process, we find the Holy Spirit brooding over the church, enjoying the *tohu bohu*, and breathing life into us as we submit to the work of God in transition.

The point is, we cannot hold on to our order and still progress to a new level of anointing. When a new paradigm unfolds before us, it will always take us back to zero. Paradigms do not build on one another; they replace each other. We start again with a new dependency arising out of fresh inadequacy. Our dependency upon the Lord has to go to deeper levels before our experience can rise to new heights. This is transition!

When He needs to, the Lord will stand up in our boat and speak peace to our situation. Peace comes from the anointing with the word that the Spirit releases to us. One hundred twenty people were having an orderly prayer meeting when the Holy Spirit blew in and created disorder and some confusion. Now, God is not the author of confusion (see 1 Cor. 14:33). However, if we do not have His perspective on the current situation, then *we* are confused! Many people are confused because they have little patience to stop and listen to God. We want to hear what we feel we need to know to get relief in our situation. We are committed more at times to our comfort than we are to our development. The Lord, on the other hand, is committed to giving us comfort in the midst of our obedience to Him in transition.

People were confused in the Acts 2 account because they did not know what God was doing. We often naively think that if the Lord is in something, there won't be any confusion. That is clearly not the case here. Frequently, God's action when entering a situation brought puzzlement. We see bewildered people throughout the Scriptures from Abraham to Paul. That is precisely because God, when He intervenes, brings a new order. A violent, rushing wind blows everyone off their feet and disrupts the meeting, resulting in people staggering about in the street where they are accused of being drunk. There is joy and laughter and the confusion of many different languages, leaving many people scratching their heads in wonderment (see Acts 2:1-13). It is interesting that it is God's order that turns the community upside down!

Firstly, there is confusion in the church until they come into alignment with what God is doing. Then their obedience and new participation creates confusion in the world (who thinks the church is predictable!), and this turns society upside down and inside out—to the point where people dare not join the church, but cannot stay away either! Confusing, isn't it?

We have managed, with all our knowledge, experience, and understanding, to make the church into a stereotype. Many churches can function quite well (at a low level) without God. He creates a divine imbalance to promote dependency upon Him. But the world sees us in our independence and assumes that we are just a stereotype organization. They put us neatly into a box so they can dismiss us as irrelevant.

The Lord is now blowing that box apart. He is dismantling the stereotypes and creating new prototypes of church. We are being made uncomfortable with the Lord. However, as we come into alignment with His present purpose, the world will become uncomfortable with us. Then they will become, in turn, either antagonistic or fascinated by what the Lord is doing. We will become a talking point for all the right reasons. Transition leads to revival, which is effective and persecuted, and definitely not ignored!

There is also something else happening that we must understand. There are times when everything we try to do does not work. There is a resistance. None of our meetings, attempts at outreach, new initiatives in prayer, or youth work seems to work. We blame it on the enemy. As a church, we fast and pray. People become more discouraged. We spend time trying to identify the enemy resisting us.

Perhaps, though, it is not entirely the work of the enemy. Possibly, the resistance is not external, but internal. It could be that our wineskin is the real problem. Perhaps God is trying to break the mold so that He can bring us into a new dimension of power and activity. We are trying to do new things out of the old structure, which is resisting us. If our structure does not work for us, it will not work for non-believers coming to us. If our wineskin is not releasing the full blessing of God for our members, our non-members will not be persuaded to try it. Wine turned to vinegar will not find a palate!

Know the Opposition

The ground of transition will be contested by an implacable enemy who will try and frustrate us at every turn. That is why the whole point of times of transition is to increase our dependency upon the Lord. We must learn how to hold on to the majesty and supremacy of Jesus.

It is so easy when we are going through change and transition to blame the enemy, to blame people, or to look at a human rationale for our situation. I believe that God wants to give us a divine rationale because, in my experience with God—limited though it may be—I have come to understand that God allows in His wisdom what He could easily prevent by His power. If God is allowing certain things, then we want to know His wisdom. Our prayer, however, may be more geared to asking Him to stop the situation than to help us understand it. When God chooses to ignore our prayer, we have to ask another question or make a different prayer—one that may be more in line with what God is doing. That is why we need the wisdom to know the difference.

God is speaking deep to deep these days. Jesus said to His disciples, "I still have many things to say to you, but you cannot bear them now" (Jn. 16:12). In other words, He was limited in what He could do in their hearts and what He could speak into their lives because of their own perception. The Lord is always trying to raise our perception of what He is doing. That is what we call *revelation*.

That could be said of the Church right now. Deep is calling to deep. I have never known a time when I have felt such a weight of Heaven pressing in on what we are doing. Angelic sightings around the world are on the increase. Demonic manifestations that are more powerful and bizarre are also on the increase. The supernatural is folding itself layer upon layer on top of the natural. Heaven is desperate to come to earth. There are more intercessors now in the earth than there have ever been in the whole of the Church's entire history.

> *Confusion is caused by a lack of alignment.*

There is a tremendous amount of intercession going up these days. Every church, no matter how small, has someone praying intensely. Many churches are coming into a place of intensity with intercession. It is easy to see that the whole world of what we are doing is shifting. There are deep things happening across the Church, some of which we don't yet understand. I believe there will be some messages coming to the Church that will come by angelic visitation because we won't be able to bear the weight of them. No one will be able to get the weight of revelation by themselves from the Holy Spirit. I believe that we will have angels coming just as we saw in the Scriptures, in both the Old and New Covenants.

Angels are heralds of eternity sent to help mankind break through when they cannot break out. They operate at the points where Heaven touches the earth, where significance needs to be broadcast, and where God's plans and purposes need to unfold with dynamic effect. They are unlooked-for occurrences. One cannot summon an angel; they do only the bidding of God. They are ministering spirits sent to give a message or support at a critical time. Their presence is increasing in the earth. This is a truly supernatural time for churches to gain that heavenly cutting edge of spiritual gifting and character.

We are breaking new ground and becoming more prophetic in a world going mad with reason. Prophetic churches pass through things ahead of time. This will make us a target for criticism. This will no doubt be good for our humility. Human opposition is designed by God to bring us into grace. Demonic opposition brings us into greater power. All opposition is designed for our benefit.

Human opposition will teach us how to be gracious and merciful. We will learn how to love our enemies, how to pray for people who persecute us, and how to bless those who work against us.

Demonic opposition is to teach us how to stand in the authority and the power of the Lord Jesus. It is designed to show us the majesty and supremacy of Jesus and to enable us to learn how to submit to God (see Jas. 4:7-8).

A prophetic church will pay a price to see the prophetic emerge in the earth. Everything that this type of church does is built on progressive truth. Revelation that is unfolding will not be understood by other churches until it is fleshed out in something visible. This takes perseverance on our behalf, so that one day our critics can have fellowship with us in spirit and truth. We need to keep praying over our detractors that the Lord will open their eyes, that what is invisible and therefore incomprehensible can be seen and apprehended. The church needs a total change of perspective to operate in the supernatural realm. We cannot indulge in the laws of reason and logic and expect to fight off the demonic. We cannot hear words concerning the future without willingly changing our practices in the present.

We will see what God is seeing; speak out what He is saying; and do what only He is doing—simply because He wills it. We will have to suspend our disbelief to share the perceptions of the Holy Spirit.

The enemy must be known, isolated, and overcome if we are to move into the realms of God that are unfolding. That is why we need the prophetic. Prophets have a profound love of God and a deep hatred of the enemy. They have always been in the forefront of any battle against untruth, deception, injustice, and oppression.

Most of the leaders in the Bible had a strong prophetic dimension to their lives. Many were prophets! Yet the notion in today's churches is that prophets and leadership do not mix (work that one out). We have a church that does not understand process and growth, largely because the people who understand these realms are not in any place of authority or real influence. Reason has replaced revelation.

I love reason. I believe that God is reasonable, except when He chooses not to be. Then we need revelation. Words of wisdom are meant to provide us with supernatural reasoning that is not grounded in human logic and intelligence.

The mind must be renewed at times in order to keep pace with God's reasoning. Things that do not make sense in the natural will unfold supernaturally by divine revelation as God communicates at a deeper level of faith and on a higher plane of thought. Our thoughts are not His...yet!

Real prophetic people (that is, those who have been disciplined and shaped) intuitively interact with God on this level of supernatural understanding by revelation. Real apostles (that is, fathers, master builders, and facilitators) have the innate capacity in the Spirit to interpret prophetic revelation into a strategy for church response and development. That is why the new prototype of Church will be founded on the partnership between apostles and prophets dependent on the Lord Jesus Christ.

Frustration Releases Impartation

Very few people understand the process of turning prophetic potential into something actual. It is one matter to have received a prophetic word; it is quite another to see it fulfilled. I personally know many individuals and churches with significant prophetic words spoken over them. All *personal* prophecy is conditional, whether or not any conditions are implied or stated in the prophecy itself. Conditional prophecy relates to the possibility, not the inevitability of fulfillment. It can be delayed or even canceled according to our response as well as by our capacity to align our hearts and lives in lifestyle obedience to the revealed word of God in the Scriptures. There is unconditional prophecy, which relates to God's overall plan for mankind. It may be adjusted but can never be prevented from coming to pass because it depends upon God Himself, not human response.

We need perseverance and patience to walk with God and see that word fulfilled according to the Lord's discretion and timing, as well as according to our preparation and placement. We will need to work with the Holy Spirit to turn our potential into reality.

Working with frustration is a key factor in turning our potential into something actual. I like frustrated people. They are one of the hopes of the church. Most people are frustrated because they care about something. However, they have a distinct responsibility to the Holy Spirit to use their frustration for the correct purpose. It is sent to provoke them to intercession. They must allow the Holy Spirit to direct their frustration into meaningful prayer and waiting on God. In this way, by the Spirit, frustration is turned into passion, which releases the prophetic to empower people before God.

> *Frustration creates an opening— for God or the enemy.*

If people abuse their relationship with the Holy Spirit, their frustration is used by the flesh to sow discord, strife, and division. They will become a dissenting voice rather than a positive prophetic utterance. Frustration reveals our true heart and releases an impartation that is either negative and destructive, or positive and empowering.

If we intervene between our frustration and God's purpose, we are tampering with the law of cause and effect. People do not guard their thoughts carefully enough, especially when under the pressure of frustration. If we leave our thoughts unguarded, the flesh can usurp what the Lord wants to do. We must understand the power of frustration if we are to avoid mis-creation. We need a genuine respect for cause and effect as a necessary condition for turning frustration into impartation.

By choosing God's purpose, we reject the potential for divisiveness to occur. Cause always belongs to God; the effect is whatever is released through the Son. Frustration is sent firstly to change us, to make us more into the image of Jesus; that is cause and effect, stage one. Stage two occurs when we allow frustration to cause us to stand in the gap and intercede for others, the effect of which is a release of impartation that empowers and inspires. Stage three occurs only through the success of the first two phases. That is, we arrive at a place of trustworthy servanthood after having passed the test of unselfishness.

The fundamental conflict in the world is between creation and mis-creation. All fear is implicit in the second, and all love is implicit in the first. The conflict is therefore between love and fear.

Do we love God enough to allow Him to fulfill His purpose no matter how much it hurts ours? Do we love other people enough to serve and help them no matter how much we want to be right? Alternatively, are we more afraid of not being recognized or proven right in this issue? Are we afraid that we will be treated just like a servant? If we have ever asked the Lord for the privilege to be His servant, then we really must not get upset if He treats us like one!

Isaac was not the cause of Abraham's prophetic inheritance to be fulfilled; he was the effect. The cause to fulfill the prophecy over Abraham was only ever going to be God Himself (see Gen. 18:10-19). Part of our frustration too is that we cannot see where our lives fit into the current circumstances unless they change. Therefore, in acting within the issue, we also are trying to create space for ourselves. We have an ulterior motive, no matter how we dress it up to hide it. Hidden agendas, no matter how benign, will inevitably lead to a mis-creation of God's purpose. Rest assured that the significant test in frustration is to determine whether we will sacrifice what is close to our own heart in order to serve God.

Can we lay our desire and our hope for significance on the altar of God and trust in Him alone to fulfill it?

It is a test—a real and great examination of our motives, desires, and true spirit of servanthood. It is here that we will discover whether we will usurp the occasion for our own ends or whether we will lay down our lives for the purpose of obedience. When Abraham was told to offer up Isaac as a sacrifice, it was a major test of his obedience (see Gen. 22). He went believing that "God will provide for Himself the lamb for a burnt offering" (Gen. 22:8).

He had the knife in his hand ready to kill what was most dear to him, before the Lord stopped him. The blessing and impartation that were released at this time to Abraham were both huge for himself and momentous for those coming after him (see Gen. 22:15-18).

We can hold on to our own dream only by letting it go in the service of God. That, perhaps, is one of the lessons of frustration that we all must learn if we are to be true servants of God. His promise and goodness are the cause of our fulfillment, not our desire to take hold of the promise and make it work.

David had to learn a similar lesson in his life with Saul. King Saul had pursued David with every evil intent to prevent his son-in-law from becoming his successor to the throne. When Saul entered the very cave where David and his men were hiding, to relieve himself, he was at their mercy. David's friends urged him to kill Saul, believing that God had ordained it. On that day, David realized that the cause of his inheriting the throne was not the demise of Saul. It was simply the will and power of God to fulfill His own word. The only person who could wreck the cause of God was David himself (see 1 Sam. 24).

In frustration, conflict is inevitable if we are not focused upon God's purpose. Our self-righteous flesh will rise up to prove its point, justifying itself in the process. The effect of our flesh is unproductive and damaging to the cause of God. In frustration we must be ready with our obedience to fulfill the cause of God. Then the effect of our frustration is an impartation of encouragement, prophecy, insight, and blessing. Readiness is a prerequisite for accomplishment.

As soon as a state of readiness occurs within us, it will be accompanied by a desire to accomplish the will of God through His Spirit. Readiness is the beginning of confidence. God knows what He is doing, and we would rather trust His faithfulness to do it than our capacity to understand it.

We know that all things become clear in the end. The God who will not explain Himself before the event will reveal His purpose after we have trusted. He does not always speak initially, but He always speaks eventually. By submitting to Him, no matter how we feel, we become ready to do His will.

> *Do we love God enough to be totally obedient, even if it kills our destiny?*

Frustration is either the spark of life that creates a new dimension or the detonation of all that we hold dear. Do not snuff out that spark, but nurture it properly. The current problem in leadership concerns time, motion, and efficiency. With so many things happening, and with so many claims on our time, it is easier and seemingly more effective (in terms of results) to police certain situations and people than it is to facilitate and develop them. It is easier to deny than to expedite.

People need to understand that, firstly, frustration is an internal matter. It will highlight where and how the Lord wants to change the individual. Leaders need to give them help primarily to rid the people of unhelpful elements. As David requested, "Search me, O God, and know my heart; try me, and know my anxieties; and see if there is any wicked way in me, and lead me in the way everlasting" (Ps. 139:23-24).

We must ensure that our anxiety (frustration) about something is not turned into anything hurtful to others. Once we have allowed the Lord to deal with our own hearts, we are free to pray effectively and to stand in the gap for others. People who would rather complain and have negative fellowship than pray do not understand that they are failing their own test to legitimize their ministry. How we deal with our frustration is a major test of our faithfulness to working with the Holy Spirit. Can He trust us? Are we committed to the fruit of the Holy Spirit or just His gifting? Are we committed to the building up of the Body or to just our own ministry?

Frustration is an elegant test to determine faithfulness and current attitude. It is a privilege to be frustrated. It means, if we handle it properly, if we prove out and achieve what is on God's heart, that a new door in the Spirit realm will open up to us. If we miss the opportunity and our frustration falls into fleshly activity, that door will close on us. It may be some time before the Lord will trust us enough to open that door again. Frustration is the potential to grow and develop.

Of course, if we are constantly and continuously frustrated, we will need some form of counseling and possibly deliverance from spiritual negativity, pride, contempt, and arrogance. The flesh will have got the better of us on a regular basis, and now we become a liability. The enemy, not the Holy Spirit, is now monitoring our frustration for the purpose of strife and division, not growth and development.

God will change us first through our frustration; then He will change people around us. Frustration will bring everyone and everything into alignment with God's purpose, if we submit to Him. Transition is essential in turning our revelation into experience. There are two things we really need here. Firstly, we need a revelation of what frustration is really all about. Secondly, we must understand that transition is the place where revelation becomes experience to us. Transition is a testing and proving ground. It is the place between promise and fulfillment where we are tested to see if we can inhabit the place that God wants to give us.

The promise made to Adam was that he would rule over the earth and have dominion in it. He was put into the Garden of Eden to see if he could rule over himself. The garden was his transition place—a smaller sphere of influence and activity that was designed to be his testing and proving ground. He missed it.

We must be honest with ourselves. How many times have we been frustrated? Has anything positive and remarkable ever occurred in those times? If we are blaming others, we have missed the point. For every finger we point at someone else, there are three pointing back at us.

Did those times of frustration lead us to greater impartation, renewed servanthood, or a test passed with flying colors? If not, then these tests will come again. Times of testing are part of the process of turning our potential into something actual. We can tell who are men and women of real substance in God. They are the ones at peace with themselves. They own nothing and yet possess all things. They are not striving, not promoting themselves. They are content to trust God. He puts things into their hands because He trusts them. Their frustration has been redeemed. In its place is a continuous flow of impartation. They have become facilitators for other people. They are not concerned with their own place in the scheme of things. Great servants always have a place. Faithfulness is its own reward.

Recognizing a Breakthrough

Breakthroughs are not always obvious. Many do not recognize their point of origin. They are like the "magic eye" pictures that we see in retail stores. On the surface, all we see is a mass of multicolored dots. However, when we concentrate and focus on looking beyond the surface, the picture hidden beneath materializes.

Breakthroughs do not begin at the point of discovery. They start much further back than we imagine. They begin at the point where we set ourselves to seek the Lord by extended, intensive prayer with fasting. Daniel had been praying, fasting, and mourning intensely for three weeks (see Dan. 10:2-4). At the end of this time, he received a visitation from an angel, who spoke these words to him:

> ..."Do not fear, Daniel, for from the first day that you set your heart to understand, and to humble yourself before your God, your words were heard; and I have come because of your words" (Daniel 10:12).

Daniel was not aware of the breakthrough or its point of origin until he was told about it. Breakthroughs occur when we begin to pray in earnest and are recognized after prayer is complete. Daniel stood firm in prayer so that his intercession could be completed before the Lord. Had he given up on prayer, that which had begun on the first day of intercession may not have been completed to the point of recognition at a later time.

> *Pressure produces a breakthrough or a breakdown, depending on our focus.*

Everything that God does is birthed through warfare and confrontation. While Daniel was praying, warfare was being conducted over the nation. Daniel was unaware of the battle or even his part in it. He had no idea what his faithful praying had contributed to the heavenly battle.

Wherever Jesus went, He provoked warfare. Demons would cry out, provoked by His presence. Healing and deliverance occurred because of the interaction between His presence and demonic forces. Some people tried to stone Him, others kill Him. If we are praying for His presence to come, provocation will come with Him! We will partake of all the warfare He provokes.

I had a phone call from a church leader who said, "We really want you to come." He kept pursuing it over several months, and finally I said, "Why do you keep pursuing it? Tell me a bit about your history." He replied, "We need a breakthrough." I said, "Well, are you ready for a breakthrough?" He said, "We need some blessing to cause us to break through." I answered, "I am sorry, but no one breaks through in blessing. You only break through in confrontation."

I went on: "Blessing gives us breadth; confrontation gives us depth. Real breakthroughs don't come in times of blessing. They come in times of warfare and confrontation. If you want me to come to give you breakthrough, you had better know that if you don't have a confrontation while I am there, you will have it soon after I have gone, because that is the nature of breakthrough. You have to have a battle to break through. You have to be in a war to break through. The enemy has to come against you so that you can break through against him. He has to come on to your defense. You also have to go on the offensive so you can break through against him.

"There has to be interaction between the Holy Spirit in you and the enemy. So if you want to break through, you must understand that it will arise out of the confrontation between God and the devil among your people. Your steadfast spirit will be the main reason that breakthrough occurs. If you quit, breakthrough will not happen. The art of breakthrough is learning to live with the God of war."

In times of war, we will see a side of God that we do not see at any other time. That is why confrontation and warfare are so important. We are not afraid of it; the truth is, we have to get to like it. That doesn't mean that we all become deliriously happy at the thought of spiritual warfare. Warfare is a sober business. We can relish the fight once we are in it, but we must count the cost before we start it. Our God is not afraid of anything; nor is He upset or provoked by anything. He is a God of war and He laughs in the face of His enemy, because God knows who He is in Himself. He has total knowledge of His own identity.

He is wanting to put all the qualities and characteristics of His own warfaring nature into the church. However, He only puts them in us on the battlefield. So we have to get on the battlefield! There are a lot of churches that are not even on the battlefield yet. We have to be good enough to be attacked by the devil. Most churches are not good enough to come into real spiritual warfare. The enemy does not have to attack them because they do a pretty good job by themselves!

The devil doesn't have to attack a lot of churches. He can simply come in and press a few buttons of the flesh: resentment, bitterness, ambition, pride, arrogance, and unteachable behavior. As long as he can press those buttons, we cannot make it to the same battlefield. We have to win the internal battle before we can win the external one. We have to win the internal battle as individuals. We also have to win it on a corporate level so that we come together as one people with one heart, one mind, and one voice. Then we are ready for real warfare, and then all hell will break loose around us. Then we will find that God will reveal Himself in a way that we never thought possible. The nature and spiritual capacity of a church changes dramatically when the God of battle presents Himself in its midst!

Jesus said these words in Luke 22:28-30:

But you are those who have continued with Me in My trials. And I bestow upon you a kingdom, just as My Father bestowed one upon Me, that you may eat and drink at My table in My kingdom, and sit on thrones judging the twelve tribes of Israel.

"You are those who have continued with Me in My trials." There is an anointing for fellowship with God in confrontation that births a bestowing of Kingdom in our hearts. Kingdom is given to us in the violence of confrontation. The Kingdom of Heaven suffers violence, and the violent take it by force (see Mt. 11:12). We need a godly violence in our heart that says, "We are not going to be moved; this is what we believe in. We are going to stand here; we are not moving. We are standing here, and we are believing God."

In warfare and seasons of trouble, there is a quality of suffering and perseverance that actually births in us a greater anointing to work the works of God. God actually trusts us, because He trusts what He sees of suffering inside our heart and life.

We cannot build anything without suffering. So many leaderships are moving away from suffering. Good leadership knows how to suffer; they know about patience and perseverance to stand their ground. People can leave, but the leaders will stand their ground. It is in that time that God learns He can trust us. He bestows something in us. Anytime God has actually increased the anointing upon my life (over the past 20 years), it has come after a time of severe battle, warfare, criticism, or suffering of one kind or another. We suddenly look back and we realize that the grace of God helped us to stand in that time. Then the blessing of God came upon us afterwards and increased the anointing. Paul said, "I thank my God that He counted me faithful, putting me into the ministry" (see 1 Tim. 1:12). There is a faithfulness there that we are both earning and learning to develop in the heart of the Lord.

Each one of us will go through that kind of transition. We need to understand the stages that God will take us through so that we don't run at the critical moment. We are going to have some interesting and critical times in church life where everything is balanced on a knife edge.

> *Many churches are not good enough to be attacked by the devil.*

We will learn about the mind of God as He teaches us to walk by faith and not by sight. We also will receive His goodness and mercy. His mouth will discipline us into the simple obedience of faith whilst His heart will comfort us in our distress of learning.

The only time God will speak to our mind is when we have sinned. Then He says, " 'Come now, and let us reason together,' says the Lord, 'Though your sins are like scarlet, they shall be as white as snow...' " (Is. 1:18). The remainder of the time He will say, "Trust in the Lord with all your heart, and lean not on your own understanding" (Prov. 3:5). The issue is if we believe, not if we understand.

In the next dimension of church, we must prepare ourselves to walk with the God of the unreasonable. He will call us to do the impossible, to take on projects that are inconceivable to our mind-sets. These projects will have their roots in the prophetic. That is why we must nurture the prophetic gift and ministry in our midst. Without it, we cannot become a prophetic church that is able to envisage all that the Lord would want to accomplish in and through us.

Without that revelatory rationale to guide and help us, we will miss the grandeur of the wider purposes of God. We will be trying to take a neighborhood while He wants to give us the city. We will be attempting to believe God about the wider locality when He wants to use us as a catalyst to take the nation.

When our own thinking has the upper mind, we interpret everything with soulish logic. We look at our own resources and the scale of the problem in front of us, and we make a rational, intelligent judgment of our chances for pulling it off. If the circumstances look too huge and awesome, we will not even attempt the matter. We will be like the ten spies who returned from spying in Canaan. We will give an "evil report" of what the opposition is like and of our chances of victory (see Num. 13:25-33).

However, when we are moving in faith regarding God's ability, we put a different complexion on things. Like Joshua and Caleb, we will give a report that is full of regard for the anointing of God, even at our own expense:

> ... *"The land we passed through to spy out is an exceedingly good land. If the Lord delights in us, then He will bring us into this land and give it to us, 'a land which flows with milk and honey.' Only do not rebel against the Lord, nor fear the people of the land, for they are our bread; their protection has departed from them, and the Lord is with us. Do not fear them"* (Numbers 14:7-9).

There are some bold faith proclamations here:

1) If the Lord is pleased with us, He will give us the land.

2) Do not fear the people of the land, for they will be our prey.

3) Their protection has been removed, and the Lord is with us!

These two men did not deny the truth of the bad report; there were giants, fortified cities, and a strong army. But Joshua and Caleb focused on the Lord and His power. The other spies did the opposite and felt insignificant and incapable as a result.

Being a prophetic church means that we live by every word that God speaks into our current situation, as it happens. We do not live on previous words, but *proceeding* ones.

There is a revelatory rationale for all that God does. In transition, He is working to prepare us for the next dimension of life in the Spirit. There is a process to follow and understand. There is a breakthrough that comes with transition. Many churches do not survive the transition. They break up under the pressure. Transition is the sternest test in a church's history. Only the best can take hold of their inheritance in the next stage. But beware, the pass mark is not what we think it is!

There are four stages to transition. First is *revelation*, which is the unfolding of God's vision and purpose. This will plunge us headlong into *confrontation* with the enemy, as the flesh wars with the Spirit within. During this dilemma, God is doing a work of *transformation* to make us into the image of Christ. Only as the result of this process is seen can the final part, *manifestation*, be revealed. This is the unfolding and fulfilling of the initial revelation that began the season of transition. We will look at these stages in more detail in the next chapter.

Chapter 11

Character and Transition

Part 2

*C*hurches are in transition for a variety of reasons. Some are changing from being an excellent local church to having a resource church anointing. This means an increase of vision and a new dimension of influence as more and more people are empowered and released. Others are gearing up into a regional context because they have a Kingdom heart that wants to see the city and the area move into a higher supernatural level.

> *The purpose of transition is to give us the character we need to live at the next level of power.*

Some churches are becoming apostolic centers where the resident fivefold ministries enable the church to have an international significance in church planting and development.

For many churches, though, transition will simply mean the process by which they embrace their corporate destiny at a much higher level. Figure 1 highlights the change both onward and upward as we follow the proceeding word of God spoken over the work.

Let's look at the first of the four stages of transition: *revelation, confrontation, transformation*, and *manifestation.*

Stage 1: Revelation

When the Lord seeks to move us into a new realm, He looks for us to have an increase of vision, anointing, and power. Along with that, there needs to come an increase of commitment and character.

The process of transition always begins with revelation (see Fig. 3), which is an insight from the Holy Spirit, possibly by prophetic disclosure. A prophetic word is released that inspires and ignites fresh faith regarding our destiny and overall vision as a church. The prophetic word may gather up previous words together with our current vision and take the whole concept much further forward. Revelation has impact. It will force us to reexamine where we are now and where we are going.

Revelation brings appraisal and scrutiny to everything we have done and are currently doing. Revelation gets under our skin, making us feel excited about what is opening up to us in the future, but also apprehensive about what it all means. Revelation means change. It is a beginning preceded by an ending (which is the paradox of transition), a closure and a new beginning, surrounded by vulnerability in the whole church.

The prophetic word makes us feel great. We become excited by the vision but sobered by the change involved.

Revelation may come by teaching. I have known several churches where new vision has arisen in the congregation because of expository teaching on the new church of the twenty-first century or new models of church. The members of that body have been caught up in faith to believe for and desire urgently to become such a church. The teaching has been a catalyst to create a different environment within which the members begin discussion and dialogue about structural changes, new vision, and a different spiritual culture.

I have known some churches where various people across the spiritual spectrum of the work have had almost identical dreams.

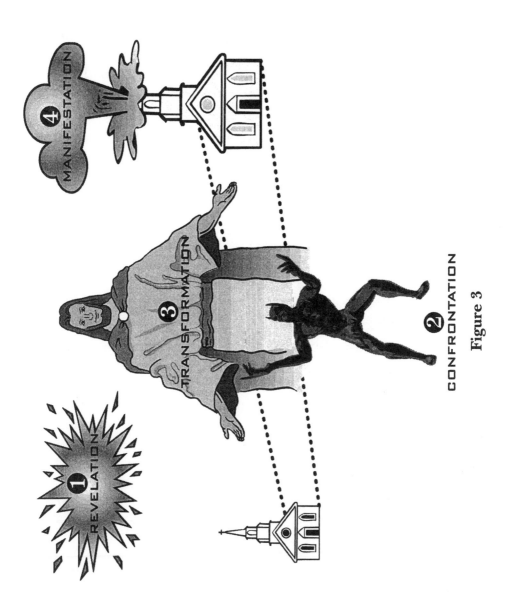

Figure 3

The dreams have been about moving to a new location, starting a new project, developing a range of new church initiatives, or a mixture of such actions.

In several places, people had dreams that followed on and built up a picture of what God was revealing from one person to another. In one instance, two of the nine people who had the same dream were actually in relational disharmony, and this event brought reconciliation! What has been interesting in these events has been the diversity of people used by the Lord. The emotional makeup, character, and relationship between these people have been markedly different. That fact itself has given serious weight to the supernatural quality of the event.

Of course, we do not change things based solely on dreams (although there is scriptural precedent to do so). However, we do use them as a catalyst for prayer, discussion, and further seeking of the Lord. We can recognize that God has sovereignly intervened, and now we need to make ourselves available to the Holy Spirit and one another.

Revelation also can come through apostolic insight and relationship. Many times there is an apostolic/prophetic visionary and a directive nature and quality to our discussions and relationship with our network friends and churches within c.net, the Cornerstone network to which I belong. We care and pray for one another. We stand together in times of tension and difficulty; we work side by side in the Kingdom, teaching, imparting, ministering to one another, and wanting the best for one another. These all act as a catalyst for fresh direction and insight into vision and destiny. Apostles can interpret events surrounding a church and give practical wisdom regarding a way forward.

As a network, we like to perform church surveys from time to time within the family of churches. This helps us prevent churches from becoming stale and stereotyped. It tells us which churches are on the move and perhaps need prophetic encouragement. It tells us which churches may need overhaul in terms of their structure and mission.

We would expect revelation to flow out of these encounters, so that we can move forward with prayerful purpose. Revelation increases expectancy in the hearts of people, which is excellent and hopefully contagious, but it also creates problems for us in the outworking of new vision. We want our people to be in faith and have confidence in the Lord. We want this new anticipation and excitement to touch as many as possible. But we must take care not to hype it up into something beyond what the Lord has spoken. Leaders often can go too far and turn anticipation into assumption in order to gather support for the new thing. If we can maintain a fair balance between excited vision and sober challenge, we will do well.

Rhythm Without the Blues

Total balance is a myth. The only time we are completely balanced is when we stand still. Walking occurs when we throw our weight between one foot and another and maintain our momentum in a sense of direction. Spiritual balance is the movement of obedience and the distribution of faith between vision and sacrifice as we move together in unison. Expectancy can be dangerous for us if we are unfamiliar with how the Lord likes to work.

Although vision and revelation combine to bring us a fresh sense of destiny, they also can inhibit our capacity for thoughtful preparation. Jesus

> **Total balance is a myth.**

tells us in stark terms to count the cost of any new thing before we attempt it (see Lk. 14:28-32). We can get caught up in the excitement and go-for-it attitude, only to get caught out when something opposite happens. Hype invalidates reflection. Assumption derides consideration.

Faith and caution are not in opposition. They are compatible soul mates—opposites attracted to the same God. Faith wants to go for it! Caution wants to do it right. Faith says, "Yes! We're going to do it." Caution says, "This is how we should go about it." Caution brings strategy to the impetus of faith so that nothing is wasted. The main difference between the two is pace. Faith wants to get there immediately; caution wants to get there in one piece!

Faith will pay the cost, whatever it is; caution does not want to pay more than necessary. Faith says, "Let's just pay it as we go." Caution says, "Let's budget for it before we start!" Caution and faith need one another. Without faith, caution will deliver a peacetime budget in a warfare situation. Without caution, faith will not have the strategy to overcome obstacles.

Faith believes it can run a marathon and can't wait to start running. Caution knows how to run a marathon so that faith doesn't run out of steam.

All runners will physically hit what is known in athletic circles as "the wall" in the marathon. Those who run with caution and belief allied together will survive the worst obstacles and finish the race.

Faith plus caution is the marriage of particular knowledge and confident belief. Knowledge in this instance is the understanding of God's ways with a grasp of strategy and momentum. Everything has a rhythm in God. When He changes the momentum, the strategy must alter. Faith goes with the movement and momentum; caution goes with the rhythm and strategy. If we can connect together in this way, we will have rhythm without the blues!

The Lord will always make sure that every group has a mixture of these people within its membership. They are opposites in perception, but necessary allies in operation. This is the balance we must seek, the friendly interaction between faith and caution that allows us to run with patience the next stage of the great race. Faith is not mindless, nor caution faithless. They are the left and the right leg of movement. We need to understand them both and get them moving together if we are to avoid doing splits!

Prophecy and Contradiction

There is a reason for this partnership. Expectation on its own will speed up our momentum to the point of launching out into the atmosphere. We may be happy to boldly go where no church has gone before in our lifetime. Expectation searches out the horizon and seeks to get to the high point of anointing and power as quickly as possible.

However, with God, at this stage the quality of the launching pad is more important than the actual rockets. We will spend time and energy making sure our rockets (faith and resources) can enable us to reach our destination (vision). The Lord seeks primarily to ensure that our launch base (character) is adequately upgraded to be able to handle the pressure of the new launch.

In expectation, we are thinking horizon, but God is thinking about foundation. When revelation comes, we want to get there as quickly as possible. We are enlivened by the prophetic power that captivates our hearts. However, there is a contradiction in the prophetic that declares to us, "You cannot get there (horizon) from here."

Contradiction is the journey from revelation to manifestation—the process of transition. Joseph received a prophetic dream that he would one day have authority above his father and brothers (see Gen. 37). The dream concerned them all bowing down to him. This prophecy was fulfilled eventually in Genesis 47, but not before the opposite had occurred. After relating the dreams to his family, instead of *them* looking up at *him*, Joseph found *himself* in a pit looking up at *them*!

He was sold as a slave and sent in chains to a distant country. His life had gone in the opposite direction to what he perhaps was expecting. Plainly, the Lord was not going to fulfill the prophecy over some empty-headed young man who did not have the sense to keep his mouth shut around some very irate brethren! After the calling comes the training. Once we have received serious prophetic input into our lives, we then need particular development before the word can be moved to a place of fulfillment.

David found a similar set of circumstances at work in his own life. He was anointed to be king by the prophet Samuel (see 1 Sam. 16). Nothing said or done at the time disclosed to David that he would be discredited and have to live in caves in the wilderness before the prophet's words came true.

Israel received a strong prophetic word from Moses (see Ex. 6:6-8) that contained seven "I will" declarations from the Lord regarding their future and their destiny. The words never mentioned their journey into the wilderness or their subsequent testing by God as part of the means of fulfillment.

This is the major part of the transitional and prophetic process. Before our destiny can be fulfilled, we must conform to all the character requirements that are a priority if we are to represent the God of Heaven. He wants all of us to conform to the image of Jesus as a prerequisite to fulfillment of prophecy. After the initial excitement of the word and the release of vision and destiny, God switches His attention to our character. Now He has to work on our personality, nature, and temperament, to elevate it to the point of approved trustworthiness. Our destiny is put on hold until the time that we are proved out in our character.

> *Prophecy may legitimately go in the opposite direction before it is fulfilled.*

After the prophecy, we are starstruck with our destiny; however, the Lord is looking at something different! He is looking at our character and gauging the work and development we will need in order to develop us to that place of high calling. This development will include a testing of our humility; our servant heart; our reliability under pressure; our truthfulness and purity; our leadership or ministry ability; our capacity to endure stress in warfare; our ability to learn from our mistakes; and above all, our conformity to His love, grace, mercy, and kindness. All these will come under intense scrutiny in the most difficult and trying of circumstances. It is almost as though, whilst we are still stargazing after the prophetic word, the Lord trips us up, throws us into a dark room, and beats the living daylights out of us! At least, that is what it feels like.

Our lives run in the opposite direction for a time as God begins to work with our character. It is here that most people let go of their vision and call. The instinctive reaction for many people, when their lives begin to run in conflicting directions to their prophecy, is to blame the prophet. It is easy to assume that because the prophet said one thing and the opposite is now occurring, then the prophecy is false. However, most accusations of false prophecy in this instance are made because of ignorance about process.

Process is a journey, a series of stages between one dimension and another. The journey is not in a straight line of upward development from the point of origin. Rather, like a bird taking off from a high point, there is a dip before there is a rise to catch the thermal undercurrent.

The process of God in developing our potential into something actual involves the releasing of revelation. This causes us to look up to determine our destiny, but it is followed by a decline in our fortunes as we plunge into the next stage of the process, which is confrontation.

Stage 2: Confrontation

Revelation leads us to a point of confrontation (refer to Fig. 3). Literally everything within our church that would prevent God from fulfilling His word to us will be examined. The bottom will seem like it is falling our from under the church. We will feel ourselves dropping into our own version of Joseph's pit. PIT, as we know, is an acronym for "People In Transition."

God never promises power without suffering. Before we receive the power of His resurrection, we must experience something of the fellowship of His sufferings. Before the release of His life, there is a conformity to His death. Paul said that death works in us so that life could work in others (see 2 Cor. 4:12).

If we want to know Him in resurrection power, then we have to know Him in the fellowship of His suffering, because the two things are combined. If God has promised us life, He will give us death first, because death works life in us. We have to understand the mind of God and the ways of God. God will always deliver us to death. Paul said, "We are always delivered to death so that the life of God can be made manifest in us through our mortal bodies" (see 2 Cor. 4:11). When Jesus was on the cross, He said, "It is finished," but He didn't ascend directly into Heaven from that point; He descended into hell. It was from hell that He went up to being seated at the right hand of the Father. Even for Jesus, that point of "It is finished" was not the end of His ordeal. What He meant was that one part was finished, but now He had another part to accomplish. He had to take back the keys and confound the enemy. He went down before He went up. He went down into hell for a purpose: to lead captivity captive, to render the enemy powerless, to take the keys of the kingdom, and to conquer death and hell.

Spirit Versus Flesh

This part on earth was finished, but the part in the spiritual realm was not finished. So He had to go down before He could go up, and we will find that the same is true for us. There are key things that have to happen in this period of confrontation. If we do not submit to God in the confrontational period, we will not experience the transformation that needs to happen so that we can occupy what God has promised.

The next thing that will happen at some point is that all hell will break loose from inside the church. We will find that instead of climbing into a spiritual dimension, we will drop into a carnal one. We will find levels of immaturity that we did not believe could exist amongst senior Christians in our midst. We will find childishness, petulance, flesh, strife, envy, and hunger for position, as the pride and ambition of people begin to surface. As the destiny of the church begins to unfold, instead of realizing our potential for greatness, we must come to terms with our capacity for carnal behavior. He gets to work on our flesh and, instead of being elevated to a new place in the spirit, we plunge into carnality. Why? Because God is determined to get rid of everything in us that is rotten. We will be plunged as a church into a period of confrontation. The enemy will attack the vision and the leadership. There will be criticism and resentment. Old power struggles will reemerge and old wounds will be reopened. Anything inside us that is unresolved will come to the surface, because that is the whole point of confrontation.

We can get into the place where God wants us to be only when we actually go via the cross. God will take us right to that. He won't take us up into the heights; He will take us down into the depths. We will go into the grave and God will deal with our flesh life. The enemy will be active all around the church, but we need to know that God is going to use him to get rid of the flesh. The blessing of God may continue to fall because the Lord will not leave us comfortless.

This continued blessing is the goodness of God at work. God is simultaneous in His actions; that is, He is always doing several things at once in our lives. These actions do not have to add up together. They can be all separate and not necessarily linked in any way. We all have known God's blessing on our lives; whilst at the same time, the Holy Spirit convicts us of personal sin. Similarly, we have experienced the power of God corporately despite internal carnality and lack of unity.

> *As our destiny unfolds, our potential for greatness is disturbed by our capacity for weakness, for a season.*

When farmers plow their fields and then level them for planting, we see a wonderful flat surface waiting for new seed. If there is a rainfall on that field, though, the next day it will be covered in stones. The rain softens the ground, allowing what is hard within it to come to the surface. In a similar way, anything that is hard in our lives will come to the surface in this time of confrontation.

If this is happening now in the church where you are serving, take heart. God is getting rid of the flesh; the vision has not gone away and the prophecy was not wrong. God has the vision safe. It will be restored to you after the process is complete, provided that you obey and submit to Him in transition. Give Him what He wants.

In transition, we are in the process of God's making us fit the word He gave us. We may feel that we are moving further and further away from the revelation that God gave us. This is no time to look at our destiny. We must behold the process and begin to look at the character of the church.

This is not a time to dwell on projects, begin new initiatives, or commit ourselves to new ventures of faith. If we are in confrontation, it is because God is dealing with something that should not be there. Depending on where the church is in the process, we do not know how many people will leave the work during this period of testing. It is better not to plan any faith ventures involving finances until after the process is complete.

Most churches going through transition will suffer a contraction in their resources. Finances, personnel, key people in ministry, and leadership may flow out of the church initially. Some will be fair-weather friends leaving us for other pastures when the going gets tough. Generally, these people may be no significant loss. We cannot lose people who were never with us in heart in the first place. Others may be more key to our progress, and losing them will hurt us. Some will go because they may move with a job change. If things were different, they may have refused the promotion or change of work situation, but now they feel it necessary to pursue church elsewhere. Some will leave to start a new work locally and may try to take others with them.

God will always reduce us to that which is precious. Of course, for some it is the right time to go because the Lord does have other plans. Generally, though, when the heat is fierce, we are burning up that which is wood, hay, and stubble. Fire always tests our quality (see 1 Cor. 3:12-15). After the process, we may have a church that is leaner numerically, but fitter in spirit.

The gifts and the calling of God are without repentance. Let God hold on to the vision and the future; we must hold on to Him and one another.

It is the age-old battle of the Spirit against the flesh. There are some attitudes, mind-sets, and approaches that simply have to change. In confrontation, the Lord will touch our selfishness, self-preoccupation, and egotistical behavior. We all will be humbled in some way before God is satisfied that He can release us to the next level of anointing.

It seems a contradiction, but it is true, that the prophetic word about expansion should cause us to enter a period of contraction. Our first stop on the confrontation process is the cross of Jesus, followed by the grave. Death must work in our midst to God's satisfaction.

In this process, we discover that both God and the devil have their own agenda. God's agenda is life, the realization of the vision, and the entrance into a deeper anointing and a more powerful spiritual dimension. The devil's agenda is the destruction of all that we hold dear at this present time. He is wandering around us like a roaring lion seeking whom he may devour (see 1 Pet. 5:8-10).

We are encountering nothing new; we are dealing with nothing that has not been the experience of countless churches. Out of this period of suffering will come the approval of God to take us on into His plan and purpose. The enemy has three strategies in mind to use against us in this period of difficulty. These are *infiltration*, *depression*, and *passivity*, which, if we succumb to them, will lead us to division and decline.

Infiltration

The problem with confrontation is often the timing in which it occurs. No time seems to be the right time, but some are more problematic than others. It is very difficult when our church is going through this painful process of transition, whereas churches around us are enjoying a laughing anointing! We are going through our worst time ever as a church while others are basking in renewal.

The most natural thing to do at a time like this is to look for something at fault and someone to blame. If we have no revelatory rationale for current events, we will doubtless interpret them from the soul rather than from the spirit man.

Instead of looking beyond the circumstances to detect the fine hand of God at work, people look for the obvious and interpret it according to their own thinking and feeling. If the facts themselves are not obvious or do not add up totally to cover the difficulty, we invent things from our imagination, supplying pseudo-spiritual reasoning to our own particular actions.

> *God will always reduce us to that which is precious.*

It is always incredibly difficult to see other churches being blessed when we are under trial and testing. People would rather believe that there is a problem in the leadership; there is sin in the camp; that we have the wrong vision; or that we are out of the will of God. They want to write "Ichabod" (no glory) over the door of the church and withdraw to a more blessed place. They do not understand the purposes of God. The same process will come to every church in some way as God cleanses the temple of the Church.

When something bad happens, it is easier to believe that it is the devil's work. It may well be true, but we do need the perspective of the Holy Spirit in order to see where the hand of God is moving. He allows in His wisdom what He could easily prevent by His power!

God is dealing with our flesh and our capacity to be carnal. The flesh is the only means whereby satan can get his hooks into the church. The flesh is a bigger problem to the church than any demonic intervention. The enemy tends to overplay his hand and his work becomes obvious. The flesh is much more insidious. It has many disguises and hiding places and can flare up in the most surprising of people.

Many churches are not yet good enough to be attacked by direct demonic activity. Their flesh is too good of a target to miss. Why assign a demon power to disrupt the church when pushing a few flesh buttons will have a similar effect? We do an excellent job ourselves in terms of disruption and division, when we allow the flesh-life to remain unchecked and nonaccountable.

Confrontation is the process by which God begins to work on our character and our lifestyle. Jesus said, "The prince of this world has come, but he has nothing on Me" (see Jn. 14:30).

Confrontation is designed to remove every hook of the flesh in our lives. The Lord will plunge us into crisis where every shameful thing hidden behind our public mask of spirituality will begin to surface. When the Spirit falls, the flesh will always rise. These two are ancient enemies who cannot abide each other's company.

Confrontation is the internal battle for spiritual supremacy. Will we see the carnal man crowned as the overriding power of our lives, or will the humility, gentleness, and meekness of Christ be fashioned within us as we submit to the Holy Spirit?

Will we stand and be faithful to God and people around us, or will we quit and move on, perhaps to repeat the cycle elsewhere? Of course, not all such outward/onward movements are wrong; there are many new alignments taking place in these days as the Lord repositions His people for growth.

Confrontation is God's attacking the flesh. It is the work of the cross in our hearts. It is about laying down personal agendas and realizing that the Lord is killing our pride, ambition, and lack of real servanthood. He is dealing with our sin nature and our sin habit. He is breaking us; crushing us in the winepress of His dealings; chastising and scourging our carnal behavior; and getting rid of the enmity within us that casts a shadow over our relationships with Christ and His Body.

Throughout all these trials and difficulties, the Lord uses confrontation to make us fit and ready for all that He has planned. Many churches will not graduate to the real battlefield. They are still in spiritual kindergarten because the flesh has not been laid to rest. God has to deal with the enemy within before He can lead us to conquer the enemy on any external battleground.

In infiltration, the enemy seeks to get between people, to penetrate relationships with his poison. Marriages are a favorite target. It is hard to concentrate on spiritual developments in the church when our home-life is a battlefield of emotional hurts. Leadership teams are a choice target. There is a simple strategy at work here: If the head is damaged, the body is made powerless. Any relationship of note and significance will come under attack in this scheme of infiltration. The devil will use ambition in people to divide and rule. He will create power struggles in key people. Unresolved issues will be encouraged to flare up again; grudges will get another opportunity to express themselves; unforgiveness will manifest itself in some pseudo-spiritual manner.

Long-standing resentments, roots of bitterness, and hidden agendas will all surface at this time. The enemy will use any ego that is unbroken, any unredeemed personality or character trait to accomplish his design. All of it will be respectfully hidden under a covering, under a veneer of spirituality. These are all points of entry where the flesh cannot resist the touch of the devil. It is what the apostle Paul termed carnal behavior (see 1 Cor. 1:10-13; 3:1-9).

The more spiritual the devil can make the flesh appear, the less likely we are to understand that we have been infiltrated. In the Corinthian church, divisiveness was revealing itself in the pseudo-spiritual dialogue of the flesh playing "follow my leader" with "I am of Paul, Cephas, and Apollos," whilst the more astute fleshly response of "I am of Christ" captures the moral and spiritual high ground. Paul wisely cut through all this nonsense to expose carnal behavior on all sides. Carnality inhibits revelation. It keeps us in spiritual infancy where we are unable to be trusted with real truth and power.

> *Carnality*
> *inhibits*
> *revelation.*

Paul also had another apostolic perspective on this type of behavior, expressed in First Corinthians 11:17-19:

Now in giving these instructions I do not praise you, since you come together not for the better but for the worse. For first of all, when you come together as a church, I hear that there are divisions among you, and in part I believe it. For there must also be factions among you, that those who are approved may be recognized among you.

Handling the potential for division is a major part of growing up as a church. God does not create this scenario, but He does allow it to happen for a purpose.

God allows power struggles so that the church can identify who are the real leaders. In the time of conflict and power struggle, we find which leaders are really concerned about the flock and which people are more concerned about their own status and position. We discover, beneath all the spiritual rhetoric, who are preoccupied with their own vision, ministry, and anointing.

People in the church are frightened of division. They will offer any compromise between factions in order to keep things together in some semblance of unity. The issue here is not unity; it is approval. On whom is the hand of the Lord resting for focal leadership? To be able to discern correctly, examine the behavior of the people involved.

Is there someone who is being domineering, controlling, or manipulative? Is there somebody behind the scenes behaving dishonorably? Is there somebody walking around getting into every house telling stories? Is there someone on the phone to everybody causing divisions and divisiveness? Who is doing the peaceful thing, and who is doing the divisive thing? In that way, the church will know who is approved of God, because those who behave righteously in a situation are approved, while those who behave unrighteously are not. Why? Because they are grabbing for power themselves. That is where the church has to learn wisdom. Times of divisiveness are actually very important in determining who are the real "called of God" leadership in this body of people. Do not be afraid of the potential for division; just look to see how people are operating. Those who behave righteously in accordance with the fruit of the Spirit and the character of God are approved; those who are doing the opposite are clearly not, because they are walking in the flesh to get their own way.

It is part of God's way of shaping us for war so that when we get on the real battlefield, we can be confident that the person leading us has the approval and mandate of the Lord. This person really cares for our soul and will not leave us when the going gets tough. We know that we have a captain at the church and not a corporal with delusions of grandeur. Most people with some semblance of anointing can usually talk the talk, but actions under stress reveal character.

Infiltration is about the enemy gaining a point of entry to get power in the church, which will lead him to his next part of the strategy.

Depression

Continuous attack upon and within the leadership has a debilitating effect upon the soul as well as on the effectiveness of the church. Internal strife leads to a depression of faith, low morale in prayer, and dispirited worship.

The enemy wants to cause as much pain as possible so that the church will be unable to carry on in its current form. The more strife he can generate at this point, the stronger a hold he has on the church both now and in the future. Even if the issues are resolved and we stay together, he is hoping that enough damage will have occurred relationally to make the possibility of further infiltration more likely. He is quite happy for us to resolve our issues as long as there is uneasiness in our hearts toward one another and the pain of the circumstances we have endured has not been healed. This gives him ammunition for another day.

This is important to understand. We must not have resolution at any cost. To compromise now is only to store up problems for later. Christians are famous for sweeping things under the carpet. We must insist on forgiveness, inner healing, and true restoration of relationships as a prerequisite for moving forward together. The activity, program, and vision of the church must be put on hold for a season in order for full restoration to be made. Otherwise, action will dilute reconciliation. This will leave gaps for the enemy to exploit at a later date. The internal war must be fully won before the real external conflict can begin. I do not want to go into real extended conflict with the enemy if people on my side are still holding grievances.

The purpose of depression is to demoralize. It is to create as much pain, hardship, woundedness, and resentment as possible; it is to paralyze the leadership into inactivity. Depression prevents active faith by setting people against one another, so that everyone becomes weary and lethargic. Its purpose is to bring the church to a place of battle fatigue and exhaustion.

Under depression, the flesh regurgitates history. We go back over the old ground we thought had been dealt with already. The enemy digs up the cache of ammunition that he buried the last time we had an internal conflict. Unresolved issues sweep through our emotions, creating further despondency and dejection. When past history is raised, our current confusion is deepened. That is why we cannot move on from our current crisis without real forgiveness and restoration.

Where there has been a breakdown of love, trust, unity, and peace in relationships, real restoration must take place. Otherwise, we just bury our emotions for the enemy to exhume later. Any promotion of disloyalty, betrayal, and unfaithfulness must be thoroughly cleansed. All behind-the-scenes sniping and negative fellowship must be fully repented of before we can move forward, or we will simply revert to type when the pressure returns.

If we care more about what we each think, feel, and want than we do about relationships in the church, we must beware! We badly need to examine ourselves before the Lord, because we are more liable to be part of the problem than the answer.

At this point, infiltration has occurred and depression has set in, pushing us away from one another and therefore away from the purpose of God. Any cliques that form will have more potential for divisiveness than unity, even if our motives are honorable. It is simply too easy to become negative even in a wholesome way in these circumstances. All of us must be very, very careful before the Lord. Things said and done now will have repercussions for years. Godly conduct and honorable behavior will enable us to reap the blessing of God for years to come. But disreputable behavior will sow discord, continuously resulting in constant reoccurrence of internal fleshly conflict.

> *To conduct effective warfare, we need a captain in the church, not a corporal with delusions of grandeur.*

Even meeting together in small groups for prayer can be fraught with hidden negativity. Emotions and thoughts in times of stress demand expression. We can find ourselves talking about the issues for two hours and praying for 15 minutes.

Ironically, it is churches that have successfully negotiated these turbulent waters that have formulated core values and principles of behavior. Our God is a God of principle. His nature is unchanging, no matter what occurs. He has core values from which He operates that provide radiant confidence to all who know Him and walk with Him. He is the same yesterday, today, and forever (see Heb. 13:8). It is this unchanging nature that is part of our inheritance within the image of Christ. Core values represent the unchanging personality of God and are what we fall back on in times of relational conflict.

Debilitating depression is what occurs when we have not properly defined our core values. We therefore will react to people and situations rather than respond to the Lord. Core values enable us to focus on God and be led by the Spirit. We do not become embroiled in the carnality; rather, we allow our response to elevate us into the nature and character of God. So we practice peacemaking, love, gentleness, self-control, and kindness.

Depression causes isolation. People leave the church in search of blessing and new beginnings. The purpose of confrontation is to create a spiritual transformation within our lives, enabling us to grow up and put on the new nature. Leaving in search of blessing may seem desirable at the time, but mostly we only confirm our immaturity and inability to move up to the next level of anointing. When spiritual depression takes hold, we are ripe for the final scheme of the devil's strategy.

Passivity

It is interesting to note that the people who tend to suffer the most in internal strife are the wives and children of leaders in the church. Most leaders are used to stress, conflict, and spiritual attack. It is their family who will come under the most direct attack. Wives in particular seem to take the brunt of relational conflict. The number of people they can talk to and confide in is at best drastically reduced if not completely destroyed. They have to be more careful than anyone else in case an unguarded word spoken in confidence is repeated by a friend who means well but acts thoughtlessly.

This is just one of the many reasons why the church must agree on an external individual or group to come and help them through the crisis. We need objectivity and a wider perspective on what God is doing. We need help to be both reconciled and restored. We need to determine our core values. External friendship and support that is impartial and anointed can enable us to emerge with credit, integrity, and destiny intact.

The team helping us through must firstly focus on character and the fruit of the Spirit before we get into the debate. Each of us must learn how to focus on our integrity, Christlikeness, and morality before we can realistically begin to debate the issues. What type of behavior does God expect of us in these circumstances?

Secondly, the team must release revelation into the church regarding the purpose of God at this time, so that we all are clear about what the Lord wants to achieve in this crisis. They must reveal the process behind the crisis so that we have a path to follow. This will alleviate many unnecessary words and feelings as we deal with them personally at the source.

Thirdly, any outstanding grievances and judgments from a previous time must be dealt with now as a priority. We must spike the enemy ammunition and render it useless. We need a declared amnesty so that old issues can be laid to rest and not become part of the current situation.

Finally, they must be allowed to arbitrate the issues to a meaningful and long-lasting settlement, at the heart of which is genuine reconciliation of relationships and restoration of vision and purpose. It is important that this external team has the broad support of the majority of the people and that they are truly capable of being objective and impartial. This is not Christian gangsterism where we get our friends in to get others to toe the line!

Without that external frame of reference, we will slide quickly into depression and passivity. If the crisis goes on too long without resolution, some will give up. A malaise will set in that hinders prayer and productivity. Some will cease trying to participate. Lateness or non-attendance in meetings will become prevalent. There will be no spark in worship because emotions are at a low ebb. Some will be hoping that a word of faith may penetrate the fog of their uncertainty. We will have lost our ability to generate faith from within our own spirit. We will become tired and dispirited, too weary even to continue talking over the same ground. We will have no energy. Everything will be a trial and a pain. We will sadly conclude that it is better for us to leave. We may search for spiritual reasons regarding why we are jumping ship—more to make ourselves feel better than to validate our actions. Some will simply fold their tents and steal away.

Our ability to focus on anything significant will be much reduced. We will feel isolated and unsure of who we can properly relate to in the church. There will be a loss of faith and initiative. Subversion and passivity will become the order of the day. Faithfulness will be discontinued by some people, particularly in the area of personal help and financial support. Key workers will lose their drive and take sabbaticals. Financial input will drop as people withhold their substance until the situation stabilizes. Unfortunately, many of these people do not store up their tithes and offerings; they just stop giving!

> *In times of crisis, we should fall only as far as our core values.*

Some will begin to choose sides in the issue or try to stay neutral. We will choose sides often on the basis of friendship rather than obedience to God or any outward signs of righteousness and morality. We will not imagine that it is possible for people to be right about the issue but morally corrupt in their behavior and how they handle the situation. I have known men to be very accurate about the issues but use the situation to feed their own selfish desires and ambition. I also have known people who have been wrong about the issue but morally circumspect in how they handled the situation. Character under stress is more valuable than an accurate diagnosis. In situations containing great potential for unrighteous behavior, always mark the people who behave like Jesus.

Passivity is destructive and will lead to division and a continuance of improper behavior, resulting in ongoing strife within the village, town, city, or region.

Determine the Origin of Your Foundations

Even the people who left the church early on in the dispute will still snipe at people from the cowardly safety of noninvolvement.

There may be a fifth column still at work within the body perpetuating the infiltration, depression, and ongoing passivity that the enemy so loves. Those who left will still want their influence to be felt in the work. They will not be under authority anymore, but they will still persist in sowing their perspective—however relevant or poisonous it may be—into the homes of people who have chosen to stay.

This type of activity could probably fall into the category of manipulation, control, and domination. If we have left, we must abandon our place in the issue. We have no voice now and must render our part in the issue inactive. If we are sought out, we must express no opinion. It is important to be scrupulously correct in our thinking, speaking, and behaving. We can pray blessing on people but must not give advice. If we have taken ourselves out, we must stay out! The wrath of God at this type of behavior will eventually catch up with us later as we reap whatever we sow.

I have known many churches to begin operation in times like this and suffer the exact same reversal. When churches are going through internal strife, it is my practice to determine the source of their beginning. How did they originate? In my limited experience, I have discovered that approximately 70 percent of churches going through internal warfare were actually birthed in similar circumstances. A number of these churches are going through legitimate transition because God has a purpose to elevate them to a new place of anointing and vision.

Other churches, however, are simply reaping what they have sown from their point of origin. If God does not own the getting of something, He cannot own the having of it! How we start dictates how we finish. Churches that began in rebellion will end in ignominy. We must determine the reason for our current distress in the church and not just assume we are in transition to a more powerful place.

It may be that our history has caught up with us, and we must determine now what the Lord would have us do. Is He allowing us a period of chastisement where we are being humbled to seek repentance and forgiveness from those we have wronged? Is He scourging us of our arrogance and ambition? Must we make an act of public repentance and contrition in order to set right the past and bring healing and reconciliation? If so, we need to appoint an external team to help us fully obey the process of repentance.

However, it simply may be that the Lord never intended our church to start. He was never in the split and does not endorse our activity. We may have blessed people individually (because God is faithful to us personally), but we have never been able to grow corporately to any level of significance. Our corporate vision has never taken off; we have found ourselves stumbling from one good idea to another, but nothing has really worked. We have a modicum of success but no sustainable breakthrough. People join and people leave, but spiritually we are not really going anywhere. Our church may have a history of continuous divisiveness and splitting. That may tell us something if we have the heart to listen. We may well be wasting our life and our substance on something that will never grow from personal blessing into corporate anointing.

In crisis, we must evaluate our history in an attitude of openness and honesty. We can fool ourselves and deceive other people, but God is not mocked. What we sow, we will reap. Some churches need to close their doors and disband. Whatever spirit of division and rebellion that we have entertained and given room to, must be driven out of the area. We must apologize to other churches. Our people must be delivered of rebellion and deception before being placed honorably with other churches. Any revenue from the sale of property and equipment plus the current account can be given to missions or sowed into the unity of the churches in the area. What began in dishonor can be terminated in full righteousness, giving no place to the enemy.

Our demise must be honorable, or we sow continuous problems into other churches through the conduct of the people we have given away. Receiving churches must be kind and merciful but firm enough in relationship to ensure that past behavior does not remain current practice.

Confrontation is the touch of God against the flesh. It is the hand of God moving unseen behind the enemy and sinful man, orchestrating the downfall of everything that would prevent Him from achieving His dream for the church. The Lord uses everything to destroy the work of the world, the flesh, and devil in our midst. However, it is not all gloom and doom. In the midst of the desperate process of change, we will see the Christ walking among us spreading His fragrance and beauty in our hearts. Heaven will come to earth as the Holy Spirit broods over our seeming chaos, effecting a transforming work in our lives. We will suffer the loss of many things, but we will gain the one thing that makes it all worthwhile: the love of Jesus...the beauty of His presence manifested among us.

> *If God does not own the getting of something, He cannot own the having of it.*

Stage 3: Transformation

Through the violence of the confrontational issues surrounding us, God does a work of transformation. In the stormy process of spirit versus flesh, He removes our old nature and soaks us in the new nature of Christ (refer to Fig. 3).

Jesus is established in our hearts as we develop the fruit of His character. The fruit of the Spirit always grows best in poor soil. When others are being unkind, the gentle nature of Christ is formed in us as we respond in kindness in return. Faithfulness grows in situations where we are tempted to walk away but choose to be loyal and stay. Peace is established within as we choose to stay in rest in the midst of the turmoil and the tumult of adversity. It is called moving in the opposite spirit to what is coming against our life. It is loving our enemies, praying for those who use us, and blessing our persecutors. As we submit to the will of God, we learn obedience through our suffering and deliver ourselves to a place where God can trust us. He trusts what we manifest of His Son.

This process does not have to be completely pain-filled and desperate. The joy of the Lord is our strength (see Neh. 8:10). For the joy set before us, we can endure this divine treatment of the cross in our lives. As we learn to humble ourselves, the Father will joyfully fill us with a greater presence of His Son. As the manifestation of Christ's presence increases, so does the fruit of the Spirit, which is the nature of God. Our pleasure in God increases and we are filled with joy, encouragement, and comfort of the Spirit. Our desire for the Lord increases with our submission, turning to delight in our daily lives.

Confrontation/transformation is a combined process engineered by God to kill off our flesh and enliven us in His Spirit. Unless we allow ourselves to submit to the Lord, we can never fully inherit the totality of our prophetic call. The process worked in Joseph but failed in Saul, whereas David's life appears to be a cycle of contradiction that constantly brought him into confrontation with God and transformation within. God eventually regretted making Saul king because it seemed that he could never grasp the significance of the process the Lord was using to change him. David, though frail and imperfect on many occasions, actually learned enough in the turbulence of his life to be called "a man after God's own heart" (see Acts 13:22).

When Israel came out of Egypt, the shortest route to Canaan was through Philistine territory. Though Israel was armed for battle, the Lord took the people the long way round because they were not ready for the fight (see Ex. 13:17).

There are shortcuts in the Spirit, but you have to be of a certain caliber and quality to endure the fight that you will find on that journey. It is not easy! There is a particular tempering that is required. The desert route was God's way of changing weaklings into warriors.

The church is looking for acts of power to provide a shortcut into a new dimension of life, love, and service. However, every move of God delivers us to the cross of Christ, from which there is no escape. The move of God within us creates a willingness to take up the cross, die daily, and follow Jesus. The cross understands the process of death to life that the Lord is establishing in our lives.

In the process of transformation, God has three strategies to combat the schemes of the devil and to establish His own will in the church. It is confrontation for a season to provide transformation for a reason. In order to occupy the high territory of the Spirit that is our inheritance, we must conform to the image of Christ and become supernatural as Christ is formed within.

We can learn to enjoy this work of God as well as endure it. Jesus, for the joy that was set before Him, endured the cross (see Heb. 12:2). This must become our response also in this direct work of the cross. God is nailing things in our lives that simply must die. It pleased God to bruise Jesus, and it pleases God to bruise us also. It is supposed to be painful. However, in transformation, we also will know incredible love and comfort as God soothes our pain and ministers to us in our distress. In the Garden of Gethsemane, an angel ministered to Jesus as He prayed to be wholehearted in the will of God, knowing the suffering that would entail (see Lk. 22:43). God is bringing us to a place where He can actually trust us with the very thing that He prophesied over us in the first place. He is doing a work of transformation.

He is purifying the temple, cleaning His house. He is pruning us, cutting us back that we might become more fruitful. We can consciously work toward His goal or unconsciously oppose it. If we cooperate, it is a short, sharp, intense, and very painful death. If we resist or fail to flow with the process of change, we unwittingly make the whole thing longer than perhaps necessary.

Out of every ten churches that have entered transition, approximately half have not made it. The flesh was too strong. The church went from revelation into confrontation, but then the church split and went back to revelation. I have seen a number of churches with a revelatory word about moving from being a good local church to being a resource church of an Antioch nature. Some of these churches are broken and very probably will never rise to that high calling. They could not endure the contradiction.

In the violence of the confrontation and transformation process, they could not stay on the cross. It hurt too much. The reason that confrontation and transformation are combined into

one process is because God wants us to behold Jesus. He wants us
to hold on to Him and be held by Him. We do not enter and
endure contradiction and then pass
through transformation. If they followed
after each other, none of us would make
it. They are a combined work of God. The
devil is loose, but Jesus is present! The
flesh is dying but the new nature is rising.
We are losing our friends in the natural
but growing in friendship with God in the
Spirit. We are shedding our old wineskin
and forming a new one.

> *We have
> confrontation
> for a season
> to provide
> transformation
> for a reason.*

The first of God's three strategies is communion with Him.

1. Communion With God

God wants to be present as we transition. How do we enter
into communion with God? The first thing we have to do is humble ourselves before God. If we humble ourselves, He will exalt us
in due time. If we exalt ourselves by not giving in to the process, it
will be harder for us later on. I can remember teaching on this in
a particular place in America. I was there for a week, and I taught
on transition for the first couple of days. One night, I arrived early
at the church before the meeting. There was a particular guy with
a group of people in the church building, and he was commenting
on this teaching of the whole death process. He was remarking
that he considered the process to be foolish, and how could we
enjoy this whole thing if God was leading us to death? He was
going to go elsewhere and enjoy life!

That was his attitude: "I am not staying around here to get
kicked around by this, that, and the other; you have got to kiss
your brains good-bye to actually live in this whole thing." That was
his whole attitude. Then he noticed me standing at the doorway
and he said, "No offense, preacher." I said, "None taken, and I
quite understand your point of view. But I want to say to you, it
pretty much doesn't matter where you go; the process is going to
follow you. You can do it either here right now or wherever you
go next. The next church is probably in the same thing too, either
by the time you get there or after the first few months of your

being there. The more you keep running away, the more difficult you are going to make it for yourself. God is going to get more and more difficult with you. Jesus put it this way: You can either stumble over this rock and be broken, or this rock can fall on you and you will be crushed. Now your attitude is, 'I am not stupid. I am not staying around to endure all this pain. I am off.' That is fine. My attitude is, 'I know that I can't avoid this thing. I would rather be broken than crushed, but I cannot avoid being hit. I want to stumble over this thing and be broken. I do not want something to fall on me from a great height and crush me.' You pay your money and make your choice, and my choice is to stay here and die right now. Hey, you live your life the way you want to, pal."

I want to be more conscious of the glory of change in transformation than I am of the pain of change in confrontation. I want communion with God, so I am prepared to humble myself so that I can please Him with all my responses. On the days when I have to grit my teeth, cry my tears, and endure, I want to hold on to Him as He holds on to me. On the days when I can smile because the pain is just a dull ache, I want to resolve to continue with God in the process.

> *My brethren, take the prophets, who spoke in the name of the Lord, as an example of suffering and patience. Indeed we count them blessed who endure. You have heard of the perseverance of Job and seen the end intended by the Lord—that the Lord is very compassionate and merciful* (James 5:10-11).

If we really are going to rise to a place where our own personal anointing and faith level is high, then we are going to need to know what real communion with God is. All ministry comes out of relationship. Power comes out of suffering, and anointing comes out of intimacy. It is in communion with God that we learn how to humble ourselves under His hand. There is no point in complaining. The most positive thing we can do in confrontation is to fast and humble ourselves before God. We then ask the Lord to let His light shine into our lives. Is there anything in our life that He would not be happy with?

In that process of building communion, we learn how to live in the character of Jesus. We learn how to make the first commandment first: "Love the Lord your God with all your heart, with all your soul, with all your mind, and with all your strength" (Mk. 12:30). It is in that time of communion that the fruit of the Spirit is established. It is always interesting to me that in a time of confrontation, people talk about gifts and power when they should talk about fruit and character. That is what confrontation is about. It is always about fruit and character, about the life of Jesus, not the power of Jesus. It is always about the life of Jesus, not the work of Jesus. When we are in confrontation, when we are under pressure, God is talking to us about fruit and character.

In communion, the Lord works a new level of intimacy into our lives. Standing still under the hand of God, wanting His will to be fulfilled no matter what cost to ourselves, is one of the most intimate responses we can make to Him. Kneeling down to kiss the hand that hurts creates an intimacy that truly glorifies the Lord.

When we choose to submit to the Lord in times of great adversity, it is because our hearts are crying out for intimacy and communion. Part of that closeness is a new level of prayer that arises out of a broken and contrite heart. We give God permission to touch anything in our lives, and we ask for His faithfulness to endure so that His will may be done.

In communion, our behavior before God is moving us into godliness and righteousness. The character of Jesus becomes our prominent desire—to be transformed into the image of Jesus. There is a constant presentation of ourselves before the Lord. We live in the edict of Romans 12:1-2:

> *I beseech you therefore, brethren, by the mercies of God, that you present your bodies a living sacrifice, holy, acceptable to God, which is your reasonable service. And do not be conformed to this world, but be transformed by the renewing of your mind, that you may prove what is that good and acceptable and perfect will of God.*

> **Broken or crushed?**
> **Life in the Spirit is about choosing your pain.**

Every day we receive His mercy, presenting ourselves to Him and asking for renewal of mind so that transformation can take place. As the pain and difficulty of confrontation abounds, so does the presence of God in transformation. Our minds are assailed by the adversity of our circumstances, but as we present ourselves humbly before His mercy, His thinking renews our mind. We live through one more day proving the will of God in transition. In communion, we learn to live in day-tight compartments before Him. As we present ourselves at the beginning of a new day, we gradually begin to experience the newness of life that God re-creates within. New every morning is His mercy and His steadfast love (see Lam. 3:21-26).

As we grow in our personal communion with the Lord, then He becomes the central issue in the transition process. We are turned around from dwelling on the pain and loss to begin to understand and experience the gain of transformation. The presence of God begins to increase upon us. Worship begins to blossom and reach for new heights. Every church should write songs that signify the love of God in the time of trial. Every church should keep a journal that details the prophecies, vision statement, and mission of the church that makes up our corporate revelation and destiny. Added to that should be a record of God's dealings with the church in the transition process.

Unity should become an issue in our hearts. We need to unite around our love for Jesus and ask the Holy Spirit to enable us to find new ways of loving and caring for one another. This will lead us into the second part of God's strategy.

2. Covenant to the House

The church is the dwelling place of God by the Spirit. He lives in our relationships, not in our meetings. It is the love or lack of it between God's people that attracts Him to us or denies Him access.

We are living stones being fitted together with others to provide a home for God in our friendships. (See First Peter 2:4-8 and Ephesians 2:19-22.)

The confrontation/transformation process has been designed by the Lord to increase the degree of fit between God's people. Transition shapes and dresses our life so that we can successfully take our place alongside others. Transition squares us up and gets rid of all our rough edges, which prevent real unity from happening.

The process destroys carnality and independence, and allows God's love to cement us together in a new bonding of love and friendship. It is so important to the Lord that we redefine our covenant together as people brought together to serve the purposes of God. Out of transition should come a new set of core values—principles of loving relationship that we can fall back on in times of adversity, so that we never again fall prey to friction and divisiveness.

Redefining our covenant walk together and reestablishing our core values are vital parts of coming out of transition into a new place before God as a church. In transition, the whole church (or as many as remain!) need to discuss together the issues of friendship and loving relationship.

We must, with great deliberation, think through what we want from our relationships and make covenant at a new level. Wherever our hearts are joined together with others, we must strengthen the ties that bind us together. Friends must talk openly of their love for one another and their desire for a stronger heart connection. Existing relationships must become more inclusive as we open our circle to involve fresh people. No one should be lonely. Those who are loners must be loved into submitting that side of their nature in order to evolve a relational lifestyle. We cannot change people's personalities. Some people are naturally more open and gregarious. However, we all have to make relational adjustments in order to build a habitation for the Lord.

> *God lives in your friendships, not in your meetings. Make Him welcome by how you love one another.*

Covenant must be redefined around openness and honesty; nonnegotiable love in times of adversity; believing the best of one another; making negative fellowship and criticism an offense against the house; looking out for one another; and considering others more important. If we looked through a concordance for all the "one another" verses and practiced them, church would be a radically different place. Do everything to make God welcome!

Redefine the servant-spirit heart of the church; talk about love and unity, sacrifice, mutual trust, and obedience to God on a corporate level. Come to the place of the early Church, who were of one mind, one heart, one accord, and all together.

Make sure that the presence of God is your priority, not just His power. God is present when covenant is made and kept. He will test our covenant, so be prepared for that. We want to build a church that is so attractive to God that He cannot stay away.

This kind of covenant can be forged only in the adversity of transition. We can design covenant at any time, but it can be made real only in adversity. It has to be tested. In adversity, real communion and covenant are forged in the house of the Lord. Testing makes it or breaks it. We must make sure that our relationships are strong enough to attract the presence of God as well as to endure the warfare that our corporate anointing will provoke.

We all will be under attack in this new dimension. That is part of the adventure and the excitement of walking in a new place with God. We get to see a whole new level of His majesty and supremacy. We must learn how to stand together and fight for one another (as opposed to against each other!). In covenant, we send out a message to the enemy: "If you attack one of us, you attack all of us. If you trouble one household, we all will come after you! Everything you do against us will only drive us closer to God and one another. We will not be infiltrated anymore. We will deal with the enemy within. You will have no place among us."

Jonathan did not make a covenant with David when everything was going well. He made it when his own father was seeking to kill his friend. It was forged in adversity. Jesus said to His disciples, "You are those who have continued with Me in My trials" (Lk. 22:28). Their relationship was developed within the warfare generated by Jesus' ministry.

Difficult times are the making of a church if we can hold together. If our difficulties drive us apart, it is probably because we did not have much in the way of relationship and friendship. Real covenant is defined in times of danger, difficulty, and diversity.

It is an unwritten law in relationships that all friendships will be tested. We have to know who are our real friends. Which friendship is only at a surface level? Which relationships are based around performance? If I am doing well and am successful, people flock around me, but if the wheels come off my wagon, do I have any real friends—those who will ride the storm with me?

We mostly make covenants or expressions of love and friendship in good times when all is well. Relational storms signify if our hearts are true.

That is why God is dealing with the enemy within, dealing with our carnality, so that He can raise us to that level where we make covenant and live it out with each other. When the church is going through profound distress because God is sorting people out on the inside, the one thing that He will want to establish in that particular church is covenant. That is what our present distress is all about—it is about us personally coming into greater communion with God and collectively coming in to covenant in the house of God. He will want to establish covenant in the time of distress. The enemy wants to split us apart, infiltrate, demoralize, subvert our relationships, divide, rule, and close down the church. God is looking for us all to come together, start standing together, and make a new covenant to the house of God.

In distress, we must redefine covenant in our midst. Don't wait until everything is going well; start looking at it right now. What is the process of covenant? Don't wait until things get better, because we could be hopelessly divided by then. The only way we move forward in this time of distress and attack the enemy is by making covenant with each other. We choose to believe the best about each other, choose to stand together, choose to understand that this whole thing is the work of the cross and nothing more, and that we must allow God to deal with our hearts. Reestablishing the core values of God will become a matter of policy in our friendships.

One of our major core values must be that we love each other no matter what is happening. Another is that in times of tension and difficulty, our love is nonnegotiable. So if we are having differences in the leadership, our love is never on the negotiating table. We love each other no matter what, and we stay together. We are just having a difference of opinion, but we are committed 100 percent to each other. Loving each other is a core value and principle.

We live together in relationships that are based on God's principles, not a worldly value system. The world values success, wealth, position, status, good looks, and charisma. If those elements diminish in the world, friendship can fluctuate accordingly.

God loves us according to His principled nature. He is unchanging in the way that He acts toward us. The loving-kindness of God is from everlasting to everlasting. It is fresh every morning. He forgives and He forgets. He is gracious and kind, slow to anger, swift to bless. His goodness and kindness enable us to apologize and be changed. He is the same yesterday, today, and forever (see Heb. 13:8). Grace is a core value with our heavenly Father. In our sinfulness and stupidity, His love is unchanging. He practices the fruit of the Spirit in our lives! This is how God treats us in good times or in bad; when we are doing well or badly. How can we be any different from Him?

In times of demoralization and stress, we must redefine our core values, for they are what we will hold onto while going through the storm. They are what will stop us from sinking into depravity and sin; they will prevent us from dividing and splitting off, breaking our covenant to the house of God. We are building relation-

> *Covenant is forged and made real in times of stress and adversity.*

ships of mutual trust and honesty, of openness and obedience to God, of integrity, of love and unity, having a fervent spirit toward one another. We are living in sacrifice and being committed to each other. We are speaking those values out, living them out, and working them out in the violence of the situation that we are caught up in.

In distress, as a church, we will discover who is really joined to us in heart and who is joined to the euphoria of what was happening in the meetings.

When churches are expanded in the Spirit realm, they have an influx, an increase of people joining. Everyone wants to be where the anointing is present. I would counsel churches not to make big plans for new buildings and expenditure too soon. Do not get carried away by the momentum of current success.

Every time of expansion is followed by a period of contraction. Wait till the storm hits. Then see who remain faithful when God is pruning the work. It is a scriptural principle that after a time of heavy fruit, pruning must occur in order to increase our potential for future success.

See who remains after pruning has taken place. These are your real disciples; anyone else was just a hanger-on. In times of blessing, all the spiritual nomads come out of the woodwork. In adversity, they will disappear. This is what we call "felt-led" poisoning. During times of blessing, people "feel led" to join us; during adversity, they "feel led" to go elsewhere. Such people are rootless and will never grow. They are clouds without rain. They have a form of godliness but no power. No root means no fruit. We simply cannot count on them. Of course, we are not denying the power of God to change such people. However, we do not start counting Christians until the storm is over! These people do not have any concept of sacrifice or faithfulness. They keep drinking out of someone else's well instead of digging their own.

It is in times of difficulty when we learn what covenant is really all about. If all we are doing when the going gets tough is going somewhere else, we will never actually put down roots. I remember a guy coming up to me at a conference and asking, "Will you pray for me? I need a prophetic word over my life." I lifted my heart to the Lord and the Lord said to me: "Don't you dare prophesy over him!" So I said to the Lord, "Okay, fine. Would You mind telling me why?" He answered, "Son, this guy has been a nomad for ten years. The problem in his life is that he has got no root system, because he never stays in a place long enough. He wants you to bless him. If you pray for him, Graham, I will bless him because you are praying for him. However, you will not be helping him because all you will do is bless him in his disobedience. He needs to stop wandering. He needs to stop this spiritual fornication that he is involved in, staying in one place only when things are good and then leaving and not taking any responsibility. He needs to stop that nomadic way of life and put down roots. The real problem with him is that he has no root system. Even what you bless him with, he cannot sustain and keep or hold. He will lose it because he has no roots."

I looked at this guy and I said, "Well, God has told me that I can't prophesy over you because you are a nomad. You haven't got any roots, and your real problem is that you keep going from church to church and you have no root system. Therefore, you are never going to hold onto any blessing that God gives you. So until the time comes when you obey the Lord, put down roots, work through all the problems that you have in your own life, and stop projecting things onto other people, you will never actually know the sustained blessing of God in your life, and you will always be rootless. When the wind of adversity comes, you will be the first one blown out. I will not prophesy over you, but with your permission, I will pray that you will put down roots and learn faithfulness to God and His people." He merely said something extremely unpleasant and left.

3. Commitment to the Leadership

Generally, we get the leaders we pray for—or not, as the case may be. In transition, the leaders are going to be particularly vulnerable. They will be the main target of demonic attack from outside and fleshly connivance from inside the church. They need love, support, and prayer at this time. Instead, they will usually receive criticism, complaints, and accusations. They will come under attack in all kinds of insidious ways.

Internally, some people may make a power play by seeking to undermine their leadership, authority, and gifting. This will usually come from within the leadership, from a particular ministry within the church, or from someone who feels that his gifting and ministry has not been promoted in the way he would like. Then there are the vultures from other churches—leaders and ministries who feed off these types of situations. On the surface, they offer a shoulder for our people to cry on—tea and sympathy with prayer and "prophetic counsel." It appears benevolent but belies the grasping power underneath. They will deny sheep stealing and simply say they are growing better grass. A thief is a thief.

Most of this activity goes on in private and secret. I believe that we should be cautious about people joining us from other churches in the locality. We do not want to deny people the right to move on in the purpose of God; however, we must make sure that it is the purpose of God. Don't steal sheep. Birth some new ones out of the world. Transfer growth seldom works effectively. It can take years to work some things through with people unless we have a move of God upon them. Better to have fresh fish than someone else's kippers.

> *Those who remain with you after pruning are your real disciples. Anyone else was a hanger-on.*

Of course, I do realize that many people have been smoked by the ungodly fires of some leaders and ministries. I do not want to deny people a place of healing. However, they must be willing to eventually get healed, delivered, and move on in the purpose of God.

In transition, there is a spirit of accusation that is dispatched to attack the leadership. Again, we must fall back on our core values in this type of situation. Most leaders will not have trod this path before, so mistakes will happen. Mistakes that arise out of ignorance and inadequacy are par for the course, entirely understandable, and easily forgiven.

Defend your leaders against the flesh and the demonic. Guard their back. We do not have to become "yes men" who live in perpetual agreement with leadership. We are allowed to have private disagreements as long as our love and commitment is not on the negotiating table if things do not work out how we want. Disagree by all means, but remain faithful to the core values of God.

Pray for your leaders. If you are having it tough, they are probably having a harder time. One of the reasons churches split is because people stop praying for their leaders in the distress that they are experiencing. Leaders are vulnerable and human and need the protection and shield of our love and prayers.

Transition is a time when we should express our commitment to leaders and act it out. They need to know who they can count on in the battle that is raging. If we withdraw in seasons of trouble, we will never gain strength as a church to attack the enemy. Write a letter, send a gift, take them for a meal, pray for their home and family. Stand with them publicly.

They will not be right about everything. That clearly would be an unrealistic expectation. They are under immense pressure and will inevitably not see some things as they should. The grace of God can cover our mistakes as we go through transition. The valley is no place for making decisions. Let us try and leave, when possible, major decisions until we regain our equilibrium.

Transition is a character issue. Our leaders are taking hits in transition. They need a prayer shield. They need friends whom they can confide in, people who will knock out the dents in their armor. Leaders will need continual expressions of love before this thing is over. Their confidence may be fragile despite outward appearances. The violence of transition may last for months. The buildup of pressure will be huge, and leaders need somewhere to vent just as we all do.

We don't have to get creepy on people and fawn all over them. Neither is this an opportunity to insinuate ourselves into any future power base. It is love for the sake of love. It is representing God's heart and capacity to bless, restore, and support.

In times of continuous stress, our leaders need the Aarons and the Hurs to hold up their arms just as they did for Moses in the fight against a resourceful enemy (see Ex. 17:8-13). Leaders need to know that God is protecting them and that people are believing the best and praying over their lives.

Commitment to the leadership now in transition will enable us to develop the authority for future warfare as we take ground. In transition, we are defending the ground that we possess, but we also are developing the authority to increase our territory in the future. Something is forged in transition between leaders and the church.

This is where God learns whether He can trust us and thrust us into the real battle for supremacy in the region. Stand together in faithfulness. Be faithful to the Lord, the vision, the house, and the leadership. The enemy will try and make you passive in your response to leaders. Be active in expression. Be visible in serving. Make it a joy for leaders to be over the church. Let your yes be a yes verbally! Expression deepens impression.

Our ability to hold together during transition will strengthen our corporate character, causing a greater flow of sanctification and godliness. This is where we will begin to rule as we earn a place of trust with Almighty God.

Receive External Help

In transition, we will need friends from outside who can provide objective support and care. We also need access to people who understand transition and process. In transition, we are redigging the foundations of the church so that the Lord can erect a bigger building and release a greater dynamic of corporate power and identity. The only people who can really help us now are apostles and prophets. They are foundation ministries.

It is inevitable in transition that our structures are going to change. New paradigms need to form as God delivers us from being a stereotype to a prototype church. Changes must come. We need prophetic insight and apostolic strategy combining together to redevelop the foundation and structure of the work.

> *In transition, our leaders will take more hits than the corporate body. They need a prayer shield.*

We will need external help to cultivate our core values and to redefine our friendships. We must suspend as much as we are able of our program in favor of meetings that will build, support, and sustain us through the process of change, for a season. The quality of relationships must improve or our corporate character will be diminished. Unity must be practiced. Trust must go to a deeper level.

We need these external ministries to enable us to work through our differences. It is not just on the public platform that we need building ministries. It is in our discussions at leadership level. The new wineskin needs to be described by prophetic input from a building prophet. There are blessing prophets who are good in public meetings, speaking and prophesying over people. Only a building prophet can speak of the future in the violence of transition and inspire people to hold on together. A building prophet will make himself available to counsel, advise, and continuously inspire the church in this difficult period.

Apostles and prophets together are the eye in the storm, bringing peace and order into chaos. They are a catalyst to provide breakthrough. By teaching, advice, prophecy, and impartation, they can furnish the building blocks to enable us to bridge the gap between where we are now and where we aspire to be.

Stage 4: Manifestation

The combined resources of apostle and prophet will bring us to the place in God where there is a release in the Spirit realm (refer to Fig. 3).

In transition, our corporate identity will be released and a new life message will form. Manifestation is the fulfillment and the revealing of all that God declared to us in revelation at the onset of the process. The Lord now trusts us enough to cause us to rise up and occupy a new place.

Transformation has worked and our character has grown before God, giving Him confidence in our capacity to live at this new level. He gave us the original word, then plunged us into confrontation and transformation to enable our character to rise to a place where that word could be released. Now we fit the word that we have received, and a whole new realm of power and anointing will open up to us.

We cannot merely pray down the presence of God; we must attract Him by the quality of our relationships. We must become living stones fitted together into a house of God. The Lord is not looking for great meetings. He is looking for a house. If we build it, He will come!

Through transformation we are made beautiful before the Lord. He becomes attracted to our holiness and love for one another. There is a blessing in unity that attracts the Holy Spirit.

354 Graham Cooke

There is a curse in disunity that attracts the demonic. Worship begins to grow in our midst because we are falling more in love with Jesus. Our corporate identity and vision is reestablished in our midst, and we inherit a season of divine acceleration. A quickening spirit is released that speeds up the new spiritual growth we need, to occupy this new place. Time that we thought would be lost and wasted in transition is now mysteriously made up as God commits Himself to manifestation in our midst. People begin to grow and accelerate in the Spirit.

Faith begins to be magnified in people's hearts as they hear the Lord in a fresh way. We come to that place in our occupation where souls begin to fall into the Kingdom. There is an anointing upon individuals to witness; there is an anointing on the church to reap the harvest that God is actually giving us. We will find that all the people round about us who God has been preparing, unbeknownst to us, suddenly start coming to the church and finding the Lord.

God starts digging us wells on housing developments where we never had a presence. He gives us property in places where we never actually thought of moving to. All sorts of things begin to happen around us. God begins to give us our inheritance—and the land along with it. He enlarges our boundaries in the natural as well as in the spiritual. Suddenly, our territory increases because, in confrontation, God transformed us and now is trusting us, actually marking out our inheritance and territory. God is the original territorial spirit. The enemy is just a copy. God is territorial. He said to Israel, "I will mark your territory from the Euphrates river down to the sea," and He gave them the boundaries (see Deut. 11:24). That is a territorial spirit at work.

The devil has never done anything original. All he does is copy God. God is a territorial spirit, so the devil wants to be one as well. God will give us our inheritance, and we will find our territory will begin to increase. Everything we come into now will come to us through the warfare of transition. Don't be frightened of this whole process, which God loves; He knows the place it will lead us to. He will walk us through it hand in hand. We will discover God in ways that we never thought we would ever know Him during time.

I have worked with churches in transition for a number of years, and I love the whole process. I find it remarkable. It is fascinating to help churches begin to see God in a way they never understood Him before. They begin to experience God and come to a place where they realize that nothing can hurt them. Nothing can touch them. This is where their anointing in warfare and battle really gets birthed in their hearts.

We begin learning about what it is to rely on the presence of God and on the person of God. When we make space for the King of kings, His presence with us gives incredible heart and faith to enable us to press through transition. When He comes, He comes in power and in faith. Even the whispers of God will cause great faith to rise. When the presence of God comes, everything comes with Him.

> *Only apostles and prophets can rebuild the church through the violence of transition.*

We are going to become a church that moves in the manifest presence of God. But first, we have to be conformed to His image—and that happens only through confrontation.

The prophecy and vision we received in revelation now begin to unfold. Divine appointments begin to happen. God is in the house and in control!

The Law of Retribution

In the violence of confrontation, there will be some people who will leave us. Some will be fair-weather friends and perhaps no great loss. Others may be leaders and ministries—key people in the work in spiritual, financial, and relational terms. We may lose friends and people whom we have come to depend on. All our resources will come under attack.

Whatever the prophetic promises about resources and anointing that God will release to us, we will suffer a contraction before we experience expansion. It is a grievous experience when we know that people who should have known better, leave us and go elsewhere—people who have a level of maturity and wisdom but cannot see the point of what is happening. Some leave because of personal ambition. Others leave for a quieter life and greener pastures. People whom we thought were anchor points are now no longer there, and we feel adrift in a sea of turmoil.

Surprising things happen in transition. Anchor people leave, and those who were drifting suddenly put down roots and are a stabilizing influence. Adversity changes people for the better as well as the worst. The devil steals people away from the work, but not everyone who leaves is deceived. Some leave legitimately in God. Many, though, are taken from us, and we cannot endorse their departure.

In manifestation, the Lord makes the enemy pay for his handiwork. In Exodus 22:1 we read, "If a man steals an ox or a sheep, and slaughters it or sells it, he shall restore five oxen for an ox and four sheep for a sheep."

An ox is a working animal and therefore represents a leader or a key gift in the church. A sheep represents a church member. I believe we have permission at this time to ask for retribution and repayment. Look back over the period of transition to people who have been lost to us. Possibly, we had to release an "enforced" church plant because a bunch of people were set on leaving and that was the most positive way to do it.

Count up all the key workers and church people who were lost. Name the types of ministries that were stripped away from the church. For every gifted person and leader, we want five caliber replacements. For every church member lost, we want four new people.

This is important! To really pay the enemy back, we must ask the Lord for replacements at the new level we are occupying. We do not want replacement people at the old pre-transition level. We want people who can be a resource now at this new level. We are asking for an increase of people with the capacity to inherit and minister in the new land of occupation. We need to make the enemy regret all that he did against us!

We must come together before the Lord in the manner of the widow in Luke 18:1-8, who constantly came to the judge for justice. He refused to give it many times. The widow finally received justice from him because of her persistence. Note that her cry was "Avenge me of my adversary!"

God is the exact opposite of this unrighteous judge. He is not unwilling to hear us. However, we need to come before Him with persistence to request that He judges the enemy on our behalf. We must ask for a restoration of new people at the new level. We must ask for retribution according to Exodus 22:1.

We want people who fit the new paradigm. We want resource church people who will fit us now and add immediate weight to current spiritual developments. Ask and keep on asking.

Some of these people will join us from elsewhere. Others will suddenly accelerate growth from within. Do not stop praying until these people are present. Enjoy this time in particular. This is our opportunity to proclaim the favor of the Lord and vengeance on the enemy (see Is. 61:2). Have fun getting revenge on the devil— make him pay. Above all, enjoy this new place in the Spirit. Learn to bask in the warmth of God's favor and blessing. This is a new day!

> *Many churches have settled for the omnipresence of God rather than His manifest presence.*

Ministry Information

If you want to contact Graham Cooke, or would like more information on his ministry, please do so by one of the following methods:

Carole Shiers
PA to Graham Cooke
PO BOX 91
Southampton
SO15 5ZE
United Kingdom

Tel/Fax: +44 (0)2380 399133
Email: grahamcooke@clara.co.uk
http://www.grahamcooke.co.uk

The following will give you a brief glimpse into the impartational equipping events from Graham's ministry that are close to his heart:

The Emerging Church of the 21st Century

The church in the city/region will be a viable part of our ministry and focus in these days, and this conference is aimed at generating partnerships to enable churches to combine together in the great commission.

The Church in Transition

A training event aimed at providing a revelatory rationale to enable your church to be turned around, implement change, and release members to become a productive corporate resource.

Who's Building the House?

This conference is designed to provide a biblical foundation for understanding the role of Ephesians 4 ministries in the church today.

Power in the Spirit

A conference aimed at provoking people to become more effective in their calling, increase their faith threshold, and develop them in a strong flow of revelation and personal authority.

Reclaiming Your Inner Territory

This is a conference aimed at empowering people to live in the spirit realm and remain in a consistent dimension of anointing and power.

Leadership Training

An extremely practical program dealing with key issues of leadership, providing a yardstick and framework to measure the skills and understanding necessary to create tomorrow's church.

Cycles of Intimacy

This conference is designed to enable people to break through into practicing the presence of God by birthing a new passion for Jesus.

The Way of the Warrior

The practical, down-to-earth training and impartation of this event will enable us to develop strength in significant areas of our lives, so that we will produce a church full of the majesty of Jesus, who are undermining the enemy, and becoming a fortress for God.

The Best Is Yet to Come

An exciting conference aimed at people over 40, it combines training, equipping, and personal ministry with prophetic impartation to release this people-group into a powerful new anointing.

Schools of Prophecy (3 levels)

1) Developing the Gift of Prophecy lays the foundations for moving in the gift and gives guidelines on its use in church.

2) Establishing a Prophetic Ministry provokes people to a greater all-round maturity and consistency in the prophetic realm and will lay a strong foundation of character for this level of prophetic activity.

3) The Call of the Prophet examines the making of a prophet, his/her role in the church, impact on the nations, and relationship with the Holy Spirit.

Other
Destiny Image *titles*
you will enjoy reading

THE GOD CHASERS (Best-selling **Destiny Image** book)
by Tommy Tenney.
There are those so hungry, so desperate for His Presence, that they become consumed with finding Him. Their longing for Him moves them to do what they would otherwise never do: Chase God. But what does it really mean to chase God? Can He be "caught"? Is there an end to the thirsting of man's soul for Him? Meet Tommy Tenney—God chaser. Join him in his search for God. Follow him as he ignores the maze of religious tradition and finds himself, not chasing God, but to his utter amazement, caught by the One he had chased.
ISBN 0-7684-2016-4

GOD CHASERS DAILY MEDITATION & PERSONAL JOURNAL
by Tommy Tenney.
ISBN 0-7684-2040-7

THE POWER OF BROKENNESS
by Don Nori.
Accepting Brokenness is a must for becoming a true vessel of the Lord, and is a stepping-stone to revival in our hearts, our homes, and our churches. Brokenness alone brings us to the wonderful revelation of how deep and great our Lord's mercy really is. Join this companion who leads us through the darkest of nights. Discover the *Power of Brokenness*.
ISBN 1-56043-178-4

ENCOUNTERING THE PRESENCE
by Colin Urquhart.
What is it about Jesus that, when we encounter Him, we are changed? When we encounter the Presence, we encounter the Truth, because Jesus is the Truth. Here Colin Urquhart, best-selling author and pastor in Sussex, England, explains how the Truth changes facts. Do you desire to become more like Jesus? The Truth will set you free!
ISBN 0-7684-2018-0

POWER, HOLINESS, AND EVANGELISM
Contributing Authors: *Gordon Fee, Steve Beard, Dr. Michael Brown, Pablo Bottari, Pablo Deiros, Chris Heuertz, Scott McDermott, Carlos Mraida, Mark Nysewander, Stephen Seamands, Harvey Brown Jr.*
Compiled by *Randy Clark. Randy is also the author of "God Can Use Little Ole Me."*
Many churches today stress holiness but lack power, while others display great power but are deficient in personal holiness and Christian character. If we really want to win our world for Christ, we must bring both holiness and power back into our lives. A church on fire will draw countless thousands to her light.
"Caution: The fire in this book may leap off the pages on to the reader. God's fire empowers, purifies, and emboldens our witness. This is the way the Church is supposed to be. Highly recommended."
—Dr. Bill Bright, Founder and President
Campus Crusade for Christ International
"The future of the Church is at stake and this book has some answers."
—Tommy Tenney, Author of *The God Chasers*
ISBN 1-56043-345-0

AUDIENCE OF ONE
by Jeremy and Connie Sinnott.
More than just a book about worship, *Audience of One* will lead you into experiencing intimacy and love for the only One who matters—your heavenly Father. Worship leaders and associate pastors themselves, Jeremy and Connie Sinnott have been on a journey of discovering true spiritual worship for years. Then they found a whole new dimension to worship—its passion, intimacy, and love for the Father, your *audience of One*.
ISBN 0-7684-2014-8

Available at your local Christian bookstore.

Internet: http://www.reapernet.com

Other
Destiny Image titles
you will enjoy reading

NO MORE SOUR GRAPES
by Don Nori.
Who among us wants our children to be free from the struggles we have had to bear? Who among us wants the lives of our children to be full of victory and love for their Lord? Who among us wants the hard-earned lessons from our lives given freely to our children? All these are not only possible, they are also God's will. You can be one of those who share the excitement and joy of seeing your children step into the destiny God has for them. If you answered "yes" to these questions, the pages of this book are full of hope and help for you and others just like you.
ISBN 0-7684-2037-7

WOMEN ON THE FRONT LINES
by Michal Ann Goll.
History is filled with ordinary women who have changed the course of their generation. Here Michal Ann Goll, co-founder of Ministry to the Nations with her husband, Jim, shares how her own life was transformed and highlights nine women whose lives will impact yours! Every generation faces the same choices and issues; learn how you, too, can heed the call to courage and impact a generation.
ISBN 0-7684-2020-2

WOMAN: HER PURPOSE, POSITION, AND POWER
by Mary Jean Pidgeon.
When the enemy slipped into the garden, he robbed Eve and all her daughters of their original purpose, position, and power. But today God is bringing these truths back to women. He is setting His daughters free and showing them their value in His Kingdom. Let Mary Jean Pidgeon, a wife, mother, and the Associate Pastor with her husband, Pastor Jack Pidgeon, in Houston, explain a woman's *purpose*, *position*, and *power*.
ISBN 1-56043-330-2

CORPORATE ANOINTING
by Kelley Varner.
Just as a united front is more powerful in battle, so is the anointing when Christians come together in unity! In this classic book, senior pastor Kelley Varner of Praise Tabernacle in Richlands, North Carolina, presents a powerful teaching and revelation that will change your life! Learn how God longs to reveal the fullness of Christ in the fullness of His Body in power and glory.
ISBN 0-7684-2011-3

Available at your local Christian bookstore.

Internet: http://www.reapernet.com

Other
Destiny Image *titles*
you will enjoy reading

Other *Destiny Image titles* you will enjoy reading

A HEART FOR GOD

by Charles P. Schmitt.

This powerful book will send you on a 31-day journey with David from brokenness to wholeness. Few men come to God with as many millstones around their necks as David did. Nevertheless, David pressed beyond adversity, sin, and failure into the very forgiveness and deliverance of God. The life of David will bring hope to those bound by generational curses, those born in sin, and those raised in shame. David's life will inspire faith in the hearts of the dysfunctional, the failure-ridden, and the fallen!

ISBN 1-56043-157-1

SECRETS OF THE MOST HOLY PLACE

by Don Nori.

Here is a prophetic parable you will read again and again. The winds of God are blowing, drawing you to His Life within the Veil of the Most Holy Place. There you begin to see as you experience a depth of relationship your heart has yearned for. This book is a living, dynamic experience with God!

ISBN 1-56043-076-1

WORSHIP AS DAVID LIVED IT

by Judson Cornwall.

This book is about David's heart and life as a worshiper. It will show you the intimacy and the necessity of God's nearness as it is discovered in a life of worship.

ISBN 1-56043-700-6

WORSHIP: THE PATTERN OF THINGS IN HEAVEN

by Joseph L. Garlington.

Worship and praise play a crucial role in the local church. Whether you are a pastor, worship leader, musician, or lay person, you'll find rich and anointed teaching from the Scriptures about worship! Joseph L. Garlington, Sr., a pastor, worship leader, and recording artist in his own right, shows how *worship is the pattern of things in Heaven*!

ISBN 1-56043-195-4

Available at your local Christian bookstore.

Internet: http://www.reapernet.com

B6:116